"THE WORLD OF HOPE"

Progressives and the Struggle
for an Ethical Public Life

FOR MY MOTHER,

ROWENE C. DANBOM,

who taught me that even a flawed system
of values is usually preferable
to none at all

"THE WORLD OF HOPE"

Progressives and the Struggle
for an Ethical Public Life

— by —

DAVID B. DANBOM

TEMPLE UNIVERSITY PRESS

PHILADELPHIA

Temple University Press, Philadelphia 19122
Copyright © 1987 by Temple University. All rights reserved

Published 1987

Printed in the United States of America

The paper used in this publication meets the minimum
requirements of American National Standard for Information
Sciences—Permanence of Paper for Printed Library Materials,
ANSI Z39.48-1984

DESIGNED BY LAURY A. EGAN

Library of Congress Cataloging-in-Publication Data

Danbom, David B., 1947-
The world of hope.

Includes index.
1. Progressivism (United States politics)
2. United States—Politics and government—1865–1933.
3. United States—Civilization—1865–1918. I. Title.
E743.D34 1987   973.8   86-14477
ISBN 0-87722-453-6 (alk. paper)

"Kentucky Hills of Tennessee" (page 3), words and music by
Michael Richards and Billy C. Farlow, copyright © 1972 Ozone
Music, administered by Bug Music. Used by permission.

"Slip Slidin' Away" (page 50), copyright © 1977 Paul Simon.
Used by permission.

CONTENTS

Introduction   vii

1   The Crisis of the Individual in Victorian America   3

2   Toward a Worldly Christianity and a Christian World   38

3   The Flowering of Christian Progressivism   80

4   The Challenge of Scientific Progressivism   112

5   Losing the Way   150

6   The Leap of Faith   192

7   The Failure of Success   219

     Notes   243

     Index   273

INTRODUCTION

This book is about the progressive movement in the United States. More specifically, it focuses on the values by which progressives attempted to live and that they attempted to inculcate in the public life of their country. It touches on culture and society, on intellectual life and family, on politics and economics, but it revolves around values, for that is what progressivism was mainly about.

My central premise is that the progressives were products of the Victorian age in which they grew up. They reflected the Victorian faith in the individual and confidence in the inevitability of human progress. They reflected also the crisis of authority in Victorian society between religious and secular modes of understanding human affairs, and the value crisis raised by the realities of a modernizing, industrializing society. These crises stimulated them to action, leading them to attempt to infuse the values of private life into public life.

I believe that the progressives looked backward rather than forward. For that reason, I disagree with the recent tendency in progressive historiography to see the reformers as modernizers, preparing American institutions for the twentieth century. Much of what the progressives did is with us still, but their purpose was to hold a reluctant society to its basic values, not to pull it into the modern age. When we see the progressives in modern terms, we lose their flavor and even, I think, their essence. In order to make progressives modern, we ignore much of what they did and most of what they said, or we assume that their rhetoric masked a larger reality. We can comprehend some of the products of their labor, but we have trouble understanding their altruism, their righteousness, their faith in people, their innocence, or their devotion to the public interest.

The reality was that the progressives were born into a comfortable Victorian world that expressed faith in the individual as the certain means to higher civilization. This faith was shaken by the social and economic crisis of the nineties. Progressivism was born in the attempt to reconcile the growing contradiction between private values and public life by inducing the latter to conform to the former. Because these values were Christian, in a broad sense, and because the reformers spoke in religious terms, I have labeled this effort "Christian progressivism." By 1910, these Christian progressives, who hoped to reform America through regenerate people, were challenged by more scientific reformers who judged truth empirically and valued efficient behavior more highly than individual character. Despite their differences, both types of reformers worked together and both had reason for optimism in the early teens, when institutions were reformed and people seemed to get better and more efficient. Ultimately their hopes were dashed by the First World War and the stubbornness of the human character. The laws they passed and the structural changes they made and even the hypocritical responses they called forth continued to exist, but these were just artifacts of their world of hope that was no more.

Rhetoric is often a weak indicator of reality, but in this book I generally take the progressives at their word. I think that most of the values and motives and goals they expressed publicly were the ones they held. This is not to excuse their faults. They suffered from their share of contradictions and hypocrisies. They were products of their class and race, and they shared the prejudices thereof. They feared much of the modern world and sought to control it. And their faults were magnified by their self-righteousness and intolerance. But they were attractive people in many ways. They were idealistic and altruistic, and they believed in the goodness of individuals and the forward movement of society. They divided among themselves, especially over the question of whether Christianity or science should be our source of authority, and eventually they failed in their attempt to reform America in a fundamental way. I recognize their weaknesses, but I am sympathetic with what they tried to do.

It may not be possible to write a comprehensive history of the progressive movement; some have even questioned whether such a phenomenon existed. Obviously I believe there was a progressive movement. It was many-faceted and complex, but I think we can learn a good deal about it by focusing on the beliefs and values of the people in it. I have not tried to write a comprehensive history of it. For example, readers will search in vain for the Hepburn Act and the Ballinger-Pinchot affair and many other political milestones of the period. Likewise, I have not attempted to cover all of the social, cultural, or economic developments of the progressive era. Hence, such things as the Americanization movement, the formation of United States Steel, the realist tendencies in art and literature, and the birth of the National Association for the Advancement of Colored People are all slighted. I have also focused on the reformers' prescriptions for public life in the economic and political realms. This emphasis necessarily slights their social reform component and the importance of women in the movement. I also chose to concentrate on published material, by modern scholars as well as by the progressives and the people who influenced them. All of these choices were dictated by my desire to maintain a focus on what I think is the essence of progressivism—the desire to force public behavior to conform to standards of value rooted in Christianity or science, to inculcate in Americans a higher sense of brotherhood and selflessness and a devotion to the public interest. I hope that the reader will understand—if not excuse—my lapses in this light. And I hope as well that the reader will come away with a sense of the progressive "world of hope" of which William Allen White wrote and which I have tried to convey.

The genesis of this book lies in conversations I had nearly twenty years ago with my graduate school advisor, David Kennedy, about the nature of progressivism. There is much in this book with which he will not agree, but it would not have been written without him. By precept and example, David Kennedy provided me with a model of what an historian could and should be and do, and for that I will always be in his debt.

A number of people read this manuscript and provided me with comments regarding it. Archer Jones was kind enough to take time from his own scholarship to provide me with a meticulous reading. In the process he endured some wretched excesses and some gratuitous assaults on some of his favorite historical figures with unfailing good humor. I much appreciate his efforts on my behalf. I also want to thank Carroll Engelhardt, John Helgeland, Larry Peterson, Mel Piehl, Hal Sears, Luther Spoehr, and Marie Tedesco for reading and commenting for me. I assume responsibility for all interpretations herein, but I think that these other people should get part of the blame for any egregious factual errors. I wish further to thank Janet Francendese of Temple University Press, who had the vision to see the book as I see it and the will to get it into print.

I also want to thank my mother, to whom this book is dedicated, for reading this historical prose with a journalist's eye. Michael J. Lyons, chair of the Department of History at North Dakota State University and friend, provided both personal support and a conducive environment for scholarship. North Dakota State University granted me leave in 1981–1982 to work on this book. Deb Sayler patiently searched out dozens of obscure and sometimes weird titles for me as interlibrary loan librarian. Joyce Grenz did the early typing for me. I wish especially to thank Janis Kirsch, who did most of the typing quickly and efficiently, and who avoided the temptation to hide when I rushed in with something that had to be done yesterday. Finally, and most importantly, I want to thank Karen. She didn't read the book, but she had faith in it because she had faith in me. I needed that more than I needed another reader.

"THE WORLD OF HOPE"

Progressives and the Struggle
for an Ethical Public Life

THE CRISIS OF THE INDIVIDUAL

IN VICTORIAN AMERICA

Progressives or otherwise, we were . . . the children
of the Victorian era. . . . We lived a contented, pro-
vincial existence.

RAYMOND BLAINE FOSDICK

Take me back to those old Kentucky hills of
    Tennessee,
Where the mockin' bird is singin', high up in the
    laurel tree.
Let the Alabama moon, shine her light on me.
Way back in those old Kentucky hills of
    Tennessee.

COMMANDER CODY AND HIS
LOST PLANET AIRMEN

In the decades after 1920 many of the old progressives recounted the
events of their lives in autobiographies. This was the twilight of that
time in America when the purpose of the autobiography was to instruct, rather than titillate, the reader. And the men and women of
prominence in the progressive generation believed their lives carried
lessons for the future.

Usually, their autobiographies demonstrated a good deal of self-
knowledge, an important asset to those who would instruct others.
They recognized clearly the forces that had shaped them, They agreed
that the Victorian culture into which they had been born and in which
they had been raised, with its strong social institutions, its strict moral
standards, its values of individual achievement, responsibility, and

rectitude, and its confident celebration of progress and civilization, had set their minds and their lives in channels from which it had been difficult to escape.

Some were wistful about their youth, remembering a comfortable, simple, and secure world of strong, patriarchal families, self-sufficient communities, confident churches, and clear value systems in which everyone believed. Yet even these agreed that the Victorian world was lost. The "simple life of my boyhood days," one of them saw in retrospect, "was a phase of a social order that had not yet felt the results of that capitalism already developing."[1] Others conceded that it was comfortable, secure, and even happy, but they questioned how well the Victorian age had prepared them for the future. "We were projected," noted Raymond Blaine Fosdick, "without preparation or time for adjustment . . . into the kaleidoscopic alterations of the twentieth century."[2] The essence of modern life is change, and Fosdick and his contemporaries had more than their share of it.

Some emphasized the narrowness, prudery, intellectual stultification, and pious hypocrisy that later generations came to identify with Victorianism. For Frederic C. Howe, who rejected many of the assumptions governing the middle-class world in which he grew up, Victorian culture was like Commander Cody's "Kentucky hills of Tennessee," a sham, a delusion that existed only in people's minds. Howe believed that hypocrisy characterized the America of his youth. Men could do whatever they wanted, could violate any social convention or standard, as long as they showed a public devotion to socially celebrated values and behavior.[3]

Whether they embraced it, rebelled against it, or strove to transcend it, the members of the progressive generation agreed they were products of a Victorian culture that had reached its zenith in their formative years. They were men and women born and raised in the Anglo-American world, mostly during the last third of the nineteenth century. They were overwhelmingly members of the middle class in a country in which most people defined themselves as members of that class and attempted to live their lives in conformity to its assumptions and values. As such, they carried Victorian culture, with all of its strengths and weaknesses, its hopes and dreams, its incoherence and contradictions, into a century in which it would be questioned, strained, and discredited until only a few tattered remnants of it would remain. These remnants of Victorianism could not unite society, even to the imperfect extent Victorian assumptions and values had done when they were robust. Yet men and women continued to cling to them, because the modern age has been more adept at shattering old verities than creating new ones. Writing in 1939, on the eve of a conflict that would further fray most of the shreds of Victorianism still existing, Hutchins Hapgood spoke for his generation:

> I am a Victorian in the modern age. The modern age which has brought me innumerable contacts that are not Victorian, and has involved impulses and imaginative tendencies quite different from those of the Victorian age; revolutions from that time in ideas and in the forms of political, economic, and marital worlds. And yet these new elements, although constantly conflicting with the old, by necessity grew out of the old.[4]

To understand the progressive generation, then, we must begin with Victorian culture in America.

I

At the heart of Victorian culture in the United States was a set of values and ideals regarding the nature of human beings and their behavior. As is the case with any value system, that embraced by the Victorians did not describe reality perfectly. Real behavior did not always conform to cultural standards in Victorian America, though the latter did provide a means of evaluating and criticizing the former. Likewise, not everybody embraced the standards of Victorian culture or attempted to live by them. American Victorianism was most closely associated with the white, native-born, middle-class, Protestant mainstream of the country. However, people with other backgrounds could and often did embrace Victorian values, and usually found it to their advantage to do so.[5]

The focus of Victorian idealism was the individual. Americans in the Victorian age embraced a religious and secular faith in individual self-determination that infused every area of human endeavor. The burden of individualism fell especially heavily on men, both because Victorians believed them to be fundamentally different from women and because women were effectively excluded from most areas of active public life. The individual, Victorians believed, was the shaper of his own destiny. His economic success was dependent upon his own efforts, as was his social position. In politics, the conscientious citizen of a republic was supposed to make his decisions as an individual, independent of self- or group-interest, on the basis of what was best for the country. People determined their eternal futures as well, choosing salvation through their faith and actions.

The belief in self-determination carried some subsidiary assumptions with it. One was the belief that self-improvement was possible. In America, where opportunities seemingly abounded, and where few social or legal barriers to individual advancement existed, the individual could and should improve himself. The ideal of the age was the man who began his career as an agricultural laborer, apprentice, or clerk and rose to proprietorship of a farm, shop, or store. As men improved themselves by rising from humble beginnings to economic or political achievement, they improved the community as well. Popular economic and political thought emphasized the notion that the self-directive individual who made his own decisions and controlled his own life was the key to economic, social, and political progress. And the impartial observer, viewing the tremendous progress of the republic and the communities that composed it, would be hard pressed to deny that, in the American environment at last, individualism and advancement seemed to be complementary forces.

A second assumption contained within the idea of self-determination was the belief in self-reliance. If the individual could determine his fate, he should determine it. If those who succeeded should benefit from their efforts, those who failed should suffer. To the Victorian mind there was nothing immoral about the notion of making individuals responsible for failures that had issued from their own actions. Men who shaped themselves must, by definition, rely upon themselves.

From our modern perspective, Victorian individualism seems simplistic at best and fatally flawed at worst. We believe that so many economic, social, biological, political, physical, and psychological factors shape the individual that his or her sphere of self-determination is, at best, quite narrow. We think that the burden of self-reliance in the absence of true self-determination is unjust and even cruel. And we recognize that the individualism of Victorian America contributed to petty economic striving, to the tendency to place material values on everything in life, to the destruction of the physical and social environments, and to the legitimation and even the elevation of human selfishness.

But individualism was attractive to many late-nineteenth-century Americans because it imparted dignity to people. Individual self-determination did not describe reality perfectly, but in a relatively open society and open economy, based broadly on small, independent farmers, artisans, and storekeepers, it was not as fanciful a notion as it is in our more modern, mechanistic, and deterministic world. Examples abounded of self-made men, and even the many who were unable to duplicate the economic or political achievements of the few could reasonably anticipate modest rises in wealth and status in the dynamic economic environment of the expanding nation. Of course, then as now the idea of self-determination served a class function, validating, legitimizing, and celebrating the position of those at the top of the structure and debasing those at the bottom. This is one of the reasons why this idea enjoys vitality today, when it is less descriptive of reality than it was a century ago. But the idea of individual responsibility also attracts us today at least in part for the same reason it attracted the Victorians, because it makes individual dignity possible and imparts purpose to individual efforts. Post-Victorian notions of heredity, environment, and psychology have amended and compromised the idea of individual responsibility for us, but in the late nineteenth century self-determination and self-reliance were burdens borne by every man. For those who failed, the physical and psychological burdens were tremendous, but the successful bore them as lightly as one bears a badge of honor.

Their emphasis on individual responsibility did not lead late-nineteenth-century Americans to believe that the individual was always necessarily good or that the actions he took to advance himself always benefitted the community of which he was a part. Even in America, where so many benefits had seemed to flow from the fount of individual volition, enough examples of cruelty and selfishness existed to illustrate the potential danger of the unrestrained individual. As George Fredrickson showed some years ago, the American Civil War indicated to many the potential dangers to society of unrestrained individualism, and the romantic, transcendental individualism of the antebellum period had been discredited as a result.[6] The problem for the Victorians was how to keep the individual from doing antisocial things without preventing him from doing those things that benefitted himself and the community. The solution—logical enough in a society that celebrated individualism—was that the individual should restrain himself by behaving in accordance with a strict, socially sanctioned moral code.

When we reflect on the morality of self-restraint in the late nineteenth century, we usually think first of the area of sexual behavior, which our Victorian forebears sought to control with an elaborate— sometimes even ridiculous—set of conventions. Rectitude, reticence, and chastity were the reins Victorians placed on lust. But carnal passions were not the only ones the individual was supposed to restrain. Diligence and frugality were urged on those drawn to self-indulgent laziness or extravagance. Honesty and integrity were upheld to those tempted to operate through trickery or sharp-dealing. Duty was enshrined as a guide to those who might shirk their responsibilities to others. Courage countered cowardice, and seriousness, sobriety, and moderation stood as reproaches to frivolity and intemperance. As Daniel Walker Howe has pointed out, the Victorians were serious people. They took duty, responsibility, and virtue seriously, and that meant a more or less continuous struggle to restrain many human impulses.[7]

The morality of self-restraint, with its emphasis on self-denial and self-abnegation, served Americans in a variety of ways. Like all moral systems it provided a sense of identity to those who held it, and that was no minor consideration in an increasingly pluralistic society. Unfortunately, it also gave the people who held it a sense of superiority over those unable to live in accordance with its principles. Its celebration by the churches and its identification with advancing civilization gave self-restraint an importance that transcended the life of the individual. Self-restraint was also viewed as the path to economic advancement, both for the striving farmers, artisans, and shopkeepers of the old, small-scale, agricultural-industrial-commercial economy and for the new, bureaucratized middle class of the emerging industrial regime. And, in a republic that prized its openness and that celebrated the absence of government control, self-restraint was an important civic virtue.

The morality of self-restraint carried many benefits, to the minds of the Victorians, but it was extremely difficult to inculcate. In the words of one historian, the morality of self-restraint was an "heroic attempt to coerce a recalcitrant and hostile actuality." [8] It was not simply that ethnic, religious, or racial groups out of the mainstream often rejected some aspects of it, but that individuals within the mainstream had such difficulty living by it. The Victorians had such faith in individuals that they thought people could overcome human nature itself. Sometimes they could, but it was always a struggle.

Most of the institutions in Victorian society enlisted on the side of those struggling to restrain themselves. The family and the church at once depended on and attempted to further self-restraint. The public school advanced it in didactic exercises. Respectable public opinion enforced it in neighborhoods and communities. Even benevolent and fraternal organizations urged their members to live by it. [9]

While people often seemed able to govern their private lives — their relationships with family, friends, lodge brothers, neighbors, and so forth — in general accordance with the morality of self-restraint, their public behavior normally fell short of this ideal. Practices in political and economic life did not approach this standard, and few serious men of affairs believed a congruence between the moral ideal and the public reality to be possible. Robert Wiebe notes that many in the late nineteenth century "preached a segmented morality that divided a man's life into compartments and judged each part by a separate standard. A gracious warmth in the living room, decent manners in the street, pious thoughts on Sunday, a formal honesty in dealing with acquaintances, and animal cunning before the rest of the world all passed at the bar of justice." [10] For Frederic C. Howe, the existence of this double standard showed the hypocrisy of the Victorians. To others, the existence of two spheres underscored the fragility of the institutions that upheld the morality of self-restraint.

The threat from the public sphere did not turn private institutions inward, for they had a public role. The purpose of those institutions that upheld the morality of self-restraint was to create "a person who would no longer need reminding of his duties, who would have internalized a powerful sense of obligation and could then safely be left to his own volitions." [11] Individuals of this sort would keep the world safe for families, churches, and communities, but they would also extend progressively the values of self-restraint into the public sphere. Early in 1890, the Congregational minister George Hubbard defined this conception of social change in the *New Englander*:

> From within outward is the invariable law of moral growth. Successful reform, like charity, begins at home. We may not begin the work of change and of purification at long range and gradually diminish our radius of operation till we reach self last of all. We must rather think of self first. We must exemplify a reform in our own lives, before we require our neighbors to practice it.[12]

This individual reform promised to be the means of continuing human progress, and to the Victorians, as one scholar has noted, "progress did not merely describe human history and predict its future; it functioned as a central moral value." [13] As they viewed their century, the Victorians could see progress toward higher levels of civilization on every hand. Material development, scientific advancement, and physical expansion were most obvious, but Victorians also noted the spread of political liberty and democracy and the abolition of slavery as important signs of progress. Even war, that most stubborn survival of barbarism, seemed to be fading before the inexorable march of civilization. Increasingly, optimists claimed to see important changes in human instincts. In an article in the *Forum* in 1890, Frances Power Cobbe, an Englishwoman who had devoted herself to the characteristically Victorian reform of ending cruelty to animals, foresaw increasing civilization in even the most private areas of life. She argued that the desire for "food has passed through many stages of progressive refinement till its grossness has well-nigh evaporated" and that "sexual love has undergone a still more celestial change, and has been transmuted, in the higher races, till it is often less an animal passion than the most exalted and delicate of sentiments." To Cobbe, further progress to even higher civilization, based on the increasingly refined individual, was inevitable:

> Above this stage of true human civilization [in which man exhibits prudence, forethought, and self-restraint] which has been . . . attained, there is yet [another] which is reached when a man's pleasures, lofty and refined as they may be, are subordinated to his sense of duty, his passion for justice and truth, his enthusiasm for humanity. The man who is willing to sacrifice, not only his present but his future, not only his lower pleasures but his highest enjoyments, to hasten the coming of the Kingdom of God, the reign of righteousness, has reached the summit of true civilization.[14]

So the Victorian age placed its burdens and its hopes on the individual. The ideal individual determined his future, improved himself, relied on himself, and restrained himself. The central tension in this construct was between self-determination, the narrow form of individualism that seemed to encourage selfishness, and self-restraint, the socially oriented form of individualism that stressed selflessness. In the minds of Victorians, this tension was more creative than destructive. Self-restraint was made both possible and virtuous by the fact that self-determination existed. And self-determination was tamed, civilized, and bent to admirable purposes by self-restraint.

Products of this value system, progressives often remarked on the tension between self-determination and self-restraint, between the self and society, between selfishness and altruism. And sometimes they explained their lives in terms of movement from one set of values to a totally different one. Graham Taylor, Social Gospel clergyman and early social worker, explained his life in terms of change and development from one value system to another:

> [Taylor saw himself changing] from an individualistic educational and religious training to a more altruistic point of view, . . . from a somewhat self-conscious intellectual and spiritual development to a more social, civic, and community consciousness, . . . from a sheltered childhood in the best home that parental love and

ability could provide to manhood's struggles for a more neigh-
borly community and a more homelike world, where each of all
the children of men may share more of the fatherhood of God
and the brotherhood of man.[15]

Yet the ideals of which Taylor wrote were less akin to polar opposites
than they were to horses working in tandem. They were not always
comfortable together, and sometimes one pulled against the other, but
neither was worth much alone. One balanced the other, and together
they were supposed to pull Victorian America down the path of progress.

II

The threat to Victorian individualism lay less in its logical inconsis-
tencies or its inner tensions than in its declining ability to provide a
satisfactory description of reality to Americans in the late nineteenth
century. The instances in human history when a close correspondence
between ideals and reality has existed have been few and fleeting. But
value systems come in crisis when the gap between the ideal and the
real widens dramatically. And in America in the late nineteenth century, industrial developments seemed to presage a world in which the
individual was unable to shape himself and unwilling to restrain himself. Modern America was rendering individualism increasingly chimerical, more and more like the Kentucky hills of Tennessee.

The outlines of late-nineteenth-century social and economic developments and the impacts of these on the reality of self-determination
have been delineated by so many historians that a brief sketch of them
should suffice to refresh the reader's memory. It is clear, first, that with
the development of a national transportation network, interregional,
national, and international markets, regional economic specialization,
the factory system of production, and growing urban-industrial centers, people became more obviously interdependent than they had been
before. Even those who had prided themselves on their independence
discovered that they needed others. Farmers, increasingly commercial
in this period, found their celebrated independence circumscribed by
their growing dependence on railroads, elevators, millers, manufac-

turers, and consumers here and abroad. For others, the fiction of independence was even more difficult to maintain. City dwellers, for example, depended on others to provide virtually every good or service they consumed, and if, like most, they worked for others, they did not even control the means through which they consumed what they needed.

Of course, Americans had always been interdependent, and the image of the individualistic, frontiersman-type is essentially a Hollywood fantasy that appeals mainly to twelve-year-olds, of whatever age. But a major difference between this emerging interdependence and that which existed before was the inequality of so many of the new relationships. The individual farmer and the village miller had needed one another, and the Dakota farmer needed the Minneapolis miller who replaced the villager. But the Minneapolis miller needed farmers as a group—not any particular farmer—and that fact placed the individual farmer in a position of increasing inequality and relative dependency. Likewise, the industrial worker and the industrialist needed one another, as the journeyman and the artisan in pre-industrial shops needed one another. But, particularly if they lacked skills, individual workers found themselves more and more in a position of powerless dependency as the factory system grew.

A related threat to individual self-determination, though a more subtle one, came from the increasingly organized nature of American life. Many of the people who organized themselves into groups in the late nineteenth century were responding to the unequal interdependency of the age. As individuals became less equal to those on whom they depended, they often compensated for their relative weakness by banding together with others facing the same problem. Hence, individual shippers joined groups to compensate for their inequality relative to railroads. Farmers, suffering from the depradations of middlemen, railroads, and banks, formed organizations to advance their interests. And workers found in unions a means of reversing the trend toward inequality and asserting some control over their working conditions, work places, and working lives.

Workers, farmers, shippers, and others organized to compensate for a loss of power and control, while capitalists organized to increase their power and control. Investors formed corporations, businessmen formed pools and trusts, and industrialists formed intricate corporate bureaucracies to increase their power and thereby render the economic environment more predictable and controllable. At the same time, other Americans formed organizations—fraternal, patriotic, or professional—that imparted a sense of identity and a feeling of community in an increasingly impersonal urban-industrial society.

Robert Wiebe has explained the formation of multi-functional groups during the late nineteenth century as a rational and comprehensible part of a "search for order" in which Americans attempted to compensate for their declining autonomy and independence.[16] But for many Americans at the time, the organizational impulse was an ominous development, especially in the case of economic interest groups. Groups may have been created in response to a loss of a sense of individual self-determination, but when individuals submerged themselves in groups and acquiesced in joint decisions, avoiding personal responsibility, a newer and more vivid threat to self-determination was exposed. Groups sometimes made claims on the individual that threatened his loyalty to traditional institutions or violated his civic responsibilities. Moreover, groups, if perhaps no more selfish in quality than individuals, multiplied the selfishness of their members, raising that troubling aspect of human nature to a new and more serious level. And self-interested organizations, when they conflicted with one another as they so often did, threatened social harmony in an America that prized it highly.

Self-reliance and self-improvement also became less descriptive of reality as economic and social change diminished the scope of self-determination. People still enjoyed economic opportunities, certainly, and the industrial economy generated many new white-collar jobs and an expanding bounty of material things for socially mobile people to enjoy. But even a qualified economic independence became more elusive for the average person. Nothing is sure in life, but in 1840 a young man could reasonably anticipate a future as a self-employed farmer, artisan, or shopkeeper. In 1890, a young man could reasonably anticipate a future of dependency in the corporate order. His material life might well be richer than that of his predecessor, but a gilded cage is still a cage. Moreover, the requirement that the individual rely on himself, predicated on the faith that he controlled his fate, became unjust and cruel when his ability to shape his life declined.

The bitter irony that underlay the deterioration of the reality of individualism was that it destroyed itself. As H. Wayne Morgan has noted, "the individualistic ethic that united Americans ironically seemed to create impersonal economic power."[17] The men who dominated the new industrial system celebrated the self-justifying values of self-determination, self-reliance, and self-improvement, even while they created industrial institutions and corporate structures that circumscribed the independence of others. That the national businessmen were the most accomplished practitioners of individual self-determination in their age was seldom doubted, and that fact disarmed, confused, and demoralized those who remained devoted to that ideal but who were disillusioned by some of its products.

Doubts about the vitality of individualism were paralleled by questions regarding the inevitability of the social progress that individual volition was supposed to bring. By the last quarter of the nineteenth century there were those who questioned whether progress was occurring in every area of life. Surely the nation was larger and richer than ever before, and material and scientific progress was continuing and even, most agreed, accelerating, but some stubborn facts simply could not be submerged in the sea of optimism. In 1879 Henry George asked in his pointedly titled *Progress and Poverty* why it was that economic progress seemed to be paralleled by an increase in poverty.[18] The question was more important than the answer, because it challenged thoughtful and sensitive Americans for more than a generation. Others focused on the evils of the factory system, the antisocial behavior of businessmen, or the conflict between capital and labor. Still others complained of low standards of civic behavior and seemingly pervasive corruption in government.

Many reasons were suggested for the ambiguous course of modern progress, and most of them revolved around individual morality. Personal behavior in the private and public spheres of life seemed increasingly to diverge. The Victorians had always recognized that, in practice, different standards applied to public and private behavior. But the morality of self-restraint, which Victorians believed shaped behavior in private life, was supposed slowly to infuse public behavior as well. Instead of being elevated, though, standards of public behavior seemed to be deteriorating. The distressing fact, as James B. Gilbert notes, was that "traditional morality, even to its defenders, appeared to hold less sway over the loyalties of modern man." [19] Industrialism had brought in its train not moral improvement, but, in Theodore Roosevelt's phrase, "a riot of individualistic materialism." [20] Men were obsessed with getting and holding wealth, property, and things, and they were not particular about how they got them. Instead of tailoring their activities to fit the morality of self-restraint, men took only the letter of the law—the statute law, the law of classical economics, or the Darwinian law of natural selection—as the guide to their behavior. Leading the way were the businessmen who dominated industrial society. Edward Chase Kirkland once pointed out that "John D. Rockefeller demonstrated the operational advantages of separating morality and business." [21] Rockefeller was not the first to make this separation, but he was one of the most successful and most emulated entrepreneurs to do so.

The core of the morality of self-restraint, "individual responsibility and self-control," seemed in decline throughout public life, as were the shame, remorse, and guilt men had once felt for misbehavior. [22] Much of the problem lay in the decline of the local community. The development of the national market brought national industry, and it also brought changes in economic behavior. When customers were unknown masses hundreds of miles away they might be treated differently than when they were friends and neighbors. And an employer's treatment of his workers might change when they were part of a faceless horde rather than trusted colleagues. As the community grew and became anonymous, as the "impersonal and tenuous ties of the market place" replaced the old "small-town solidarity," the good opinion of one's neighbors was no longer an important determinant of one's behavior. [23] At the same time, one's peers became important arbiters of behavior, and their standards might diverge sharply from those of the community. Certainly, this should be clear enough to us today. We recognize that people who violate community standards—by using drugs, for example—often do so in order to gain the approval of a narrow peer group whose acceptance they cherish. Anonymity and the development of peer groups apart from the community, holding values different from those of the community, combined to contribute to a moral deterioration in economic behavior in the late nineteenth century.

The erosion of self-restraint was as ironic as was the diminishing reality of self-determination. The men who dominated the economy — and who thus did so much directly and indirectly to cripple self-restraint — were their society's most accomplished exemplars of many of the specific components of that value. They were man who had overcome themselves, mastering their impulses to be lazy, to spend, to waste, to shirk duty. Those aspects of the morality of self-restraint that were most applicable to economic success — hard work, thrift, sobriety, a serious view of life — were strongly represented among the new lords of the American economy. Unfortunately, most were not as successful when it came to restraining their avarice, ambition, aggression, materialism, or gluttony. Moreover, the ability of some people to benefit from restrained behavior might prevent others from doing so. This phenomenon can be seen with particular clarity in the case of the work ethic. As Daniel T. Rodgers notes in *The Work Ethic in Industrial America, 1850–1920*, the development of the factory system represented the strength and power of the work ethic: "The work ethic helped impel the restless personal energies of the Northern manufacturers, blessed their enterprises with a sense of mission, and gave them a transcendent sanction." [24] And yet, for the people who worked in the factories, machine-tending stripped work of its satisfactions and sapped its moral content, and the growth of large-scale industry diminished the extent to which practice of the work ethic would lead in the future to economic independence.

The fact that the men who dominated the economy personified so many admirable values disarmed their potential critics. Big businessmen showed that self-determination, self-reliance, self-improvement, and self-restraint worked, even while their actions weakened these values and diminished their reality for others. The men and women of the late nineteenth century were confused. Material progress was occurring, but social and moral progress were much less clear. Standards of private behavior seemed high, conforming to the morality of self-restraint, but in public the individual appeared to be acting in a more self-indulgent manner. This disturbed thoughtful Victorians, who wanted to reduce the divergence between private and public standards, and it led some of them to fret that, instead of private standards infusing public life, public standards—or lack of standards—might begin to infuse private life.

Americans were particularly concerned that the selfish materialism of public life would invade the home. To Victorians, the family was the first and most important product of human progress, and it was the key institution in the effort to civilize a barbarous world. In the home, the morality of self-restraint was supposed to reign and to be implanted in the children, who would gradually civilize the world by practicing elevated moral standards.

The middle-class home, as it was evolving in the nineteenth century, seemed especially well suited to playing this civilizing role. Urbanization, commercialization, and industrialization brought changes in family function, family role, and sex roles of family members, especially in the middle class. Work came to be separated increasingly from the home, making it less of an economic institution. The diminished economic function of the home was paralleled by declining family size. The average couple had fewer children, had them over a shorter time span, and deferred them from work for longer periods.[25]

These changes had an especially important impact on women. The removal of adult males from the home for most of the day and the home's diminished economic functions turned it increasingly into a social institution over which women exercised power. The home came to be seen as the province of women and the core of female life in a civilized society. Ideally, women were to turn homes into safe harbors of care and affection to which men could retire after their daily struggle in the cruel seas of public life. Women were also to use homes as schools for inculcating the morality of self-restraint in children. As successive generations of children ventured into the world, they would tame and civilize it, extending the influence of the home beyond its walls.

The effect of the ideal of domesticity on women is a matter of considerable debate among historians.[26] Unquestionably, stress on the role of the female in the home limited women's potential in the public arena. At the same time, it gave women avenues for more or less exclusive action that had not existed previously. The Victorians did not question the ideal of domesticity. To them, it elevated women and gave them primary responsibility for functions to which they were especially suited. While men were thought to excel at self-determination, women were commonly believed to exhibit superior powers of self-restraint. To Victorians, control of the home by women had a tremendous reformatory potential, for it promised to civilize the world.

But the deterioration of self-restraint in the public sphere that the late nineteenth century witnessed raised the spectre of the opposite possibility—that the home would be barbarized when standards of public behavior infused it. The increasing separation of the home from the world had carried the promise of its emergence as an independent, reformatory institution, but that same separation rendered it more vulnerable to aggression from without. Portents of the destruction of the home by the values of public life were there for those who wanted to see them.

Life in the Victorian home was supposed to be based on the same morality of self-restraint that the home was expected to inculcate. As one historian has noted, husbands and wives anticipated that "their partners would make certain sacrifices, fulfill specific obligations, and conform to a pattern of behavior appropriate for maintaining a tranquil home." [27] When these expectations were not met, when men failed to support their families, or showed brutality toward them, or gave full rein to self-indulgent passions such as drinking or lust, families broke down and divorce or, more often, desertion sometimes resulted. Family disintegration indicated to Victorians that the selfish standards of public life were threatening to consume the selfless standards on which the family was based.

One component of individual self-indulgence that threatened the home was materialism. Social commentators recognized the growing "commercialization of the home," but they seemed unable to stop it. [28] As the home came to be suffused with material values, as it became an arena for the collection of things, as it filled with the material gadgetry of modern industrialism, its role as an institution embodying non-economic, spiritual values was diminished.

American business, then as now the most revolutionary force in society, encouraged the transformation of the home into a materialistic institution. For example, the life insurance industry, which Viviana Zelizer studies in *Morals and Markets*, shifted the basis of its appeal to customers after the 1870's from an emphasis on the duty men owed to their loved ones to an emphasis on the material benefits that insurance would convey. "As the selfish economic interests of the premium payers were acknowledged and even encouraged," Zelizer notes, "earlier appeals to their altruism were disregarded as unrealistic."[29]

Americans were ambivalent about national developments in the late nineteenth century. Material progress was everywhere evident, and those most closely identified with it exemplified the multi-faceted individualism America cherished. And yet material progress was paralleled by the appearance of social and economic ills, by the erosion of American values, and by the rise of an aggressive materialism and an increasingly selfish individualism. Confused and disturbed, many Americans turned to the church for guidance, assurance, and explanation.

III

The churches responded to the challenges of the late nineteenth century. Few churchmen questioned the appropriateness of addressing problems that were, superficially at least, social or economic in nature. To the churches, most social and economic problems were basically moral, and it was the special responsibility of Christians to address them.

Religion—especially Protestantism—carried forth the values of Victorian culture and was central to Victorian society. The churches spoke directly to their members but they indirectly addressed the nation as a whole, touching most Americans in the process. Ministers were respected members of communities with political power and social influence. Their sermons were respectfully reprinted by newspapers on Monday mornings, and their opinions were solicited regarding virtually every issue. The mainline Protestant denominations—the Presbyterians, Congregationalists, Baptists, and Methodists, in particular—saw themselves virtually as state churches, identified with the nation and its ideals and especially qualified to guide and instruct the people and their secular leaders in the maintenance of those ideals. At a time when national media and national organizations were developing but were still primitive, the churches served as truly national institutions. This function was facilitated by the fact that the churches spoke a common language, among themselves and with the citizenry as well. No one could deny that churches and their parishioners were divided among themselves by social class, region, or theological and doctrinal points, but they shared a broad ethical foundation and a collection of sacred literature. And they spoke to an out-of-church citizenry that was more familiar with the ethics, myths, traditions, and literature of Christianity than is the unchurched population today.

One student of the clerical response to industrializing America has characterized it as reflecting "an aggressive, dynamic form of Christianity that set out confidently to confront American life at every level, to permeate, evangelize, and Christianize it."[30] This characterization captures the confidence with which the churches attacked the problems of late-nineteenth-century America, but we can also see a measure of defensiveness in that enterprise. Part of this defensiveness derived from the fact that the churches were attempting to maintain positions of social leadership against the challenges of wealth and science, but there was another factor at work here as well. The churches, like the family, were supposed to spread their principles to the larger society. But, again like the family, the church itself was threatened by the intensifying forces of selfish individualism and materialism in society. The church faced a dual challenge. It had to maintain itself and its principles, and it was obligated to extend those principles to society. In theory, the first was dependent on the second, but in practice it often became necessary to emphasize one or the other.

Some of the internal problems of the churches were relatively new. Science, natural and social, threatened religious explanations of the nature and development of man. Darwinism presented the challenge that we first think of, in part because the controversy it spawned between science and religion is still with us. In *The Origin of the Species* (1859) and in his later works, the most important of which was *The*

Descent of Man (1871), English scientist Charles Darwin argued that animal species, including man, had evolved into their modern forms through a process of natural selection. By the 1880's Darwinian theory had been embraced by most natural scientists in America, as well as by many in the developing fields of social science. Darwinism disturbed Christians initially because it seemed to make the creation of man dependent on the blind forces of natural selection rather than upon God's actions. Moreover, when applied to human behavior Darwinism implied that actions were neither moral nor immoral, but simply appropriate or inappropriate responses to a particular environment. It seemed to indicate, further, that true self-determination did not exist. Applied to society by enthusiasts here and in England, Darwin's theories served to excuse the vicious individualism that already alarmed the churches and others committed to self-restraint.

More subtle, but also troubling to thinking ministers and laypeople, was the threat of social science, in the forms of historical criticism of the Bible and the comparative study of religions. The very fact that scholars would look at Christianity and its sacred literature as fit subjects for scientific inquiry carried ominous implications for the social consensus regarding the nature of the sacred. And, of course, when scholars questioned portions of the Bible or emphasized similarities between Christianity and other religious systems, the churches often felt threatened.

The combination of natural and social sciences corroded belief. The former represented a new source of authority; the latter raised doubts about the old. "In 1850, the intellectual ground of belief in God had seemed like bedrock," James Turner has noted; "by 1870, it felt more like gelatin." Together, the new challenges to religious authority created what Paul Carter has called "the spiritual crisis of the Gilded Age."[31]

The churches all grappled with the social and spiritual problems of the age, but the denominational complexity of American Protestantism decreed that they would do so in different ways. The churches most faithful to the Calvinist tradition provided the most unbending resistance to the challenges of science. They also tended to emphasize that social regeneration depended on individual salvation. More liberal clergymen, such as Lyman Abbott and Washington Gladden, looked to accommodate challengers and stressed social action. But in practice social action among Protestants might mean anything from welfare work with the poor to support for such social control measures as prohibition and the required reading of the King James version of the Bible in the schools.

Differences among denominations, significant as they were, should not obscure for us the fact that most churchgoers wanted their churches to address the problems of society or the fact that most ministers believed that to be an appropriate function. The two religious leaders who, if popularity is an indication, dealt with the troubling questions of late-nineteenth-century life most successfully before 1890 were Henry Ward Beecher and Dwight L. Moody.

Henry Ward Beecher was the foremost proponent of liberal Protestantism in the late nineteenth century.[32] The theological principles that he propounded for a generation from his Brooklyn pulpit reflected eclecticism, optimism, and an individualism that appealed strongly to troubled Protestants in the Victorian age. Like most successful leaders, he told his followers what they wanted to hear. He assured people worried about social divisions, economic change, and the direction of the country that all was well, that progress was both good and inevitable, that perfection could be achieved, and that the United States was at the cutting edge of human advancement. Beecher told those concerned about self-determination that people controlled their own fates, both in this world and in the next, and he assured them that self-improvement and self-reliance remained valid concepts. He also urged the Victorians not to forget the importance of self-restraint, noting that they must "humanize the nascent industrial-capitalist order by infusing it with social responsibility, strict personal morality, and high cultural standards."[33] People, Beecher stressed, had duties to others in society, particularly to those less fortunate.

Beecher set the pattern for liberal Protestantism by emphasizing similarities rather than differences among denominations, by minimizing the conflict between religion and the social and biological sciences through his emphasis on faith as a sufficient justification for religious belief, and by painting God in friendly and benevolent hues. Lyman Abbott, who bridged the gap between Beecher's Victorian Christianity and the Social Gospel of the early twentieth century, emphasized the importance to himself of Beecher's view of God:

> When I came to Brooklyn in the spring of 1854, my Christian theology was something like this: I regarded God as the Moral Governor of the Universe, the Bible as a Book of Laws, Jesus Christ as the giver of a law more spiritual and more difficult to obey than the laws of Moses. Sin was disobedience to those laws, redemption was remission of deserved penalty. Under Mr. Beecher's ministry I came to regard God as a Father, whose character and attitude toward me was interpreted by my own father; the law, whether the Ten Commandments or the Sermon on the Mount, as an interpretation to me of God's ideals for his children; Jesus Christ as the supreme manifestation of the Father; and redemption as a new and divine life of faith, hope, and love which he inspires in all who desire to receive it.[34]

Beecher's theology is not above reproach. It skirted many of the theological and social problems of the age. It is even possible to see in it hints of the kind of happy-face, have-a-nice-day religion, void of intellectual content, that sometimes passes as Protestantism today. But it did provide hope, assurance, and moral guidance to many members of a troubled generation. Moreover, as Paul Carter notes, for people like Abbott, raised in Calvinist orthodoxy, "the 'gospel of love' . . . was about the most relevant and liberating message they could have heard. Only one step beyond . . . was . . . the Social Gospel in the next generation, condemning the old orthodoxy not only for its theological inhumanity but also for its social regressiveness."[35]

Dwight L. Moody, the leading revivalist of his generation, came to the ministry after an early career in business and lacked formal theological training.[36] His message, like Beecher's, was individualistic, though he was more faithful than Beecher to orthodox Calvinism. Moody emphasized the ability of people to assure their own salvation, and he stressed the importance of individual self-restraint of "passions which might be corrupted by alcohol, sexual impulses, or lust for money, fame, and power."[37] Impatient with theological disputes and doctrinal nit-picking, and poorly versed in the fine points of both,

Moody urged the churches to cooperate in the great work of evangelizing the nation. And, unlike some revivalists past and present, he stressed God's love for humanity rather than attempting to make people fear God.

Moody's message, like Beecher's, has been criticized. Even his rather sympathetic biographer has condemned "the glaring inadequacies of an individualistic social ethic in an age of consolidation and growing interdependence." [38] But it was Moody's individualism that made him popular and relevant in the Victorian age. Moody saw individual purification as the means to community purification. As individuals became regenerate, as they restrained their dangerous passions and proclivities, and as their hearts were purified, they would reform the economic, social, and political systems through their contact with others in the world. [39] Moody displayed an intuitive grasp of popular notions of individualism, individual responsibility, and the relationship between the individual and society. Moreover, though Moody lacked a sophisticated understanding of the modern age, he did inspire people to attempt to come to grips with its problems. No less a Social Gospel figure than Shailer Mathews believed that the roots of socially conscious Christianity in modern America lay in Moody's evangelism. [40]

Beecher and Moody both ministered to the urban population, and their careers reflected the growing concern of Protestants with the nature and future of urban America. The problem faced by urban Protestants was two-fold. On one side it was an institutional problem. Protestantism simply was not thriving in the late-nineteenth-century city. Part of the reason was immigration. The relatively large number of Catholics and Jews in the city reduced the numbers on which Protestant churches could draw. But even urban Protestants seemed to show much less interest in attending and supporting churches than did their rural co-religionists. Working-class Protestants were particularly uninterested in attending church. The churches attacked this problem on a broad front, through such devices as missionary work, the Salvation Army, the Young Men's Christian Association, urban revivals, and the expansion of community-service activities. Despite these varied efforts, it is difficult to disagree with Martin Marty's conclusion that "Protestantism did not come up with adequate or satisfactory new forms for ministry to the cities." [41]

A couple of facts help to place this failure in perspective. First, at the very least, the churches did minister to the needs of the middle class in the cities, consoling and reassuring it and holding before it the values of self-determination and self-restraint, helping it adjust to a strange and frightening environment. Second, the urban church could never recreate the social dimension of the rural church simply because it had so many competitors for popular time and interest. All voluntary institutions depend in part for support on those who simply want something to do. By providing a variety of leisure-time activities, the city destroyed the monopoly that churches in rural society continued to have on social recreation and enjoyment. The church also suffered from the declining sense of community. The increasing numbers of Americans who felt a loss of autonomy and community during the late nineteenth century responded in one of two ways. Most often they formed new groups, based on some economic or social identification, that promised to recreate a sense of community and a feeling of efficacy. But sometimes their feeling of powerlessness and their lack of a sense of community resulted in a pathological alienation from all institutions and forms of community. Established institutions, of which the church was the most prominent, suffered from both phenomena.

The second challenge the city presented was to Protestant values. The city of the late nineteenth century seemed to represent everything that Victorian Protestants stood against. It mocked the notion of self-determination; it was the scene of social division and disharmony, the place where social irresponsibility was most pronounced, the center of selfish individualism, self-indulgence, corruption, vice, cruelty, and brutality. The city exemplified all of those contradictory developments that vexed the Victorians. Material progress, technical advancement, and the highest refinements of civilization existed side by side with social regression, moral deterioration, and the growing spectre of barbarism. The churches faced the city with some confusion. The temptation was always there to hunker down, to turn inward, to insulate the institution and its members from the encroaching world, and the churches occasionally surrendered to it. On the other hand, Christians were responsible for themselves and for others as well, and flaws in the world called for correction, not for withdrawal. Once again, the

Victorian duality appeared as Protestants shifted their emphasis between the private and public spheres of life.

Many of the Protestants who felt a strong sense of social responsibility turned to charity work, an area in which the church had always been vitally interested. Charity developments in American cities in the late nineteenth century reflected two contradictory tendencies of the age. As Nathan Huggins notes in his book about Boston charities in the late nineteenth century, *Protestants Against Poverty*, the developing "national charity organization movement combined the moralistic charity of the past and the scientific spirit of the time."[42] The latter tendency was embodied in the new, centralized bureaucracies, usually called charity organization societies, that emerged in most major cities in the last quarter of the nineteenth century. These societies centralized and coordinated the efforts of churches, charities, and philanthropic agencies that had previously operated more or less independently of one another.

Organized charity promised several advantages over the unorganized variety. Recipients could be screened by professional charity workers and the undeserving could be weeded out, problems could be identified and attacked in a coordinated fashion, and waste and duplication could be eliminated. To some extent, the development of charity organization societies reflected the increasing problem of dependency in an urban-industrial society in which the production of poverty and despair kept pace with the production of material goods. But the charity organization movement also reflected the trend of the time—seen with particular clarity in business—toward organized and efficient institutions operated scientifically by professional bureaucrats.[43]

In their structure and in their emphasis on system, bureaucracy, and efficiency, the charity organization societies pointed to the future, but their assumptions were rooted in the past. They assumed that poverty resulted from the shortcomings of individuals and that individuals could pull themselves out of poverty if they were aided by other individuals who were motivated by a sense of social responsibility. The charity organizations assumed that people could determine their fates, but in order to do so they had to restrain their tendencies toward individualistic self-indulgence. Waste, laziness, undependability, intemperance — these were the causes of poverty. Consequently, poverty would be overcome when the poor learned self-restraint, when the habits of thrift, hard work, dependability, integrity, and sobriety replaced the self-indulgence into which they had fallen.

Charity workers thought their clients were weak, but they did not believe that the poor were entirely to blame for their situation. To the minds of charity workers, "the urban poor had degenerated morally because the circumstances of city life had cut them off from the elevating influence of their moral betters." [44] In other words, the sense of community concern and the power of public opinion that had once supported the morality of self-restraint was no longer operative in the growing cities.

As a substitute for the friends and neighbors who had once helped maintain self-restraint in the weak, the charity organization societies created the "friendly visitor." The friendly visitor idea was developed by Octavia Hill, a London charity reformer who was widely admired in America, and by 1890 most of the charity organization societies had adopted it. The friendly visitor was a middle-class volunteer who would go periodically into the home of a family receiving charitable aid and provide a combination of friendly advice and pseudo-parental direction. Taking the advice and direction of this kind-hearted individual, the poor would presumably correct their deficiencies of character and rise from their self-imposed poverty.

The shortcomings of the system were serious. The friendly visitors often showed a smug self-satisfaction as they attempted to induce the poor to adopt middle-class values. And the poor, who needed the charity, sometimes responded with an hypocrisy that eroded whatever pride they had. But the system did reflect a recognition that the collapse of the sense of community was a serious urban problem and that environmental factors impacted on some aspects of urban poverty. It also provided a means for many of those with a sense of their duties to their fellows to exercise social responsibility.

Another effect of friendly visiting was to give middle-class reformers periodic contact with the poor, and in this interaction some of them developed new ideas about the causes of poverty. A few came to believe not only that poverty persisted because of urban environmental factors but that these conditions helped cause it in the first place. Those who embraced this insight joined other urban reformers who believed that environments could be created in cities that would facilitate the fashioning of strong families and an enhanced sense of community.[45]

By 1890 those who were concerned about the poor in the cities were sometimes mixing environmental explanations for poverty with traditional condemnations of failures of individual character. In a parallel development, some were viewing the poor in the context of the economic structure and mechanism of the city—and even the nation—as a whole, seeing poverty as a problem that was at least partially social in origin rather than wholly individual. But it remained the case in 1890 that the primary thrust of charity thought was toward individualism—poverty was an individual problem resulting from individual moral failings, and its cure lay in individual regeneration with the help of concerned individuals.

This view of poverty in the late nineteenth century was consistent with the popular assumptions of mainline American Protestants regarding self-determination, self-reliance, self-improvement, and self-restraint. Not surprisingly, American Protestants viewed wealth from the same perspective.

Historians have traditionally viewed the relationship between the Protestant churches and the wealthy in the Victorian age in an unsympathetic manner. For example, Eric Goldman assured the readers of his *Rendezvous with Destiny* that "America of the late nineteenth century, whether reformist or standpat, was a religious America, and the key link in the conservative chain of ideas was the religious sanction for the status quo." And Sidney Fine went so far as to assert that "the Protestant minister, like the businessman, gave his support to laissez faire and the *status quo*. He provided religious sanction for the businessman's views." [46]

There is much to recommend theses of this sort. Successful businessmen were often viewed by the churches as exemplars of the complex values of individualism. They had shaped themselves in honorable callings. They had improved themselves in the accepted way, by restraining their impulses. The best of them had succeeded because they triumphed over their own shortcomings, not because they mistreated others. As they succeeded they benefitted the community, providing jobs, products, and admirable role models for others to follow. There was no necessary contradiction between the common canons of Victorian Protestantism and capitalism, in theory at least, particularly when the latter was of the pre-modern, community-centered, friends-and-neighbors variety.

Cords of interest also bound the churches to the business community. In no state had churches received direct public contributions since the early nineteenth century. The loss of state support had imparted a higher level of vitality to many churches, but it had also forced them to rely upon private financial support. Many churches became increasingly dependent on the wealthy for financial backing. Even if churches had wished to criticize the business community as such, their growing dependence would probably have restrained them. It takes great courage for people to bite the hand that feeds them, particularly when they are responsible for others who also are fed.

Ironically, the more activities of a charitable or philanthropic nature in which the churches came to be involved—activities necessitated by the cruelties and dislocations of industrial capitalism—the more dependent they became on the industrial capitalists themselves.[47] The churches could not escape the pattern of dependency that spread throughout society as industrialism advanced. Nor could they escape the materialism and commercialism of the age. This does not mean that the churches immersed themselves in the profane world of commerce. But it was true that churches created hugely expensive edifices, that congregations held stocks and bonds and owned slum properties as parts of their endowments, and that ministers assured the faithful that it was moral to buy life insurance, among other products. These were not major moral failures, but they indicate that the churches were vulnerable to the corruptions of the world.

When the churches criticized the wealthy, they focused on the failings of businessmen as individuals. Businessmen who derived their wealth from human weakness—liquor dealers, for example—were usually condemned in the mainline churches. So too were businessmen in more acceptable pursuits when they behaved immorally. The problem was that in the modern economy it was increasingly difficult to connect social effects with individual causes in a clear manner. That was not the only failing of the individualistic point of view. It also prevented the churches—and the Victorian society of which they were such an important part—from analyzing the economic system in which individuals operated from a critical perspective.

In another sense, though, individualism could become a powerful force for social change, because an important component of the morality of self-restraint was individual responsibility. As the unattractive aspects of industrial capitalism became increasingly apparent and serious, Protestant concerns about individual selfishness became more prominent. In *The Public Image of Big Business in America*, Louis Galambos points out that, in the years between 1879 and 1892, Protestant ministers "balanced . . . an appreciation of . . . [economic] accomplishments . . . [with] a growing concern about corporate irresponsibility. Achievement, like sin, was ultimately a personal matter, and the Protestant minister had a deep concern for the responsibilities of man to man, or man to country, and of man to God." [48]

The responsibilities the wealthy owed to others were expressed in the ancient and compelling idea of stewardship. In theory, men of wealth had been given what they possessed by God, and he in turn expected them to be his stewards, to use their wealth wisely for the benefit of others. This idea had a venerable existence in the United States, and it continued to thrive in the Victorian age, despite its implicit contradiction by the notion of self-determination and its explicit contradiction by classical economics and Social Darwinism. Stewardship represented a possible solution to many of the problems of the industrial age—particularly those of poverty and the relationship between capital and labor—and one that enjoyed wide popularity. The inevitable by-product of popular veneration of the wealthy and aversion to governmental solutions for social problems was the expectation that those who dominated society would address its ills. Virtually all religious bodies—Protestant, Catholic, and Jewish—explicitly embraced stewardship. In this social and religious atmosphere, many businessmen were attracted to stewardship as well.

The most prominent business spokesman for stewardship was the steelmaker Andrew Carnegie, whose "Gospel of Wealth" appeared in the *North American Review* in 1889. Carnegie's version of stewardship was explicitly secular rather than religious, but it did not diverge in essential outline from the Christian conception of the social responsibilities of the wealthy. Carnegie contended that "the problem of our age is the proper administration of wealth, that the ties of brotherhood may still bind together the rich and poor in harmonious relationship." He believed that the individualistic, competitive, capitalist system was the regime that best produced wealth and social advancement. The problem was that it also produced class divisions and fear, envy, and hatred between the rich and the poor. The way out of this problem lay in the activity of the benevolent rich man who, after providing "moderately for the legitimate wants of those dependent upon him," would spend his wealth for public purposes, "becoming the mere trustee and agent for his poorer brethren, bringing to their service his superior wisdom, experience, and ability to administer." When this occurred, the poor would see clearly the advantages of the existing economic system, and "the reconciliation of the rich and the poor—a reign of harmony" would result.[49]

Carnegie reflected the conflicting attitudes of a generation in the throes of mammoth economic and social changes. Admiring the wealthy and the material wonders they had wrought, he worried about their misbehavior, their extravagance, and their social irresponsibility, all of which contributed to widening the gulf between rich and poor. In the common Victorian fashion, Carnegie called forth self-restraint, in the form of stewardship, to save self-determination:

> Thus is the problem of rich and poor to be solved. The laws of accumulation will be left free, the laws of distribution free. Individualism will continue, but the millionaire will be but a trustee for the poor, intrusted for a season with a great part of the increased wealth of the community, but administering it for the community far better than it could or would have done for itself.[50]

Carnegie's secular stewardship carried with it ample quantities of arrogance and elitism, an air of condescension and noblesse oblige, and a fear of the poor that stripped it of much of its moral content. But it was a popular idea with Victorians.

Carnegie was unwilling to prescribe the means through which the wealthy should exercise their stewardship. He suggested projects—such as the creation of libraries and universities—that would improve humankind, but he had too much respect for those he viewed as superior people to go beyond suggestion. Stewardship, lacking central direction or tight definition, was exercised in a variety of ways. Self-styled stewards varied from those who argued that their provision of jobs and goods to the community was stewardship enough, to those few, like Carnegie, who devoted their last years to spending their fortunes for public purposes. Contributions to churches, missionary societies, philanthropic organizations, and charitable agencies all went under the name of stewardship. So, too, did the creation of parks, libraries, playgrounds, bathhouses, and institutions of higher learning.

Sometimes activities passed as stewardship that really were not — such as the model tenement movement, a great philanthropic enterprise in a number of cities in the late nineteenth century. Housing reformers hoped to show that home environments could be created for the urban poor that were clean, healthy, and uplifting. But by 1895, when the office of the United States Commissioner of Labor undertook a study of model housing, reformers had concluded that it was not sufficient to appeal to the investor's sense of stewardship. The would-be steward of the poor had to be assured of a profit. In *The Housing of Working People* government investigator E. R. L. Gould exhaustively studied model housing for the poor in Europe and America, noting the ways in which a better environment and close supervision would help the poor to improve their characters. But he was forced to admit that the improvement of the character of the poor was not a sufficient inducement to call forth the efforts of wealthy stewards:

> Will improved housing pay? This is a question of cardinal importance, and only in case an affirmative response is forthcoming can we auger a successful issue to the housing problem. If the solution to the problem is to depend upon philanthropy alone it is safe to say that very small progress can be made. If city dwellers are to be better housed better housing must pay.[51]

Thus we see one of the major shortcomings of stewardship in practice. Appealing to the wealthy as stewards might be sufficient to induce them to build a college, fund a missionary, or support a soup kitchen. But major problems, such as working-class housing, could not be addressed through pure stewardship. Moreover, this attitude of "philanthropy and five per cent," in the phrase derisively quoted by New York reformer Jacob Riis, drained the concept of stewardship of much of its moral content.[52]

Other exercises of stewardship were also sullied by mixed motives. This was particularly true of activities undertaken by employers in behalf of workers under the inclusive label of "welfare work." Welfare work included everything from factory beautification and the provision of plant lunchrooms, on one end of the spectrum, to the creation of workers' housing and the institution of a measure of industrial democracy on the other. Employers hoped that welfare work would benefit their employees, but their own interests were never far from their minds. As one scholar notes, "company welfare was merely an inducement offered by enlightened employers who, long before the fashion of industrial psychology, realized the value of making the workers happy." [53] Before 1900, most businessmen confined their welfare work to a bit of plant improvement and perhaps to the provision of religious services for workers. A flower bed by the gate, a hotplate in the lunchroom, periodic visits from earnest fellows from the Young Men's Christian Association urging them to work hard and be sober—these were the results most workers saw from the meager stewardship in which their employers indulged. But some employers, such as George Pullman, went farther, illustrating more shortcomings of stewardship in the process.

Pullman was famous for two things. He developed comfortable sitting, sleeping, dining, and club cars for the railroads, and he created a model town, which bore his name, for his workers near Chicago.[54] Pullman had a number of ideas in mind when he created his community of model houses, with its church, library, stores, and hotel. He viewed himself as a responsible steward. His planned community would improve the lives of the workingmen and their families and elevate their characters. It would foster a sense of community and lead to cooperation between capital and labor. It would show that there was no necessary contradiction between competitive capitalism and Christian responsibility. At the same time, Pullman would profit, both because his town would produce happier, better, and more efficient workmen and because he would charge rents that guaranteed a profitable return on his investment. This stewardship on the American plan, this "philanthropy and five percent," worked well enough when times were good, but it failed when times were bad. Intent on returning a profit and paying dividends to stockholders, Pullman laid men off and cut wages while leaving rents high during the Depression of 1893. A bitter and desperate strike resulted, the ramifications of which were felt through much of the nation. After the strike was broken with the use of federal troops, Pullman withdrew himself from the community business.

"The great problem of this age is how a new system shall be established, with perfect justice to capital and to labor, recognizing the moral forces at work contemporaneously with the industrial forces," argued United States Commissioner of Labor Carroll D. Wright in 1894. "I feel so sure that this problem will be solved on the broadest business basis, through the practical application of moral principles with economic laws, that I have little anxiety for the industrial future of the country." [55] But if the Pullman Strike indicated anything, it was that "moral principles" and "economic laws" had little in common, and that they even conflicted with one another under many circumstances. The rickety bridge between capitalism and Christianity, between money and morals, that the celebrants of stewardship were striving to maintain, seemed ready to collapse.

Another unhappy lesson of the Pullman affair, for those with the courage to be instructed, was that the basic assumption of stewardship —that the steward enjoyed self-determination—was invalid. Pullman was no free agent. His actions were shaped by his view of capitalism, to be sure, but they were also determined by the demands of shareholders and the exigencies of the competitive system. How could the individual determine to serve the demands of God and function successfully in the capitalist economic environment at the same time? After Pullman, it seemed virtually impossible to do both.

Capital and labor drew other lessons from the Pullman affair. Businessmen saw in the Pullman problems evidence that welfare work did not produce quiescent workers. Other events pushed them toward the same conclusion. The relatively conservative but highly publicized experiments in employee welfare work undertaken by John Patterson at the National Cash Register Company did not prevent labor unrest. And even the radical innovations of plumbing manufacturer Nelson Olson Nelson, designed to give workers ownership of their plant, failed to produce totally tractable employees. These and other events contributed to growing employer suspicion of innovations in worker relations by the turn of the century. And workers, disliking the paternalism of some welfare programs and distrusting the motives of employers, tended increasingly to see collective bargaining as their salvation. For those interested in infusing the social and economic order with Christian love, these reactions seemed to portend an unfortunate shift toward greater selfishness on the parts of both capital and labor.

IV

By the 1890's the challenges to the values of Victorian America were becoming clear. Americans continued to cling to the old verities: individuals determined their futures, they could and should improve themselves and rely upon themselves, they should restrain their impulses. As individuals improved themselves, society would improve; material progress and moral and social progress paralleled one another. These comfortable assumptions formed the bases of the economic and political systems, of society, and of religion. But reality kept intruding. Scientific, technological, and material advances were not clearly paralleled by moral and social progress. Economic change brought with it social dislocation and conflict, dependency, and low standards of public behavior. Self-determination and self-improvement seemed less and less descriptive of reality, more and more chimerical and elusive, increasingly like the Kentucky hills of Tennessee. Self-reliance appeared less and less just, and the social cruelty that underlay it showed through. Self-restraint seemed to be weakening too, raising fears that the standards of private life would deteriorate as the standards of public life seemed to be deteriorating.

Americans turned to those they admired for explanation. Their statesmen, their heroes, their industrialists, and their ministers all assured them that their values were still valid. Progress was inevitable, based, as always, on self-determination and self-restraint. The problems that existed were transitory and could be solved by individual reform, social responsibility, and stewardship. It took a crisis to force Americans to come to grips with what had happened, to see the divergence between their values and reality, to face the challenge to individualism. The nineties provided the crisis.

TOWARD A WORLDLY CHRISTIANITY
AND A CHRISTIAN WORLD

> The thing lay on me like a monstrous burden that
> seemed more than I could bear. I believe that at that
> time in my experience I felt . . . the horrible blunder
> and stupidity of our whole industrial system that
> does not work according to any well-established plan
> of a brotherhood of men, but is driven by forces that
> revolve around some pagan rule of life called 'supply
> and demand' or a 'market' or a 'condition', rather
> than around a combined and intelligent effort of
> human beings who have a mutual interest in one
> another instead of a cunningly devised scheme to get
> something out of one another.
>
> CHARLES M. SHELDON

> Let all the poisons that lurk in the mud hatch out.
>
> ROBERT GRAVES

The crisis of individual self-determination and self-restraint reached
a climax in the 1890's. All of the poisons lurking in the mud of Victorian America, in the arresting image Robert Graves has the emperor
Claudius make, hatched out in the nineties.[1] The inability of individuals to control their lives could no longer be ignored. Self-interested
groups of capitalists, workers, and farmers tore at one another with
rising intensity, showing little regard for the good of society as a whole.
An industrial depression brought home the fact of a new and more
comprehensive dependency to millions of Americans and led them to
question whether material progress was inevitable. The consolidation

of industry accelerated, and business showed less regard than ever for workers, consumers, and investors. The corruption, poverty, and brutality of the age grew in proportion to the erosion of self-restraint, casting further doubt on the reality of moral progress. By the middle of the decade, most of the values and assumptions of Victorian America faced serious challenges. The decade proved to be one of anxiety, confusion, guilt, and self-doubt, in which men and women struggled to understand the problems of their society and to fashion solutions for them.

Some felt only the anxieties, and they attacked scapegoats in order to gain temporary psychic relief. It had usually been the case that blacks suffered when whites got anxious, and so it was in the nineties as an average of nearly two Negroes were lynched every week, mostly in the South. Temporarily tiring of hanging Negroes, the citizens of New Orleans lynched several Italians in 1891. This was one of the more serious manifestations of scapegoating applied to immigrants in the decade in which a staunchly anti-Catholic and anti-immigrant organization, the American Protective Association, thrived. At the end of the nineties, the whole country was given the opportunity to displace its anxieties on a foreign scapegoat, and the resulting war with Spain provided a cathartic experience for much of the nation.

Others saw the problems of the age in a more rational way, but they attacked symptoms rather than causes. If trusts are being created, abolish them. If labor is restive, repress it. If vice thrives in the cities, end it. If prices are low, raise them. Those who concentrated on symptoms often saw a single answer to the nation's problems. Adopt a particular money standard or tariff policy, close the saloons and brothels, outlaw the trusts, institute the eight-hour day, restrict immigration or disfranchise the Negro—every policy had champions who assured a confused public that they had the panacea.

Then there were those, such as Charles Sheldon, who recognized that society's problems went beyond superficial irritants such as the gold standard or the immigrants or the trusts, that the nation's basic difficulty lay at the very core of its values. As he mingled with the unemployed and homeless men of Topeka, Kansas in the first winter of the decade, Sheldon came to realize that the main problem of the nation was the deep contradiction in its values between private, Christian values based on the brotherhood of man and public, capitalistic values based on individual selfishness.[2] For Sheldon, this realization had the force of a conversion experience, and it inspired him to write *In His Steps*, a powerful exploration of the divergence between public and private values, between the morality of capitalism and that of Christ.

Sheldon was not the only person to perceive this essential moral problem. Throughout the nation men and women concluded that the problem of the individual and the problem of society lay in the divergence between public and private standards of morality. And in their attempts to reduce that divergence, to make public behavior conform more closely to private standards, the men and women of the nineties laid the foundation for the first, the most idealistic, and potentially the most revolutionary stage of progressive reform.

I

The crisis of Victorian values became increasingly difficult to ignore during the nineties. But the existence of a value crisis does not determine the method of its resolution, or even assure that it will be resolved. Sometimes when values are threatened people hold even more tightly to them, ignoring the fact of their divergence from reality. Counterfactual belief has always enjoyed some degree of popularity, especially in times of crisis, because it allows people to cling to the comfortable and to deny that a crisis exists. Its effect is conservative, because it places the burden on the individual, who may be the victim of threats to values but who is seldom their author. The conservatism of counterfactual belief makes it attractive to those who dominate society, and they encourage it in others.

Another common way to address the divergence between values and realities is to attempt to alter the latter to align them more closely with the former. Though its implications can be revolutionary in some circumstances, this strategy is essentially a reformatory one that attempts to preserve core values.

The final strategy—and the least common one—for dealing with the gap between values and reality is to alter values to fit reality. This strategy is practiced on a broad scale only in times of severe cultural crisis. Rapid and permanent changes in values do not often occur, but when they do the effect is revolutionary rather than reformatory. The Bolshevik Revolution is an example of dramatic value change in a society in crisis.

All of these strategies were pursued during the 1890's and the progressive period that followed. Complicating the problem of adjusting values and reality was the fact that the values often contradicted one another. In particular, the material progress in which everyone believed seemed to threaten moral progress, and the self-determination and self-restraint practiced by some seemed to threaten the validity of those values for society as a whole. Value confusion and the simultaneous pursuit of different strategies to reduce the divergence between values and reality make the nineties appear a bit chaotic, but disorder itself is a clear indication of a crisis in values.

Those who inspired and led the first phase of progressive reform recognized the divergence between values and realities and hoped to force the latter to conform more closely to the former. They did not always perceive the problems developing in society at exactly the same time. Henry George had fashioned a powerful, value-based critique of some of the emerging contours of American capitalism in the 1870's. Edward Bellamy, Josiah Strong, and Washington Gladden followed in the 1880's. Charles Sheldon grasped the divergence between values and realities in the windswept prairie town of Topeka in the winter of 1889-1890. Anyone who has spent much time in the Midwest knows that winter is the season for reflection, and Robert M. LaFollette "began to see really for the first time" the problems of the developing capitalistic system during the Wisconsin winter of 1890-1891.[3] As is so often the case with politicians, LaFollette had discovered that an electoral defeat had facilitated his powers of analysis and introspection immensely. But most of the men and women of the progressive generation did not come face to face with the crisis of American values until the Depression of 1893.

The Depression of 1893 was not the first economic downturn to strike the United States, but it was by far the most serious the nation had suffered up to that time. The depth of the depression—as measured by such cold indices of misery as bankruptcy, foreclosure, unemployment, and bank failure — was reached in 1894, but hard times continued to plague the country for several years thereafter.

The experience of many individuals in this collapse illustrated the chimerical nature of the notion of self-determination. Because English capitalists panicked, Kansas farmers, Seattle grocers, and Pennsylvania miners lost their homes and livelihoods. They did not often grasp the intricacies of why it happened, but many could see they were not the authors of their own misery.

Hardship was capricious. The moral, the immoral, and the amoral alike were plunged into economic despair. Painful ironies resulted. Men devoted to home and family rode the rails in search of work. Law-abiding citizens lined up for the privilege of spending the night in a warm jailhouse. The sober clutched the nickel that bought them a beer — and the privilege of eating the free lunch the saloonkeeper put out. In the absence of self-determination, self-reliance was exposed as a cruel joke played by society on the weak.

The crisis weakened the institutions people held dear. Communities learned that they were not autonomous entities that could control what happened to them. Families were torn by the unemployment of breadwinners, which poisoned the well of affection with guilt and reproach and which contributed to increased labor by women and children, to alcoholism, to suicide, and to desertion. More than ever before, the viciousness of public life threatened to engulf the private refuges of virtue.

And the public life was vicious. Businessmen found themselves in the throes of a grim irony, victimized by the same system that normally bestowed rewards on them. Initially, businessmen in many places played their accustomed role as responsible stewards, organizing soup kitchens, raising funds for relief of the unemployed, and so forth. But many soon found themselves in their own desperate struggle for survival. In the savage environment that developed some businessmen exhibited a shocking ruthlessness toward workers, consumers, competitors, and investors. In Wisconsin, for example, as David Thelen has shown, the railroad, power, water, and traction companies on which the people depended maintained high rates, diminished the quality of service, avoided taxes through the corruption of government, and arrogantly disregarded public health and safety.[4]

The political system seemed to parallel the descent of the economic system into barbarism. Corruption was rife, slander, bribery, and sometimes violence characterized campaigns, and the maxim that the ends justify the means seemed, in practice at least, to be replacing the more traditional and honorable political principles of the republic. In the West and South, the old parties considered that the destruction of the Populists justified even the most extreme actions. In Georgia, riots and lynchings, used a few years before to maintain white political supremacy, now served to maintain upper-class control. In the West, Populists and Republicans armed, and in Kansas they struggled for physical possession of the legislature. In North Dakota, a Republican clerk lost a number of reform bills between the Populist legislative chambers and the desk of the Populist governor.

Under the pressure of the deteriorating economic situation, social harmony and cohesion diminished. Racial, ethnic, and religious hatred flared as Americans sought out scapegoats for their problems. Unattached, sometimes desperate men wandered about the countryside looking for work. By 1894 the unemployed were forming into "industrial armies" that went to Washington to request relief, sometimes commandeering trains to get there. The government viewed suggestions for the relief of the unemployed as dangerously radical. Reflecting the Victorian belief in self-reliance, President Grover Cleveland argued that it was the job of the people to support the government, not the job of the government to support the people. Thus Cleveland held the government on its traditional course, unconsciously highlighting the critical divergence between values and realities in the process. No doubt some people took comfort from Cleveland's support of traditional values. But urging those who had no control over their lives to rely on themselves was insensitive and insulting at best.

Those who had jobs were not secure, for they faced possible unemployment at any time and were presented periodically with take-it-or-leave-it wage cuts from employers who could replace unhappy hands from the growing pool of unemployed. Workers usually took what was offered, but sometimes they fought back. Bitter and often violent strikes were the result. Already in 1892 an ominous struggle had occurred at the Carnegie Steel Company's works in Homestead, Pennsylvania. After a protracted strike in which a number of people had been killed and the state militia had intervened, the workers returned to the mills on the company's terms, their union broken. In a chilling aftermath to the conflict, Carnegie's manager at Homestead, Henry Clay Frick, was attacked and wounded by an anarchist gunman, Alexander Berkman, whose proficiency with lethal weapons did not match his hatred for the system Frick symbolized. In 1894, a walk-out by workers at the Pullman Palace Car Company escalated into a general rail strike that paralyzed the Midwest and that was broken, with substantial loss of life, when President Cleveland dispatched federal troops. Apparently Cleveland believed that self-reliance applied to individuals, not to railroads.

Pullman and Homestead drew a lot of national attention, in part because they revealed the nature of the new clothes worn by the two great emperors of stewardship. But there were severe outbreaks elsewhere, as well, including a bitter series of mining strikes in the Rocky Mountain West, especially in Cripple Creek, Colorado and Coeur d'Alene, Idaho. The struggle between capital and labor was as barbaric in the mines as in any area of American industry. The owners had never pretended to be Christian stewards, and their relations with the hard-rock miners were characterized by brutality and violence as often as not. That the mining industry enjoyed a healthy freedom from hypocrisy, however, did not provide much comfort to Americans shocked by the high level of social disharmony.

All of the poisons that had lurked in the mud for a generation, festering and growing, were hatching out. Shocked, frightened, and anxious, increasing numbers of people asked what had gone wrong with their society and what could be done to right it. Most of them found answers to their questions in two separate but related groups — secular thinkers who yearned for a more Christian world, and religious thinkers fashioning a more worldly Christianity.

II

Of the secular thinkers who hoped for a more Christian world, none was more important than the journalist and self-trained economist Henry George. During the 1870's, George had been struck by an apparent contradiction. The more the world progressed materially and technologically, the more human misery seemed to appear; the more wealth increased in society as a whole, the more desperate poverty became for the lower classes. "Out of these bounteous conditions" of the modern economy should have issued the "golden age of which mankind have always dreamed," but instead the bloated wealth of the few, the hopeless poverty of the many, and sharp antagonism between the few and the many had resulted. Human greed continued to flourish, even though there was wealth enough in society to provide for the comfort of all.[5]

In his great analysis of this problem, *Progress and Poverty*, published in 1879, George argued that the difficulty was socially determined and that it could be solved by society. He believed that the source of the problem was the unearned increment in the value of the land, which took resources from capital and labor, which were productive, and gave them to a privileged elite of landowners who produced nothing. George proposed to solve this problem with a confiscatory "single tax" on this unearned increment that would shift resources away from speculators and to producers, allowing society as a whole to better enjoy the benefits of industrial progress.

Henry George inspired a whole generation of reformers, particularly when the nineties forced more people to come to grips with the problems he had addressed in the seventies. For some, such as Ohio progressives Tom Johnson, Newton Baker, and Louis Post, his inspiration was direct. The single tax remained a vibrant reform idea, and the criticism of the unjust privilege enjoyed by landowners was extended to others—such as franchise owners, railroads, and industries protected by tariffs—on which a flawed economic system had heaped special advantages. To George and his followers, privilege of any kind was deplorable because it elevated some people over others and divided the community. It threatened the harmony, altruism, and mutual care on which civilized and Christian human relations must be based.[6]

Perhaps the most significant thing that George did was to criticize existing economic arrangements and suggest alternatives to them. In so doing he challenged and angered those businessmen and orthodox academic economists who smugly contended that economic practices were natural and immutable. George believed that people had created economic arrangements and that they could change them if such alteration would advance human happiness. He was broadening the scope of self-determination, arguing not simply that people could shape themselves in accordance with certain economic principles but that they could also shape those principles. George subtly shifted the burden of social advancement from the individual to society as a whole. Rather than arguing simply that social progress derived from individual progress, he held that "the advances in which civilization consists are not secured in the constitution of man, but in the constitution of society." [7] Thus he anticipated a favorite progressive compromise on the question of how people related to the environment—that people can change the environment but that, at the same time, they are subject to it.

Henry George, then, was a towering figure in American reform, inspiring much of the progressive generation either directly, through his theories, or indirectly, through his willingness to question the goodness and immutability of things as they were. He was also a moralist, accepting without question the simple ethical truths of Christianity and "appealing," as reform editor B. O. Flower put it, "to the moral idealism or sense of justice and right in the heart of man." [8] George's criticism of the system did not endear him to the likes of Henry Ward Beecher and Dwight Moody, intent as they were on assuring their audiences that everything was all right. But his willingness to criticize society from a moral perspective and his devotion to the ideal of social justice made him an important figure for the next generation of socially active Christians.

George was a critic of privilege, not of competition. Had it been the other way around, the conservatives might not have hated him so. He saw no necessary contradiction between competition and social justice. For others who hoped for a more Christian world, however, competition was at the heart of society's problems. With its emphasis on self-aggrandizement, struggle, and conflict, competition directly contradicted the Christian principles of love, brotherhood, and social harmony. It became commonplace for reformers to look forward to the replacement of the competitive system with a cooperative one.

Some assumed that cooperation and capitalism were compatible, even complementary, while cooperation and competition clearly were not. Edward Everett Hale asserted in 1888 that "the principle of co-operation . . . so essential to all Christian civilization, . . . has asserted itself with . . . signal success in many of the walks of industry." Hale's romance *How They Lived at Hampton* detailed a capitalist-cooperative arrangement in which profit sharing under expert management brought prosperity, harmony, and temperance to a woolen-mill town while elevating its moral standards, behavior, and tastes. Hale recommended his scheme to those wishing "to carry out Christian law in Christian love" by finding "in the Gospel the direction for daily life." For those rugged individualists wedded to competition, Hale recommended not the Gospel but "the cold-blooded maxims of the economists." [9]

Far more popular was Edward Bellamy's utopian romance *Looking Backward, 2000–1887*, which envisioned a cooperative commonwealth in which neither competition nor capitalism existed. In what John Thomas has called "a religious fable, an account of the triumph of the sacred over the secular forces of evil," ex-clergyman Bellamy used a fantastic meeting between a Bostonian of 1887 and one of 2000 as a device for criticizing contemporary society and pointing to a better future.[10]

The old society's problems were numerous—the competitive system was cruel, brutal, capricious, and wasteful of the nation's resources, the many were at the mercy of the few, economic hardship was widespread, and cities were sinks of misery, filth, and horror. In the Boston of 2000, however, all of these problems had been solved. The systems of manufacture and distribution were owned and operated by the state at a high level of efficiency, everyone contributed to the functioning of the economy and each person received an equal share of the nation's product, people worked for the community and one another rather than in opposition, and all lived lives of material comfort and security, spiritual elevation, health, cleanliness, and well-being. Cooperation, in the practical sense, had replaced competition. Though the new society was dramatically different, Bellamy's Bostonian of 2000 pointedly indicated that it did no more than operationalize values the Victorians talked about:

> If I were to give you, in one sentence, a key to what may seem the mysteries of our civilization as compared with that of your

age, I should say that it is a fact that the solidarity of the race and the brotherhood of man, which to you were but fine phrases, are, to our thinking and feeling, ties as real and as vital as physical fraternity.[11]

Solidarity and brotherhood were apparently attractive values to many Americans in the anxious years after 1888, for *Looking Backward* enjoyed phenomenal popularity. Bellamy's cooperative commonwealth idea, which he called "nationalism," was widely studied, and tens of thousands joined the Nationalist Clubs that sprang up throughout the nation to promote it.

From the sobering perspective of the late twentieth century, we can see disturbing hints of modern totalitarianism in Bellamy's voteless industrial army and his gerentocratic elite.[12] Bellamy could not foresee the future. What he did see was the selfish individualism of his countrymen and the need to bind, control, and redirect it if a true sense of brotherhood was to be nourished. And he remembered that this selfish people had submerged individualism only when the Civil War necessitated sacrifices of blood, treasure, and traditional freedoms. It was common for members of Bellamy's generation to associate selflessness, sacrifice, and even brotherhood with the military.

Another shortcoming was Bellamy's vagueness regarding how, exactly, the new utopia would come about, a tendency that characterized many of the well-meaning reformers of the age. In *Looking Backward*, the concentration of industry simply continued until there was one huge trust, which was coincidental with the nation. The replacement of the former with the latter was at once natural and painless, and it did not demand much conscious human action. This optimistic fuzziness carried over to real-life Nationalists, who had difficulty formulating viable plans to advance the cooperative commonwealth.[13]

Despite the problems with his system, Bellamy was a key reform figure. Like George, he saw the economy not as a natural or a divinely ordained mechanism, but as a construct that humans had created and that humans could change. George and Bellamy also shared the belief that economic and social problems were basically moral, as were their solutions. Moral values that informed private behavior, such as brotherhood and devotion to community, could and should control public life as well.

Like most of the other reformers of the period, Bellamy and George were what Steven Kesselman refers to as "monists."[14] That is, they were men who responded to the increasingly complex problems of industrial society with simple and straightforward solutions grounded in traditional American values. To modern people, this monism makes them seem simple-minded, innocent, and even reactionary. But their ideas raised a response among people caught in the throes of change, facing a growing divergence between their values and social reality, and searching for means, however vague or fanciful, of applying the former to the latter.

The tendency of reformers to see the problems of industrial capitalism as moral ones, and to address them in moral terms, intensified during the crisis of the nineties. The agrarian-reform-oriented Populist party framed problems in Christian moral language. James B. Weaver, the party's standard-bearer in the presidential campaign of 1892, reflected this tendency in his criticism of the economic system. To Weaver the key economic problem lay in the immoral behavior of those who dominated the system. "The Trust," he explained in 1892, "is organized commerce with the Golden Rule excluded and the trustees exempted from the restraints of conscience." While individuals attempted to live their lives according to the dictates of Christianity, "the Golden Rule is rejected by the heads of all the great departments of trade, and the law of Cain, which repudiates the obligations that we are mutually under to one another, is fostered and made the rule of action throughout the world." For Weaver the solution to the problem was simple. If the people were good, the system could be reformed by an increase in the power of the people. "Thanks to the all-conquering strength of Christian enlightenment we are at the dawn of the golden age of popular power. We have unshaken faith in the integrity and final triumph of the people."[15]

Liberals today are wary of religious moralism in political discourse. Some historians have applied that attitude to the past and have thereby condemned the Populists for bigotry. But most Americans a century ago understood, analyzed, and ordered their world in Christian terms.

Christian ethical concepts formed a common intellectual currency in the age. And in a society in which most people remained committed to individualism, capitalism, and class harmony, Christianity provided a means of understanding and judging social and economic problems infinitely more satisfying than that provided by pluralistic liberalism or scientific socialism. If anything, the stresses of the nineties, combined with the symbolic significance of a century ending, strengthened the tendency to perceive and explain the world in Christian terms.[16]

One of the major reformers in the nineties who analyzed the developments of industrial capitalism from a Christian moral perspective was Henry Demarest Lloyd. Lloyd's *Wealth Against Commonwealth*, published in 1894, was one of the most important reform volumes of the late nineteenth century, ranking nearly on a par with *Progress and Poverty* and *Looking Backward*. Through a study of John D. Rockefeller and the Standard Oil Company, Lloyd explored what he saw as the central problem of the age, that of the operation of wealth, in individual hands, against the interests of the community. Lloyd conceded that economic individualism and selfishness had seemed to benefit the nation when wealth and power were widely dispersed and broadly based, but their concentration in a few hands presented a threat to society. The problem was that the values upheld by society and upon which social institutions were based were in direct contradiction to those that guided individual economic behavior. Society, to Lloyd's way of thinking, was based in Christian values:

> Society is society, and lives its day solely by virtue of having put into actual routine and matter-of-fact application the principles of Christ and other bringers of the same message. Imperfect and faulty though the execution, it is these principles which are the family, the tribe, the sect, the club, the mutual-benefit society, [and] the State, with their mutual services, forebearance, and guarantees. The principles of Christ are the cause and essence of society.[17]

But the "principles of Christ" on which society was based were countered by the principles on which the economy was based:

> We have chartered the self-interest of the individual as the rightful sovereign of conduct; we have taught that the scramble for

profit is the best method of administering the riches of the earth and the exchange of services. Only those can attack this system who attack its central principle, that strength gives the strong in the market the right to destroy his neighbor.[18]

Out of this divergence was issuing an "irrepressible conflict" between the individual and society, between the law of the jungle and the law of Christ, between barbarism and civilization. Americans had it in their power to vindicate and uphold commonwealth against wealth, but Lloyd believed they must reform themselves if they were to do so. Americans spoke of Christianity, of social responsibility, of selflessness and love, but in their economic relations they behaved as Rockefeller behaved, albeit on a smaller scale. Those who dominated the economy were "by . . . our ideals and consent . . . made Captains of Industry over us. . . . We, who profess the religion of the Golden Rule, . . . divide our produce into incalculable power and pleasure for a few." Americans talked a good Christianity, but the shrewd took "their cue not from our lips, but from our lives," seeing that the people were "liars and hypocrites." [19] But men could change themselves and society as well:

> The time must come in social evolution when the people can organize the free-will to choose salvation which the individual has been cultivating for 1900 years. . . . We must bring the size of our morality up to the size of our cities, corporations, and combinations, or these will be brought down to fit our half-grown virtue.[20]

The cooperative commonwealth, for Lloyd, would come not through the beneficent action of Hale's capitalists or through Bellamy's hidden hand. It would come as a consequence of the conscious actions of a regenerate citizenry. "We are about to civilize industry," he concluded. "Mankind is quivering with its purpose to make men fellow-citizens, brothers, lovers in industry, as it has done with them in government and family." [21]

Henry Demarest Lloyd reflected the main currents of Victorian reform thinking clearly and faithfully. Like his contemporaries, he saw the essentially ethical and moral nature of the problem of behavior in the developing industrial-capitalist system. He recognized that two different and contradictory standards informed private and public behavior, and he expressed the belief that either one or the other must predominate. He associated the Christian values of private life with the advance of civilization, and he pointed to a future in which they would overcome the barbarian values of the marketplace. He held the individual responsible for the organization of society, and he stressed that individual regeneration was the key precondition of social change. Lloyd's emphasis on the regenerate individual and his appeal to a personal sense of guilt regarding the direction of society made him one of the spiritual patriarchs of those progressives—particularly the muckrakers—who traded heavily on the feelings of shame and responsibility held by the average citizen. In this way, Lloyd pointed to the progressive reform of the early twentieth century even while he mirrored the Victorian age.

The late-nineteenth-century reformers who yearned for a more Christian world were supplemented by Protestant ministers who wanted a more worldly Christianity. The "Social Gospel" movement that emerged from this impulse was a response to both social and institutional challenges to Protestant churches. On the one hand, social and economic developments in the late nineteenth century directly challenged Protestant values and leadership. At the same time, social and natural science, increasing religious pluralism, narrow denominationalism, and spreading unbelief threatened the credibility and the relevance of the churches as institutions.

The Social Gospel was an attempt to respond to social challenges in a positive, active manner that upheld Christian values and reasserted the leadership function of the church in America. But those attracted to the movement also hoped to transcend the growing problems faced by churches as institutions. They tended to see the institutional problems of the church as secondary, important mainly because these hampered the church's ability to address the moral problems of American industrial capitalism. Thus, they sought to remove these concerns from center stage in churches. They dealt with natural and social science by accepting most of their specific elements and integrating them into the Protestant belief system in Protestant terms and by stressing the importance of faith in God as opposed to a reliance on scientific "proofs" of God's handiwork. And they dealt with religious pluralism, denominationalism, and doctrinal conflict with an ecumenical spirit that stressed points of agreement rather than points of conflict among groups and denominations.

The key element in the attempt of the Social Gospel movement to deal both with institutional and with social problems was the stress it placed on the broad and humane ethical principles embraced, in theory at least, by all Christians and, indeed, by most people in Western civilization. The Christian law of love—of people for God and for one another—and the Golden Rule—that people should govern their behavior toward others on the basis of how they wished to be treated—were the ethical principles that the Social Gospel movement stressed.

Those attracted to the Social Gospel believed the Golden Rule and the law of love provided Christianity with its best and most consistent way of addressing the nation's problems and expressing social unity. Here were principles to which all Protestants, as well as Catholics, Jews, and unbelievers, could be loyal. Here was the ethical distillation of Christianity, apparently invulnerable to assaults from natural and social science and to denominational and theological wrangling. And, most important to the Social Gospelers, here was a Christian message of relevance to secular society, a means of dissolving "the artificial barriers between the sacred and the secular," a key to solving the social and economic problems of Victorian America.[22]

The impact of the Social Gospel movement remains of matter of controversy today. While some historians praise it as a bold attempt at "social salvation," others see it as a sort of halfway house on the road from orthodoxy to unbelief.[23] Both points of view have validity, but at the time the Social Gospel was significant mainly for providing inspiration and promise and for stimulating "adventurous thinking."[24] It was motivated by an acute sense of crisis and an optimism that the crisis could be surmounted. The crisis the Social Gospel addressed lay in the materialism and selfish individualism of industrial society and in the threat these posed not only to Christian values in society but to the churches themselves. Either the Christian values that informed private life would infuse society, or the brutality, amorality, and even immorality of industrial society would destroy Christian values. Graham Taylor, minister and social worker, reflected in 1930 on the atmosphere of crisis in which the Social Gospel developed:

I was led to the conviction that the evangelization of industrial and social conditions is necessary to the evangelization of the soul, still more of the world. Gradually such conditions proved to be as subversive to the Christian ideal of life among the richer as among the poorer people I knew. . . . Therefore, for the sake of religion's self-defense it more and more seemed necessary to seek to make livelihood tributary to, rather than subversive of, the Christian life; to impress the inconsistency of trying to live the religious life on the higher plane of Christian altruism, while either glad or sorry to labor on the lower level of an industrial order, which is pagan when unrestrictedly competitive.[25]

The Social Gospel movement provided a convincing analysis and an attractive prescription for social ills Taylor and others saw. It promised to bridge the gap between the sacred and the secular, to bind disparate individuals, groups, denominations, and classes together, to return the churches to social relevance and even leadership, and to provide a practical guide for daily living as well as a utopian goal for human life. It expressed the sense of crisis felt by increasing numbers of Americans while optimistically providing the solution for it. Small wonder that it proved to be the most important and vibrant development in American Protestantism between the Civil War and World War I or that it inspired so many in the progressive generation.

Though the Social Gospel movement had a number of founding fathers, the most popular was Josiah Strong, whose book *Our Country*, published in 1885, has been compared with *Uncle Tom's Cabin* in its tone and significance.[26] *Our Country* is a complex and interesting book, because it encompasses so many of the diverse impulses of late-nineteenth-century Protestantism. On the one hand, it is riddled with fear — of Catholics and Mormons, of an ungodly West and irreligious immigrants, of cities and immorality and socialism and much more besides. On the other hand, it is a book of hope and affirmation and confidence regarding the country and the future of Protestantism in it.

Strong's wide and sweeping approach, and his moralism and bigotry, has often deflected historians' attention from his pointed criticisms of the behavior of those who dominated the developing industrial economy. He complained that capitalists too often shirked their duties to those who depended on them and that workers and consumers suffered unjustly as a consequence, particularly during hard times:

> Some employers . . . in times of depression . . . run their factories for months at a daily loss to themselves, rather than throw their workmen out of employment. But such capitalists are as rare as they are noble. More do not hesitate to enter in to combinations powerful enough to command the trade, and then stop work for weeks and months in order to inflate prices, already fair.[27]

He worried that the growth of a massively wealthy class and a desperately poor one threatened society, and he cautioned that "the enormous concentration of power in the hands of one man is unrepublican, and dangerous to popular institutions." Strong further warned that "there are signs of an excessive individualism among us; a certain self-assertion, a contempt of authority which forgets that duties are co-extensive with rights." Excessive individualism and the growth of wealth created a situation in which men exercised power but showed no sense of responsibility. "The capitalist can arbitrarily raise the price of necessaries, can prevent men's working but has no responsibility, meanwhile, as to their starving. . . . We have developed a despotism vastly more oppressive and more exasperating than that against which the thirteen colonies rebelled." Strong damned materialism as well, complaining that it threatened morality, and he expressed the fear that "self-gratification" might "outgrow the power of self-control."[28]

Strong believed the responsibility for addressing and solving these problems lay with the church. To Strong, the immorality of the wealthy operating in the economy was no different from the problem of the saloon, of unregenerate immigrants, of the vicious poor, or of the irreligious West. All were moral problems and thus the province of the church. "The Church is responsible for public opinion on all moral questions, and no great question . . . can be settled for the world until Christian men come into right relations with it."[29] His evaluation of economic behavior by the standards of private morality and his demand that the church address the problem placed Strong in the vanguard of the Social Gospel movement.

Our Country projected Josiah Strong beyond his Cincinnati pulpit into a position of leadership in the Social Gospel movement. Rather than shrinking from the demands placed on a founding father, he relished the opportunity to move American Protestantism in a new direction. In the stream of articles and books that succeeded *Our Country*—a stream that, unfortunately, continued to show the tincture of fear, bigotry, and cramped moralism—Strong reiterated the theme of Protestant activism. The churches must "reconstruct society on Christian principles," thus "conquering the world for Christ." If they failed, they would "lose their opportunity of leadership and with it their great opportunity to regain their lost hold on the masses and to shape the civilization of the future." [30] Strong was not a great theorist or formulator, he was a goader, a prodder, an agitator, constantly pushing the church in a new direction. He was the Sam Adams or Patrick Henry of this would-be revolution, the Social Gospel. The Thomas Jefferson of the Social Gospel was Washington Gladden.

The genesis of Gladden's social Christianity lay in a religious crisis in his youth. Growing up in rural New England before the Civil War, Gladden was distressed by his inability to have an emotional conversion experience indicative of his reception of God's grace. This failure led him to question the whole thrust of orthodox Calvinism. To his mind, the church concentrated too much on the individual sinner, in whom it attempted to stimulate fear of damnation:

> The business of religion was to fill the hearts of men with fear.
> . . . It concentrated the thoughts of men on their own danger, and
> their own safety. . . . If force and fear are moral motives, they are
> certainly among the lowest moral motives; the conduct which
> they inspire must be an inferior kind of conduct.[31]

This religious practice repulsed him because it attempted to stimulate self-centered terror rather than altruism, it stressed that God should be feared rather than loved, and it plunged those—such as Gladden—who did not receive certain knowledge of salvation, into a "slough of despond." [32] From his Congregational pulpit in Columbus, Ohio, Gladden advanced a theology that stressed the love and friendship of God and people for one another and of people for their brothers and sisters and that attempted to stimulate human altruism rather than fear. These principles—love, brotherhood, and altruism—shaped Gladden's response to the challenges of industrializing America.

Gladden was particularly disturbed by the conflict between capital and labor, which he addressed at length in his appropriately titled *Applied Christianity*, published in 1886. Gladden thought industrial strife proved that anti-Christian principles had pervaded the industrial system. While Christian society was an organic one based on cooperation and mutual benevolence, industrial conflict indicated that the American economy was based too much on competition and individual selfishness. Moreover, industrial conflict spilled into non-economic areas of life, threatening family, church, and community. The conflict between capital and labor "destroys the moral wealth of the nation even faster than its material wealth. It tends to make men bitter, suspicious, cruel; it turns neighbors against each other; it keeps the embers of resentment and hate all the while smouldering." [33]

The solution for the "social problem," as Gladden and many others called the industrial conflict, and for the larger systemic moral deficiency it indicated, was not the destruction of individualism or of the capitalist system, but "the application by individuals of Christian principles and methods." It was the responsibility of the church to inculcate the truth in industry that "the economic law, like the moral law, can never be fulfilled without love." [34]

Applied Christianity exposed tensions that continued to characterize Gladden's thought. He tried to reconcile his commitment to Christianity with his belief in capitalism, cooperation with competition, social responsibility with individualism, "benevolence," in his terms, with "self-love." [35] Far from being an individual peculiarity, this tension characterized the mainstream of the Social Gospel movement as well as the middle-class public to which social Christians spoke. Gladden's ambivalence reflected the ambivalence of a society clinging to competition, individual self-determination, private property, and materialism while it yearned for self-restraint, benevolence, and brotherhood.

By the 1890's Social Gospel themes were being repeated with enough frequency that a broad movement within American Protestantism can be seen to have emerged. As with any movement, the Social Gospel had its divisions, the most important of which developed around the question of whether primary emphasis should be placed on individual or social reformation. Most Social Gospelers, drawing on a rich religious and social heritage of faith in self-determination and self-restraint, emphasized the primacy of individual regeneration, agreeing with Shailer Mathews that "a perfect society cannot be created from imperfect people." [36]

Moving further from Victorian and Protestant orthodoxy was a small band of Christian socialists who stressed the reformation of society as the surest means to individual regeneration. The most important of these theorists was George D. Herron, who provided intellectual leadership to Christian socialism until a personal scandal at the end of the century forced him from his Iowa college presidency and into voluntary exile in Italy. Between 1893 and 1895 Herron delineated his philosophy in a series of books, *The New Redemption*, *The Christian Society*, and *The Christian State*.

The New Redemption was a stinging attack on the capitalist system and on the church that, Herron believed, upheld it. Herron argued strenuously that the laws of nature and the laws of God were ignored by an economic system that emphasized "the triumph of cunning over character, and the conflict of selfish interests." To Herron, the absolute selflessness of Christ's Sermon on the Mount should serve as the standard to which Christians must conform. "The Sermon on the Mount is the science of society," he emphasized; "it is a treatise on political economy; it is a system of justice." The nation had come to a crisis and would have to decide whether to follow the laws of God or the values of capitalism. "It cannot be stated too plainly," Herron held, "that either the people will become atheistic, or wealth which is in Christian hands must obey the social laws of the Sermon on the Mount." [37] In *The Christian Society*, published in 1894, Herron elaborated on the nature of a society that operated in conformity with the Sermon on the Mount, contending that "justice procured through love" was "the ground of civilization." [38]

In his third major work, *The Christian State*, Herron argued that "the social salvation of our nation through Christ will by no means wait for the conversion of each individual . . . to the divinely coming social order. . . . The principles of the Sermon on the Mount may organize the economic relations of men long before every individual is converted to these principles." For Herron, the state provided the means for Christianizing society, and Christians should use it:

The state [must] become Christian, [and] Christianity . . . must become political. The only way by which Christianity can, in the largest sense, be put into practice is through possessing the state as its organ. . . . Christianity needs the state for its realization as much as the state needs Christianity for its redemption and perfection. Christianity can supply the only forces that can procure social justice, and the state is the only organ through which these forces can work constructively upon and within the whole people.[39]

To us, Herron's conception of a Sermon-on-the-Mount state conjures up chilling visions of totalitarian moral control. Among others in the Social Gospel movement, however, a close relationship between church and state was not objectionable in and of itself. Herron's ideas were more distressing to most social Christians because of the stress they placed on environment as the cause of human problems and the means to salvation. Most people in the Social Gospel movement recoiled from such a drastic de-emphasis on self-determination and self-restraint.

The churches were strongly affected by this new Social Gospel, which called upon them to fulfill public duties and which promised to revitalize Protestantism and return it to a position of national leadership. Most popular initially among Episcopalians, Congregationalists, and Unitarians, Social Gospel ideas quickly spread to Presbyterians, Methodists, Baptists, and beyond.[40] As they developed a broader conception of appropriate behavior, churches engaged in new activities, reaching out through special organizations and "institutional" facilities to the poor, to labor, and to others they had not traditionally dealt with intimately. Clergymen engaged in reform activities on a broader scale. In Buffalo, New York, for example, ministers "who accepted the implications of the social gospel took an active part in almost every reform movement, voicing their opinions from the pulpits, joining committees, and backing legislation." Not restricting themselves to the "temperance and charity work" in which Protestant clergymen traditionally engaged, they "could be found vocally advocating civil service and charter reform, opposing child labor, and championing the cause of unions."[41]

The public impact of the Social Gospel was less certain. The poor and the working class did not stream into Protestant churches because of social Christianity, nor did the out-of-church middle class. On the other hand, the Social Gospel appealed strongly to the morally earnest young people from whom progressivism drew much vitality. For people like those studied by Robert Crunden, the Social Gospel provided an analysis of social ills and a guide for social action that comported well with the Victorian value system in which they were raised.[42] In his autobiography, the famous Kansas newspaper editor William Allen White remembered his "awaking to the deep spiritual truths in the Christian Bible" at the turn of the century:

> When I . . . saw Jesus . . . as a statesman and philosopher who dramatized his creed by giving his life for it, then gradually the underpinning of my Pharisaic philosophy was knocked out. . . . I saw the Great Light. Around me in that day scores of young leaders in American politics and public affairs were seeing what I saw, feeling what I felt.[43]

That it could influence this smug young conservative Republican, whose claim to fame at that time was an insensitive editorial attack on the Populist party, was a great tribute to the force of the Social Gospel.

In American society as a whole, the analysis of and prescription for social ills suggested by the Social Gospel seemed to become more compelling as the nineties went on. One indication of this was the popularity of two vigorous calls for Christian social action published in the mid-nineties, *In His Steps* and *If Christ Came to Chicago!*

In His Steps, written by Topeka minister Charles M. Sheldon, was a simple fantasy about a town in which the citizens decided to act in their relations with one another as Christ would act. Patterning their behavior on the Golden Rule and the law of love, the townspeople found themselves in a Christian utopia in which disharmony, vice, and the sharp dealings of the market had all disappeared.[44] Published as a book in 1896 after serialization, *In His Steps* became a phenomenal best seller, with more than 20 million copies printed in dozens of languages. The simplicity of Sheldon's idea was undoubtedly an attractive feature of the book, but, as Henry May points out, there had been many "earlier and less successful specimens of the genre."[45] It is difficult to avoid the conclusion that by 1896 people were ready to see social problems as moral problems that demanded moral solutions. Sheldon's simple social criticism and his simple Christian remedies were attractive in this time of confusion and anxiety.

If Christ Came to Chicago!, by British journalist William T. Stead, exploited the popular sense of guilt deriving from the divergence between social and economic conditions on the one hand and Christian principles on the other. Stead wondered what would happen if Christ made a tour of this supposedly Christian city to see how well his principles were being followed. Acting as Christ's surrogate (and thus showing a degree of arrogance excessive even for an Englishman), Stead found an unchristian and hypocritical city. Vice flourished unchecked, brotherly love was approximated only in the self-interested political parties and the corrupt city government, desperate poverty abounded, the wealthy dominated the city, and Chicagoans honored "a trinity of their own of whom they think a great deal more than they do of Father, Son and Holy Ghost, . . . [capitalists] Marshall Field, Philip D. Armour and George M. Pullman." [46] And, worst of all, the churches refused to take responsibility for any of these shortcomings.

If Christ Came to Chicago! inspired a torrent of imitators, and Christ was kept busy for the rest of the decade going from town to town, exposing sin and hypocrisy wherever his train stopped (for some reason the authors usually had Christ on a regular—not a celestial— railroad). Stead was also one of those who, along with Henry Demarest Lloyd, pioneered the technique of stimulating popular guilt that the muckrakers later used so effectively. Taken together, *In His Steps* and *If Christ Came to Chicago!* tell us something about the relationship between more sophisticated social Christians and American society. During the 1890's, social Christianity, with its moral analyses and solutions to social problems, drew strength from the very anxiety, confusion, and guilt that it attempted to address.

III

Social commentators around the turn of the century remarked often on two contradictory tendencies they saw in the modern world. In some ways, a trend could be seen in society toward greater complexity and diversity, while a contrary tendency toward greater unity could also be perceived. Among reformers, the trend toward unity was illustrated by the emergence of a broad consensus regarding the nature and solution of social ills. The problems of society, secular reformers and social Christians seemed to agree, were moral ones that had their genesis in a false separation of public and private values and behavior, and their solution lay in the application of the values informing private life to public behavior.

Still, the growing complexity of American society and its problems encouraged some to look beyond the simple truths of Christianity to new sources of authority. The most attractive new source of authority that responded directly to the need for explanation in an increasingly interdependent and complex society was social science.[47]

Social science developed in the United States in the years after the Civil War. Most early social scientists were essentially moral philosophers who tried to apply concepts from natural and biological science to human affairs. They were generally evolutionists, reflecting the prominence that Darwin's theories had imparted to that concept. The majority of "Social Darwinists" were conservative followers of English evolutionist Herbert Spencer who saw a social world analagous to the natural world and who did not believe conscious human action could change the former in a creative way. Even the "Reform Darwinists," such as Lester Frank Ward, who believed society could direct itself in positive ways, accepted the truth of Darwinian science and saw it as a substitute for religion in the direction of men's lives. "The great moral and religious systems," Ward argued, "have been grand successes in so far as exerting an extraordinary influence and absolute control over the wills and acts of men is concerned. They have been signal and complete failures in so far as the amelioration of the condition of society is concerned."[48] Social Darwinists did not enjoy wide influence. Though their ideas were used to buttress conservative interests, their public impact was diminished largely because their analysis was so distasteful to people who continued to depend on Christianity for explanation and direction.[49]

By the mid-eighties a new generation of social scientists—the most prominent of whom were academics such as John Bates Clark, Simon

Patten, Franklin Giddings, Albion Small, Richard Ely, and E. A. Ross
—had risen to challenge the Social Darwinists. These scholars differed
from their predecessors in important ways. For one thing, they were
professionally trained and the leaders among them possessed doctorates
from German universities. This training gave them confidence and a
degree of deference from colleagues, and they took advantage of this
circumstance to shape their disciplines and the standards thereof. Their
German educations also gave them a distaste for some of the accepted
principles of Anglo-American social science. Specifically, they believed
British and American social scientists placed too much stress on the individual and failed to recognize the primacy of society, which German-
trained academics saw as an organic, cooperative endeavor without
which the individual had no meaning.

Believing in society and in its ability to direct itself, the new social
scientists tended, as Mary Furner has shown, to be activists.[50] They
believed that human beings could and would alter their lives and their
society to conform more closely to scientific truth, and the duty of the
social scientist was to discover and promote that truth. As one academic argued in the *American Journal of Sociology* in 1896, "it is the
function and duty of the social theorist to keep attractively before
'practical men' all the known and tried methods of obtaining the elements of human well-being."[51]

Social activism attracted the German-trained generation because
they believed they could help society find authoritative explanation
and direction. They differed from the Social Darwinists in that their
quest for truth did not involve a rejection of religion. Most of the
activist social scientists saw Christian and scientific truths as supple-
mental to and supportive of one another.[52] They tended to be drawn to
social Christianity, seeing in it universally valid truths as well as a
corrective for the antisocial individualism that beset Victorian society.
Of those academics who found the new social science complementary
to social Christianity, none was more important or influential than
Richard T. Ely.

Ely illustrated the compatibility of early social science with social
Christianity in his early work. Indeed, he became at once a leader in
the discipline of economics and a major theorist of the Social Gospel.
Ely believed that the church had adopted a view of its social function

that was too narrow and restrictive, accepting the pernicious notion that "things are divided into things sacred and things secular." [53] The results of the church's acceptance of this false dichotomy were unfortunate:

> The prayer for all is: "Thy kingdom come, Thy will be done on earth." Yet the church has so failed to instruct us in regard to the will of God in earthly matters, that professed Christians seem at times to lose all distinction between right and wrong in affairs of this life, and occasionally one hears it said that Christian ethics have nothing to do with practical business. [54]

Ely believed the church must redirect itself and accept the truth that "it is the mission of Christianity to bring to pass here a kingdom of righteousness and to rescue from the evil one and redeem all our social relations." It must inculcate in Christians "the constant manifestation of love to our fellows in all our daily acts, in our buying, selling, [and] getting gain." And it must recognize that "it is as truly a religious work to pass good laws, as it is to preach sermons; as holy a work to lead a crusade against filth, vice, and disease in slums of cities, and to seek the abolition of the disgraceful tenement-houses of American cities, as it is to send missionaries to the heathen." [55]

Ely brought to the Social Gospel an organic view of society and of sin. He argued that people must begin to recognize "that there is no such thing as a purely individual sin." By this he meant not simply that in sinning individuals transgressed against society, but that sin was socially shared. "Social solidarity signifies not only that man needs association with his fellow-men, but that he shares with them their sins and their sufferings," argued Ely in 1896. "Our sin is sin for others; their sin is our sin." [56]

Ely's social organicism and his conception of shared sin reflected his German training, and it carried powerful reformatory potential. At the same time, it placed him on the side of the Social Gospel movement that stressed the primacy of social rather than individual regeneration. Most socially active ministers believed society had no existence apart from the individuals who composed it.

Ely saw the state as the public incarnation of society and an engine of social advancement. In the platform he proposed for the infant

American Economic Association in 1885, Ely's first principle was that "we regard the state as an educational and ethical agency whose positive aid is an indispensable condition of human progress." [57] At times Ely seemed almost to say that the state created individual morality. "Laws establish the conditions of social life and make social life possible," he argued in *The Social Law of Service*. "Now God has made man a social animal . . . and it is only in society that man can accomplish his destiny and attain to true moral development. Laws in making possible human society make possible morality." [58] Ely stopped short of claiming that the state was moral in and of itself, but one can see in his thought the seeds of that reductionism among social scientists that flowered after 1900 into a sort of narrow and uncritical statism.

Secular reformers, social Christians, and "new" social scientists developed a critique of American society during the last two decades of the nineteenth century that was remarkably consistent. All agreed that the problems accompanying industrialization and urbanization were less technical than moral and that regeneration—of the individual, the state, or both—was the solution. They looked forward neither to a jungle society, based on struggling individuals, which they saw rising about them, nor to a pluralistic society in which the clash of interests determined the public good. Instead, they wanted a more cooperative, less competitive society, in which the standards of behavior informing private life informed public life as well and in which the self-indulgent impulses of individuals were restrained.

Reformers differed on specifics, of course, but their analyses of social ills and their prescriptions for them showed a remarkable level of consistency. Reformers could achieve this level of agreement because they shared a set of Christian ethical standards and a common moral language, not only among themselves but with the larger society as well. Later, this morally united reform outlook would be challenged by a supramoral scientific socialism on the one hand and an amoral interest-group liberalism on the other. When this happened, American reform lost its unity, consistency, and sense of direction, and it lost its touch with the people as well. But in the eighties and nineties reformers spoke the moral language and appealed to the moral concepts that most Americans shared. This does not mean that most Americans responded to the reformers, but when events increased popular doubts about the nature and direction of American society, anxious people could turn for answers to reformers who believed as they believed. And during the nineties, increasing numbers of people were asking for answers.

I V

One of the by-products of the Depression of 1893 was an explosion of locally based and locally oriented reform, as citizens, bound together in new coalitions, struggled to uphold the community interest against the social and economic forces of selfishness. Throughout the country, citizens were victimized by corporations during the economic hardship. In Wisconsin, for example, "public service" corporations callously raised rates and cut service to compensate for temporarily diminished profits. In Kansas City, fire insurance rates leaped dramatically, not because there had been more fires, but because the depression had cut company receipts.[59] In hundreds of other places, the pattern of corporate selfishness was repeated.

The rapacity and selfishness of business shook people out of their lethargy. Threatened in their own communities, they could no longer let things slide, hoping for the best. Suddenly, for many middle-class Protestants, the depression "brought the sobering realization that good intentions were not sufficiently powerful to reform an unchristian civilization."[60] As a result, "a powerful . . . 'moral awakening' stirred the urban middle-class, generating new reform energies and strategies."[61]

In local communities middle-class people reached out to the others, such as workers, who were already discontented, overcoming social divisions of class, ethnicity, and religion in the process. They found that they had much in common. All felt victimized by the selfish and irresponsible corporations that dominated their localities and by the politicians who were time-serving toadies of those corporations. All agreed there should be a community interest, or "public interest," which was apart from and superior to the interests of private individuals. And they found as well that they were united by a vague but powerful belief in "the Golden Rule of love among neighbors."[62] Religion, so long a source of disunity in American society, suddenly became a source of harmony when expressed in the broad ethical principles of social Christianity. In many towns, a sense of community was being recreated or, in some cases, created for the first time.

In their communities, people were taking responsibility for social problems. The old idea of two distinct spheres of activity — public and private — each with a different standard of behavior, was breaking down. It was becoming apparent that one of two things would happen. Either the values of church, family, and community would overcome those of the countinghouse and the statehouse, or they would themselves be overcome. The power to determine the result of this struggle lay in the hands of the people. The message of Henry Demarest Lloyd, W. T. Stead, and others was clear: Viciousness, selfishness, and materialism in society were the responsibility of the people in society, and no amount of hypocrisy or avoidance of the issues would change that fact. If the people took responsibility and acted they could change the direction of society. If they refused, the future would be their fault. The progressivism that flowered on the state and national levels after the turn of the century was rooted in local reform of the nineties, in its coalition, its moral critique and standards, and the compelling sense of social responsibility and guilt that fueled it.

The values of the reformers and the crisis that galvanized them into action imparted a sense of urgency and a tone of moralism to municipal reform. That flavor was furthered by the presence of many clergymen in reform coalitions. In New York, for example, the reform movement was led by a Protestant minister, Charles Parkhurst, who Lincoln Steffens later credited with being one of the fathers of progressivism.[63] Parkhurst's premise was that most questions in the traditional public sphere were moral in nature. "A very large percentage of the great questions that are always under discussion — social questions and political questions — . . . are nothing more or less than crystallizations about an ethical nucleus." And it was the duty of moral people to address these problems. "Say all you please about the might of the Holy Ghost, every step in the history of an ameliorated civilization has cost just so much personal push," argued Parkhurst. "You and I have something to do about it."[64] In Baltimore, the remarkable Vrooman brothers formed a "Union for Public Good." This organization, as well as its parent body, the national "Union for Practical Progress," attempted to mobilize churches and parishioners in a wide-ranging municipal reform effort.[65] In town after town, throughout the country, the same general pattern of moral reform was repeated.

Virtually everywhere reformers viewed the defeat of incumbent municipal administrations as the necessary precondition for local reform. Throwing the rascals out was an ancient and honorable American political tradition. It was attractive because it was a simple solution to difficulties that were complex and sometimes insoluable and because it allowed people to personify problems. Moreover, Richard L. McCormick has suggested, attacks on officeholders serve a cathartic function, relieving the anxieties of the attackers.[66] For reformers searching for scapegoats, turning the incumbents out was sufficient. But for most people involved in municipal reform, it was merely a necessary first step toward major alterations in city life.

Most cities were run by political machines, presided over by bosses, that were concerned primarily with personal profit rather than with public service. At their best, machines could be seen as pluralistic political organizations that brought a measure of efficiency to city government and that were decent and humane to workers and immigrants.[67] They were also usually undemocratic; they robbed taxpayers, cooperated with selfish corporations that cheated consumers, and protected organized crime and vice. To reformers, bosses conformed to a selfish standard in political and economic behavior rather than to the selfless values of private life, threatening the latter in the process. As Paul Boyer notes, "for municipal political reformers of the late nineteenth century, the worst thing about a corrupt and thieving municipal government, or one linked to vice interests, was that it poisoned the moral atmosphere of the entire city." [68]

In their attacks on the bosses, municipal reformers often found themselves allied with good-government advocates who had been fighting machine rule for some time. The motivations of these "goo-goos," or "mugwumps," as they were usually called, were complex. They worried about the moral tone of the city, they believed men in public service should have high characters (and, often, be members of the social elite), and they were attracted to structural reforms, such as civil service, that would make the city operate more honestly and efficiently. Morally motivated reformers did not oppose the general idea that some people should rule while others should not, nor were they averse to structural reform. But they were less likely than goo-goos to see structural reform as an end in itself. For them, an honest and efficient government was the first—not the last—step toward a morally regenerate community.[69]

The morally regenerate community reformers visualized was one in which high standards of personal behavior obtained. The late-nineteenth-century city, with its open gambling and prostitution, its brutal and immoral amusements, and its flourishing liquor and drug trade, presented them with a broad field for action. Once the alliance between government and vice was broken by the defeat of the machine, reformers usually turned to a strict enforcement of existing laws and the passage of new ones. These law-and-order campaigns were marked by offensives against gambling, prostitution, racketeering, and the police corruption that allowed these to thrive, strict enforcement of prohibition or of laws controlling saloons, the abolition of immoral amusements, such as lewd shows, prize fights, and dog- and cock-fighting.

The attacks by municipal reformers on behaviors of which they did not approve exposed their unattractive side. They tended to be intolerant, to exhibit narrow prudery, class, ethnic, and racial bigotry, and a penchant for the control of those they considered dangerous.

It is important to remember, though, that in the crisis atmosphere of the nineties, behavior reforms were seen as means of protecting private life from the viciousness of public life. Certainly, one need not be a blue-nosed authoritarian to agree that alcohol abuse *is* a problem that *does* threaten the family, or that the family might also be imperiled by open prostitution and white slavery, or that such things as cock- and dog-fighting could lower the moral tone of the community. For some behavior reformers these were society's only problems, but others came to see them as part of a social context in which women were mistreated, in which working people were poorly paid, housed, and entertained, and in which self-indulgence and materialism were honored economic values. For reformers with the broader perspective, personal behavior was but one aspect of society that had to be regenerated. Perhaps the difficulty we have in understanding them and sympathizing with them derives from the fact that modern reform has a split personality. Those who believe personal behavior should be reformed usually take a laissez-faire position on the economy, while those who concentrate on economic reform usually show little interest in controlling personal behavior. To most Victorian—and progressive—behavior reformers, selfishness, brutality, and materialism were antisocial forces to be resisted wherever they appeared.

Some behavior reformers looked to physical alterations in cities that would reshape human character. For these, urban planning and beautification promised to create an environment that would help elevate people, lifting them to higher standards of behavior. As Judd Kahn has shown in *Imperial San Francisco*, urban planning promised so many things that it was able to mobilize a broad spectrum of support.[70] A beautiful, well-planned city was supposed to revitalize commerce and industry, inspire the civic pride and cooperative spirit of the residents, and unite a diverse, heterogeneous citizenry.

Comprehensive city planning failed in San Francisco because of the strength of the very forces it was attempting to overcome—narrow and selfish economic individualism and social heterogeneity. But the failure of massive, coordinated plans did not deter those who worked on a more modest level. Cities and towns did undertake successful beautification campaigns. Inspiring government centers and public buildings were constructed. Zoning laws were enacted, waterfronts were cleaned up, and improved sewage and water systems were created. Parks, playgrounds, and other public recreational facilities were developed. Modification of the urban environment did not alter the individual character to an appreciable degree, but it did help make city life a bit more pleasant and stimulated a measure of civic pride. Faith in city beautification and some degree of planning did not fade after 1900, and they remain with us today, though their purpose is much more clearly commercial than it was then.

To a considerable extent, the urban poor were the objects of the behavior reformers, who were often motivated in part by fear of the lower classes. During the nineties the problem of urban poverty was "discovered" by increasing numbers of middle-class Americans. In part this increased awareness was due to the depression, which seemed to widen poverty, extending it to the virtuous and vicious alike. In towns in which a fourth or a third of the labor force was out of work, it was difficult to attribute poverty to the character flaws of individuals.

Even before the depression, though, poverty was drawing the attention of an increasing number of reformers, and Jacob Riis' sensational book *How the Other Half Lives*, published in 1890, stimulated further interest. Riis' account was rather narrow, in more ways than one. He showed a high level of ethnic prejudice, he derided the poor for being "shiftless, destructive, and stupid," and he saw housing as a virtual panacea for the myriad problems of the poor.[71] But he also argued that the difficulties faced by the poor were rooted largely in the greed of the rich and that it was the duty of society to address them.

Other studies followed, the most interesting of which was Benjamin Orange Flower's *Civilization's Inferno*. B. O. Flower, as he styled himself, was the editor of the *Arena*, a participant in numerous reform movements, and a constant critic of the church from a social Christian perspective. In *Civilization's Inferno* he lambasted the church for having "become, to a great extent, subsidized by gold . . . [and for having] signally failed in her true mission—that of establishing on earth an ideal brotherhood," and he argued that, when Christians learned the realities of urban poverty, they would abolish it. After his exploration of the problem, he challenged Christians to address it. "If Christianity meant half what Jesus intended it should mean," he contended, "this state of things could not endure for a single day."[72]

Already some humanitarian Christians were responding to the call of conscience with commitments to the poor that went beyond those of the workers in organized charity. The Salvation Army, imported from England in 1880, caught the imagination of a number of sincere Christians because of its atmosphere of self-sacrifice, its willingness to address the physical and spiritual needs of all the poor—even the most desperate and degraded—and its broad ecumenicism, which emphasized the spirit of brotherhood and downplayed theological differences.[73] In 1884 Vida Scudder, who later became a prominent Socialist, was drawn to the Salvation Army when she was in England. "Fifty years later I presume it would have been the communists whom I should have wished to join; but their day was not yet."[74] Scudder's comment is instructive because it indicates the strong appeal of Christian action groups to idealistic young people, as well as capturing the spirit of devotion and self-sacrifice demanded by the Salvation Army.

Most of the devices for dealing with the urban poor in the late nineteenth century were imported from England. The Octavia Hill method of "friendly visiting" and the Salvation Army were cases in point, as were the settlement houses that attracted so many young idealists in the nineties and after.

The first settlement house in the United States was Hull House in Chicago, founded in 1889 by Jane Addams after a visit to England had allowed her to observe Toynbee Hall, a London settlement.[75] Addams was part of that generation of late-Victorian, middle-class women that was inspired with a sense of social responsibility and a desire to serve others but that found few socially acceptable occupations in a society that maintained a restrictive view of women's public roles and activities. Accepting their role as agents of civilization but unwilling to devote themselves to families, some of these women found occupations —such as teaching, social work, and reform activity—that allowed them to operate outside the home in socially acceptable ways. Addams can thus be seen as one of the women who broke paths that would later be broadened as women searched for equality in American society.

The idea of women extending the values of civilized private life to a barbaric public world was very much in step with Victorian values and roles. It was also very much in step with the social Christianity of the age, which emphasized social responsibility and stressed broad humanitarian sentiments. For Addams, who saw herself as part of the "renaissance going forward in Christianity," a commitment to brotherhood was a basic motive.[76] Religious values remained a major motivation of settlement house workers for years to come. In 1905 a survey of settlement house workers revealed that "nearly all admitted that religion had been a dominant influence on their lives."[77]

Hull House was designed to provide a sense of community in its neighborhood, and most of the settlements founded after it had the same goal. It could be a focus of community in a limited geographical area and, because it allowed lower-class neighbors and middle-class settlers to interact, in a broader social sense as well. In addition to counteracting social and class divisions and allowing middle-class people to fulfill their sense of social responsibility, the settlement house provided services for the poor, ranging from nursing services to day care to the maintenance of employment bureaus. There was, inevitably, a certain amount of condescension and uplift spirit manifested by the settlers toward the neighbors, particularly in the early years. This diminished as time went on, and some settlers became about as good neighbors as people from starkly different social and ethnic backgrounds could be expected to be.

Settlement house workers also contributed to the development of a different view of poverty from that held by the charity organization societies. Living among the poor, settlement workers became sensitive to the environmental factors that contributed to poverty, and they stressed the necessity of ameliorating these instead of concentrating exclusively on individual character. Settlement house work led many into social justice reforms designed to relieve environmental pressures on the poor, such as public housing, public health, occupational safety, and social insurance. And the settlement experience helped shift traditional poverty workers toward a greater environmentalist emphasis.

A final strain of municipal reform during the nineties derived directly from the depression experience. The depression opened the eyes of many people to the problem of economic privilege in the form of public utilities—railroads, traction companies, light, power, gas, water, and telephone corporations. People of every class recoiled at their displays of rapacity during the economic crisis. Soon politicians such as Tom Johnson in Cleveland and Hazen Pingree in Detroit rose to challenge the privileged position of the utilities and to blame most of the problems of urban America on them. These reformers were often able to build broad and viable coalitions behind plans to regulate fare and rate structures, to limit the terms of operating franchises, and, increasingly, to have municipalities own and operate essential utilities.

There were, then, a number of strains to municipal reform during the nineties. Clean government, planning and beautification, behavior reform, concern for the poor, and the fight against privilege were all elements of reform, and they were not as incompatible as they might seem. It was common for the same people to have all of these interests, and to work for all of them. There were problems of emphasis from time to time, and some elements of reform coalitions would press measures others would not accept. For example, in Detroit Mayor

Pingree concentrated on the fight against privilege, alienating structural reformers, who believed the city's primary problem lay in an ineffective administration, and behavior reformers, who wanted the mayor to attack the liquor trade.[78] And in Cleveland businessmen who were quite pleased to see clean government did not want that government to attack privilege.[79] Coalitions could be bound by a vague moral analysis and a sense of social responsibility, but they were strained when questions arose regarding what to push and how far to push it. Despite these problems, the moral awakening of localities during the nineties produced some exciting politics, some promising possibilities, and some interesting political figures. No political figure of the period was more interesting than Samuel M. ("Golden Rule") Jones, reform mayor of Toledo, Ohio.

Samuel Jones came to politics rather late in life, having spent most of his adult years in industry. He was a self-made man who owned his own business, the Acme Sucker Rod Company, which manufactured a piece of oil-drilling equipment Jones had invented. Deeply affected by the suffering that accompanied the Depression of 1893, Jones determined to run his business by the Golden Rule. He instituted the most advanced features of contemporary welfare capitalism—paid vacations, the eight-hour day, hot lunches for workers, kindergarten for workers' children, cooperative insurance, and a stock-option plan—made all work self-directed, removed the time clock, and abolished all work rules except the Golden Rule.[80] That someone would emerge from the petroleum industry who actually believed in the Golden Rule is a phenomenon curious enough to warrant some comment, but Jones went beyond his company and attempted to apply his principles to the whole city of Toledo. In three terms as mayor, Jones battled privilege, worked to improve the lots of the poorest and most degraded residents of the city, and attempted to create a physical and social environment that would allow the natural goodness of the individual's character to predominate.

In 1899 Jones published *The New Right*, in which he explained his beliefs in expanded form. He argued that the capitalistic system prevented Americans from realizing the ideal of brotherhood because it was "individualism gone mad." It also prevented people from living in accordance with the Golden Rule. "A strictly Christian life, according to the life and teachings of Jesus, is incompatible with what is known as 'success' in business," Jones believed. "No man can succeed in business to-day and be Christian." Nor did he see much reason to discriminate among businesses. "Profit, not morals, is the purpose of business," he said, reminding his readers of a truism too often forgotten. "The saloon is run for the same purpose that railroads, stores and factories are, — to make a profit." And the spirit of profit was completely counter to the spirit of love and brotherhood upon which the family was based and upon which a Christian society should be based:

> No well-regulated, loving family would give one of its members a special franchise to make profit from the labor of the other members; neither would any member of the family desire any such franchise, but he would find his delight and pleasure in rendering such service as he could for the benefit of all, realizing by his experience that service brings its own reward.[81]

People would begin to treat one another as brothers and sisters, society would begin to operate as the family operated, and the Golden Rule would become the guide to behavior only when the economic system was changed. "Our trouble is not with the bosses, with the aristocrats, with the corporations or the Standard Oil Company," argued Jones, "but with a system that denies brotherhood and makes a weaker brother the legitimate prey of every strong man." When the public owned essential services, and when the rule of cooperation came to replace competition, the by-products of a vicious capitalist environment would pass away. Selfishness, degradation, slums, and even the saloon would go when the system that created them was abolished. And Jones was sure a new, cooperative system was coming, and that America would lead the way to its realization:

> After thousands of years of slow evolution and discovery, we have reached the banquet hall of a new civilization. The feast is spread before us, and there are plates enough and to spare; but we have not yet been able to overcome the old instinct of strife, and we are upsetting the tables and trampling on the food in our mad haste to get our share. The old instincts of the forest sur-

vive in us still, but they are becoming less and less powerful, and we are gradually learning to trust the higher motives which we have hitherto confined to the narrow sphere of the home. We are learning the wisdom of extending the spirit of family life to the state and nation.[82]

Jones' combination of Christian moralism and economic radicalism sounds strange to the modern ear. He was ahead of most of his contemporaries, but he spoke their language. They, too, took Christianity seriously. For them, Christianity was a way of defeating alienation, not a mode for expressing it. They, too, applied moral judgments to their economic system and to their political system. They, too, wanted a more Christian and homelike world. And they, too, were optimistic that such a world would come, particularly as the crucial decade of the nineties drew to a close.

V

In 1895, historian Albert Bushnell Hart published a gloomy appraisal of public life that sounded what was a common theme of the late-Victorian generation. "While in the ordinary private affairs of life moral standards are on the whole advancing, the old standards no longer apply to the political and social matters which now absorb so much attention," Hart observed. "Yet politics and government and labor questions and public order are as dependent as religion upon the average idea of what is praiseworthy and what is iniquitous; they are all moral questions."[83] A mere eight years later the *Independent* could rise to great heights of optimism as it surveyed the future:

> Just behind us are great organizations of capital and labor, and just ahead is the cooperation of these two forces in the creation of an era of universal good will. Already . . . the Golden Rule is quoted as workable. . . . Just behind is a dissolving of sectarian conceit and bigotries; not far ahead is a mighty organization of the wealth and moral force of Christendom, to sweep out the baser thought and the selfish purpose. We shall soon see an American

church, with the creed of love for man and the code of honor for God. In the twentieth century war will die; despotism will die; sectarianism will die—but man will live. For all there will be but one country—that country the whole earth; for all there will be but one hope—that hope the whole of heaven.[84]

The greater optimism of the *Independent* was not simply an editor's quirk. Many commentators around the turn of the century could sense a shift in American society, a movement away from selfishness, materialism, and brutality and toward higher, more Christian standards of behavior.

What was happening in American society was a double-edged "revitalization movement," though people of that generation did not use that term. As defined by anthropologist Anthony F. C. Wallace, a revitalization movement is "a deliberate, organized, conscious effort by members of a society to construct a more satisfying culture."[85] Revitalization is necessitated when social realities become so far separated from social beliefs and values as to create stress, in individuals and in society as a whole. There can be no question that a serious contradiction between values and realities existed in Victorian society by 1890, and that it created stress. The Depression of 1893 heightened this disjuncture, made it more difficult to ignore, and precipitated the revitalization movement.

Americans were unwilling to revitalize by altering their values to fit more comfortably with the new, distasteful realities. But they were willing to consider alterations in the thrust and direction of their institutions in order to respond better to the challenge they faced. Thus, the Social Gospel movement envisioned a change in the emphasis and direction of the church to render it better able to devise a socially relevant doctrinal response to change. Josiah Strong observed that the shift in emphasis was taking hold:

Men are not looking so far afield to find God and heaven and duty. Religion is dealing less in futures and laying more emphasis on the present. There is less spurning of earth to gain heaven, and more effort to bring heaven to earth. Men are beginning to see that right relations with man are as real a part of the Christian

religion as are right relations with God, and that the establishment of such relations should be a conscious object in religious
effort.[86]

By emphasizing the broad ethical principles of Christianity the church
could increase its social relevancy and provide a measure of social
unity, and it could also revitalize itself, recapturing its traditional position of social leadership. "If the church wishes to save itself from
extinction," Washington Gladden pointedly noted, "it must send out
its light and its truth into the community."[87]

The revitalization impulse was not confined to the churches. In
cities and towns around the country, Americans were attempting to
carry out revitalization by forcing the practices of public life to conform to the values of private life. Increasingly, people were applying
private moral standards to social, economic, and political behavior.
And people were decreasingly willing to accept the old conception of
two separate spheres with two separate standards of conduct. This was
a revitalization that aimed to universalize values—not alter them—
applying them to every aspect of life. "In countless movements for
social reform," noted L. G. Powers of the Minnesota Bureau of Labor,
"ideals are being marshalled in the warfare which the enlightened
conscience of the race is beginning to organize against the evils of a
purely materialistic civilization."[88] And teacher and Social Gospeler
Francis Greenwood Peabody noted, with some wonderment, that "whatever aspect of it we approach, we find the discussion and agitation of
the present time turning in a quite unprecedented degree to moral
issues, and using the language and weapons of a moral reform. The
social question of the present time is an ethical question."[89]

What the revitalizers of the turn of the century were promising was
nothing less than the fulfillment of the Victorian dream. They were
promising a happy, harmonious, and united society at the peak of civilization, bound together by a single standard of values. And as the old
century drew to a close, there was much optimism that the new century would see social progress unprecedented in human history. As
they celebrated the nineteenth as a great century of material progress,
commentators looked forward to the twentieth as a century of human
advancement. "That our new century will eclipse or even equal the

nineteenth in its material progress I think is extremely doubtful," argued B. O. Flower in 1901, "but that the oncoming age will leave a legacy of general happiness, resulting from a higher and nobler civilization, I believe is highly probable." [90]

So Golden Rule Jones was not so eccentric after all. His ideas and attitudes were shared by many of his contemporaries. His hopes and dreams, and those of Bellamy and Addams and Gladden and Flower and the others, sprouting from the doubts of the eighties and growing in the depression-ridden nineties, blossomed after the turn of the century in the progressive movement. It was in the early years of the century that progressives attempted to revitalize America in accordance with the Victorian vision. This was the golden age of Golden Rule reform.

THE FLOWERING OF
CHRISTIAN PROGRESSIVISM

> It was with difficulty that realism got lodgment in
> my mind; early assumptions as to virtue and vice,
> goodness and evil remained in my mind long after I
> had tried to discard them. That is, I think, the most
> characteristic influence of my generation. It explains
> the nature of our reforms, the regulatory legislation
> in morals and economics, our belief in men rather
> than in institutions and our messages to other peo-
> ples. Missionaries and battleships, anti-saloon leagues
> and Ku Klux Klans, Wilson and Santo Domingo are
> all a part of that evangelistic psychology that makes
> America what she is.
>
> FREDERIC C. HOWE

> We are building our pyramid of civilization. . . .
> But it must rest upon its base, or fall; and its base
> must be the practical Christian living of the people
> in their daily lives.
>
> WILLIAM ALLEN WHITE

Christian progressivism, planted by the Bellamys, Lloyds, and Gladdens
of the Victorian age, and nurtured by the crisis of the nineties, flowered
after the turn of the twentieth century. For a time Christian progressivism was the dominant strain of reform. By the teens it was no
longer dominant, because reformers were fixing on new solutions for
American problems based on different, and more self-consciously sophisticated, analyses of the nature of these problems. But even then,
as Cleveland progressive Frederic Howe noted, the ethical concepts

that had influenced the early movement remained an unextirpated force, shaping the response of reformers to their world.[1]

Christian progressivism makes us uncomfortable. The reformers' indignation, moralism, and righteous rhetoric offends the tastes and grates on the ears of many modern people. As early as the 1930's, interpreters of progressivism were pointing to its moralism as proof of naive innocence or narrow bigotry. More recently historians have tended to ignore it altogether, implying that moralistic rhetoric was irrelevant to the real goal of reformers, which was the modernization of America.[2]

However, as Frederic Howe indicated, to ignore the progressive value system is to ignore the essential aspect of the reform experience. For the reformers interpreted their world, its problems, and its solutions in moral terms. This was especially true in the early stages of reform, but it never faded away completely. Paul Boyer has noted that "almost every Progressive cause had its moral dimension."[3] If we are to understand these causes fully, we cannot ignore that dimension.

By the end of the nineties it was no longer easy to ignore reality. One set of standards, essentially Christian in nature, seemed to govern the behavior of men in private, while another guided their behavior in public. The Victorians had hoped that the values of the home, church, and community would come to suffuse politics and the marketplace, but the opposite seemed to be occurring. The narrow selfishness, materialism, and hedonism of the public world were threatening private life. A sense of crisis emerged in the nineties. Either American society would be revitalized by the universalization of Christian values, or those values would be destroyed. For Christian progressives, the choice was that clear.

Christian progressives believed the choice would be made by individuals. For them, the individual was at once society's hope and its peril. America's problems were seated in individuals and could be solved by them. Individual selfishness, materialism, and hedonism had brought America to its state of moral crisis. But individuals could shape themselves, reverse their direction, and in the process change society. If people governed their public relationships by the Golden Rule and the law of love, which presumably informed their private relationships, society would be transformed. "We are building our pyramid of civilization," wrote William Allen White in 1905. "And its base must be practical Christian living of the people in their daily lives." [4]

The Christian progressives embraced comprehensive principles. The Golden Rule and the law of love promised to be the means to unite a complex and heterogeneous society and the means of solving all social, economic, and political problems, as well as being the ideal but attainable goal of society. The comprehensive nature of Christian progressivism imparted both strength and weakness to it. Its principles were easy to understand, widely held, and compelling. But in practice they did not always provide sure guides to human behavior, nor could they be translated easily and clearly into public policy. Moreover, practical outcomes sometimes developed from reformers' efforts that were not in line with their premises.

In the end, they succeeded neither in regenerating the individual nor in fundamentally reforming society. But their effort to do so deserves our attention, not least because of the basic decency and nobility of their conception and their undertaking.

I

The Christian progressives did not see new problems in American life. There was nothing new about criticizing the unrestrained individual or pointing to the divergence between public and private values. These were common themes in American social criticism during the late nineteenth century. What was new was the growing acceptance of this critique of American public life. Suddenly, the public became receptive to reform journalists—the muckrakers—who focused in a moralistic fashion on misbehavior in government and business and who blamed the public for allowing shortcomings to exist. Soon, politicians who criticized economic or political figures in moral terms enjoyed spreading grassroots support. As Arthur Link and Richard McCormick have observed, "the dynamics of progressivism were crucially generated by ordinary people" aroused to action by particular events—"a sensational muckraking article, an outrageous political scandal, an eye-opening legislative investigation, or a tragic social calamity." [5]

Reformers believed the public response indicated that a great moral awakening was sweeping the country, that men and women were hearing those who criticized public behavior from the perspective of private behavior and were accepting their analysis. The spiritual revival observers had perceived at the end of the nineteenth century was spreading. An increasing number of people felt "a sense of divergence between their consciences and their conduct," noted Jane Addams. "They desire both a clearer definition of the code of morality adapted to present day demands and a part in its fulfilment."[6]

The reformers drew sustenance from the nineties. Henry Demarest Lloyd and B. O. Flower laid the foundation on which Ida Tarbell and Lincoln Steffens built. Theodore Roosevelt and Woodrow Wilson drew from the well tapped by William Jennings Bryan and Golden Rule Jones, though they would have been loath to admit it. Most important, the Christian progressives were sustained by "ordinary people" newly attuned to moral criticism, buffeted by the horrors of the nineties, confused and troubled about the direction of the nation, and anxious to hold traditional values in an age of change and uncertainty.

Then there were the reformers themselves. As Robert Crunden has noted, the Christian progressives had not only "internalized Protestant moral norms" of Victorian society, but had made a conscious attempt to apply these norms to "the very real social, industrial, political and aesthetic problems" of American life.[7] They were the finest products of Victorian culture in America. They took Victorian values seriously and thought these should be universalized. A generation earlier, most of them would have gravitated to the ministry, but the declining intellectual rigor of orthodox Protestantism and deteriorating assurance regarding its dogmas pushed many of them into "useful careers that satisfied demanding consciences. They groped toward new professions such as social work, journalism, academia, the law, and politics. In each of these careers, they could become preachers urging moral reform on institutions as well as on individuals."[8]

To many Americans, the Christian progressives' goal of extending a single moral standard from private to public life was impossible. "In the field of private morals we have little difficulty in dividing people into good and bad," noted Yale President Arthur Twining Hadley. "But in public morals, whether commercial or political, the case is quite different. The ethics of the situation are not generally clear." [9] But for reformers, the existence of different standards was more a social defect than an impediment to action. "We have as many moral standards as there are varieties of pursuits and professions among men. There is a separate and often inconsistent code of ethics for every range of human action, every plane of human conduct," admitted Charles Williams, a member of Cleveland's reform administration, in *McClure's* in 1905. "What we need is . . . the bringing up of our standards in all the various regions of our life and conduct to the same high level of the moral ideal: in other words, we need the unification and integration of a divided and disintegrated conscience." [10]

For Williams and for other Christian progressives, the injunction that one should love others as brothers and sisters and should treat them as he or she would be treated was a universal principle, made feasible by basic human goodness. "Is it not a Utopian dream that the principle of Good Will will supplant the principle of *Laissez faire* in industrial society?," asked Washington Gladden in 1909. "Can we rationally expect that such an ingrained tendency of human nature as that which is represented by the maxim 'Every man for himself,' will yield to the other-regarding motive so that men will learn to identify their interests with those of their neighbors?" The Columbus minister concluded that "the answer is that when men see that Good Will is the law, they will learn to obey it." [11] "Moral rights and duties formed upon the relations of man to man are applicable to all situations," added Jane Addams, "and to deny this applicability to a difficult case, is to beg the entire question." [12]

Christian progressives believed that as men and women put the law of love into operation in their daily lives as voters, workers, employers, consumers, and neighbors, the problems of public life would disappear. "The Christian spirit is in its essence an entirely attainable ideal of kindness and of justice," William Allen White believed, "and only as men live the Christian spirit consistently, in their simple first-hand relations with one another, will the public morals of the nation improve, and will the political and economic problems which reflect the condition of public morals be nearer a solution." [13]

Putting the law of love into operation demanded that the individual develop a greater social consciousness. It was necessary that people behave in their broader relationships as they theoretically acted toward family and friends. If the individual showed "character" and thought in terms of "service" to others, the problems of viciousness, selfishness, and social disharmony could be conquered.[14]

A redirected individualism carried a new conception of rights and duties. The *Outlook* held in 1905 that "we are born, not into rights, but into duties, . . . duty to nourish the social life that nourishes our life, to subordinate private to public interest, to seek first of all the common good in which our own is involved." [15] Some Christian progressives went so far as to obliterate popularly accepted definitions of individualism, submerging them totally in society. "The highest type of goodness is that which puts freely at the service of the community all that a man is and can," Walter Rauschenbusch believed. "The highest type of badness is that which uses up the wealth and happiness and virtue of the community to please self." [16]

Christian progressives defined social problems and solutions in moral terms, and they spoke the rhetoric of Victorian Protestantism. They understood their task in terms of a spiritual revival. First, it was necessary to acquaint the individual with his or her social sins of commission or omission and then bring about an alteration in character that was reflected in a higher standard of public behavior. On the local level, this involved efforts—often by churches or voluntary religious groups, and just as often by organizations lacking denominational ties—to draw public attention to the problem of poverty, child labor, prostitution, poor housing, or some other social ill. Often these efforts resulted in an ameliorative response by a guilt-stricken public. That the appeal to public guilt was an effective one was illustrated by the spectacular national success of muckraking journalists.

Exposure of corporate or civic misbehavior was the main occupation of muckraking, but a prominent strain in reform journalism was the indictment of the public for allowing the immorality to continue. Were cities corrupt? Was the Senate a bastion of privilege? Did corporations oppress labor, poison consumers, or cheat investors? All of it was the fault of the voting, working, consuming, investing public, which allowed it to happen.

The public responded to this phase of muckraking. Lincoln Steffens set out in his tellingly titled book *The Shame of the Cities* "to sound for the civic pride of an apparently shameless citizenship,"[17] and the cities involved threw out their bosses. Vice was attacked, franchises were municipalized, politicians were ousted, investigations were held, and reforms were carried out. Public indignation, spurred by guilt, was becoming a major social force. "Both the corrupt public official and the unscrupulous business man dread the searchlight of public opinion, which is becoming more and more effective as a regulator of conduct," noted progressive political scientist J. Allen Smith.[18]

Realizing they had touched a sensitive nerve, the muckrakers pressed the theme of popular guilt to extremes. It was a short step from indicting the people for allowing evil to accusing them of sharing it or, worse, of authoring it, and it was a step muckrakers were quick to take. Grafters were corrupt, agreed Steffens, but so were we all: "There is no essential difference between the pull that gets your wife into society or for your book a favorable review, and that which gets a healer into office, a thief out of jail, and a rich man's son on the board of directors of a corporation."[19] Some were even willing to argue that the public was the cause of the offenses against it. Fremont Older, a newspaperman whose efforts helped put San Francisco boss Abe Ruef in prison, reflected that "it was not Ruef who had made these conditions. It was we, the people, who had made them. . . . We were responsible for the environment in which Ruef found himself, we had set up the standard of success which he tried to reach."[20]

Steffens' and Older's formulations were arresting, but each was flawed. Steffens failed to see that the degree of evil might alter it in kind. Henry Ford and Adolf Hitler were both anti-Semites, but that does not make them the same or render them equally guilty for the holocaust. Older blamed the victim for the crime, implicitly excusing the perpetrator. One might be murdered because he behaves irresponsibly or because he refuses to take precautions, but that does not relieve his murderer of responsibility. The universal guilt motif characterized Christian progressive thought, and it was a valuable stimulant to action. At the same time, it had the effect of turning indignation inward, of exonerating the most guilty and allowing them to participate in some vague process of regeneration. It served to confuse reformers, complicate their search for answers, and vitiate their strength.

Their concentration on individual guilt and stress on individual character did not mean that the Christian progressives ignored environmental factors. They commonly argued that physical surroundings —housing, neighborhoods, saloons, brothels, whatever—influenced the individual's development. They were particularly concerned about the impact of environment on children—at a time when children, as special people with special needs, were being discovered in this country—and they were willing to support educational reforms, juvenile courts, carefully structured retreats, and other attempts to fashion favorable environments for children. As LeRoy Ashby shows in *Saving the Waifs*, reformers whose efforts centered on children hoped especially to fashion familial or communal environments in which attractive individual characters could be created.[21]

Christian progressives were also willing to support the removal of environmental factors that created bad characters in adults or that, more accurately, allowed the ignoble in people to outweigh the noble. Virtually all of them wanted to rid the nation of the saloon, for example, because it was a scene of sin and degradation and also because it was an environmental influence that encouraged weakness in the human character. Many were willing to go much farther. "There are many things that the State can do and must do if it would be approximately Christian," contended one reformer. "It will seek to remove all conditions that make for human weakness, and will exert its authority to provide those that make for human well-being."[22]

But Christian progressives recoiled from the conclusion that environmental conditions are responsible for all character flaws. One problem with complete environmentalism was that it created what Ross Paulson calls "the classic liberal dilemma of change in a democratic society: that in order to change the social system they [reformers] had somehow to change men's attitudes first. But if men's attitudes are a product of their environment, . . . how could they break out of the cycle?"[23] The second, and more serious, problem with extreme environmentalism was that it violated all of the assumptions of Christian progressivism. If human character and behavior are shaped entirely by the environment, then self-determination, self-restraint, regeneration, sin, and salvation are all meaningless concepts. If environmental determinism was true, the Victorian religious and ethical system was false.

Christian progressives made concessions to the environment, but they always returned to the individual. "A washed pig is still a pig and will return to the wallow at the first opportunity unless his piggish nature is changed," argued one Social Gospel minister in colorful fashion. "Even though one should fill up the wallow, still as long as the pig is given water to drink and earth on which to tread, it will make a wallow and transform these necessities into filth unless one inspire it in less piggish ideals and a less piggish nature." [24]

Even those who recognized the importance of surroundings usually argued that the regenerate individual was the means to a regenerate environment, not the other way around. From her perspective at Hull House, Jane Addams certainly recognized the impact of social conditions on individuals, but she firmly held that the individual could and should be the source of social advancement. "Social changes can only be inaugurated by those who feel the unrighteousness of contemporary conditions," she concluded. [25] Another figure who never slighted environmental influences, Christian socialist Walter Rauschenbusch, agreed that "the greatest contribution which any man can make to the social movement is the contribution of a regenerated personality." [26]

The concentration of Christian progressivism on the individual — with his or her conscience, character, and regeneration — helps us to understand many of the particular characteristics of the progressive movement. Its rhetoric of morality, its stress on duty, and its dependence on voluntary action are all easier to understand when we recognize the centrality of the appeal to conscience. As people unconsciously engaged in a revitalization movement, Christian progressives often seemed satisfied just with touching the conscience. Robert Crunden has suggested that the muckrakers regarded the exposure of evil and the appeal of guilt as ends in themselves. "Conversion was a self-justifying event," he argues. "Good works would presumably follow." [27] In 1906, a contributor to the *Outlook* praised the disclosure of political corruption, business misbehavior, and social evil not because it led to systemic changes, but because it contributed to "a real 'bracing' of the average American, making him a little more scrupulous in his own dealings and giving him a little stronger sense of personal responsibility." That, the author concluded, "is an achievement incomparably more important than the jailing of a few rascals, the replacement of a few bad officials by good officials, and the writing of a few model laws upon the statute-books." [28]

The preoccupation of Christian progressives with character helps explain their relative disinterest in legislation and in modifying economic institutions in a significant way. For them, legislation would be effective only if it was grounded in a regenerate public moral charcter. "Any permanent and useful advance in legislation is dependent on the previous creation of moral conviction and custom," Rauschenbusch argued. "If the law advances faster than the average moral sense, it becomes inoperative and harmful." [29] Philadelphia reform leader Franklin Spencer Edmonds believed laws were not too important in the final analysis:

> However long the reform movement may continue, its results are first measured by the legislation which it secures. But in the long run, the test of its success must be found in its effect on the character of the people. If it finds the people sunk in political sloth, and leaves them in the same general condition, then, even if a body of legislation has been enacted, it will not be long before political conditions are as bad under the new laws as they were previously under the old. [30]

Now we can understand the progressive attraction for regulation, for depending on public-spirited people of good character rather than legislation. A perfect social system, they believed, would not work with imperfect people, but perfect people would purify an imperfect social system. Our "concern is not with the machinery of society," argued Washington Gladden, "but with the moral motive power." [31] Consequently, when they turned their attention to the economy, the Christian progressives concentrated on individual moral regeneration rather than systemic change.

II

Those progressives who analyzed social problems from a Christian ethical perspective concentrated much of their attention on American economic behavior. Industrial development in the United States had stimulated pride and enhanced the material standard of living. At the same time, the rise of the trusts, declining equality of opportunity, growing interdependence, urbanization, corporate irresponsibility, and friction between capital and labor were unwelcome by-products of economic change. All of these problems seemed to intensify during the nineties, spurring an early version of Christian progressivism in dozens of communities.

Developments after 1900 indicated that the behavior of corporations had not been altered for the better by the flurry of local protest. The anthracite coal strike, the Northern Securities Case, the life insurance scandals, and the revelations of impurities in food and drug products were but the most spectacular evidences of continuing corporate misbehavior toward workers, investors, and consumers that were exposed in the first few years of the new century. Christian progressives who concentrated on economic behavior thus found a viable critique, a receptive public, and a large stock of suitably egregious examples.

The criticism that Christian progressives leveled against the economic system and those who dominated it differed little from what had been said by moralists who addressed the same problem ten, or even twenty, years before. The central problem of economic life was moral in nature. While men tailored their private lives to fit, generally, the Golden Rule and the law of love, they governed their economic behavior by statute law, at best, or by the law of the jungle at worst. Christian progressives argued that men could not have it both ways. Either the laws of God would tame the marketplace, or the laws of the market would come to govern every area of life.

This theme was explored particularly fruitfully after the turn of the century by Walter Rauschenbusch, the Baptist clergyman who replaced George Herron as the leading American exponent of Christian socialism. To Rauschenbusch, the relationship between public life and private life was delicate and fluid. "Our capitalistic commerce and industry lies alongside of the home, the school, the Church, and the democratized State as an unregenerate part of the social order," he argued, "not based on freedom, love, and mutual service, as they are, but on autocracy, antagonism of interests, and exploitation." This situation had developed slowly, over the ages, as the institutions of private life had been won to a Christian ethical standard. Rauschen-busch argued that private institutions had worked a beneficial effect on public life. "Our business life has been made endurable only by the high qualities of the men and women engaged in it. These personal qualities have been created by the home, the school, and the Church."[32] But he believed that society now faced a crisis. Either the Christian standards of private life would come to govern public behavior, or the amoral standards of public life would poison private institutions:

> There are some departments of life which are to some degree under the actual dominion of the Christian principle, especially personal morality, the family life, and neighborly social intercourse. But the principle incorporated in business life is so deeply affecting the methods of action, the points of view, and the philosophy of life as preached in the press and in conversation, that it is encroaching even on those realms of life which have hitherto been blessed by Christ's law. If Christianity cannot advance, it will have to retreat even from the territory already claimed by it.[33]

The strength of the Christian progressives was in their compelling ethical conception. Their weakness was exposed when they moved beyond general principles to deal with the question of where, *exactly*, the immorality of the system was seated and the question of how, *specifically*, it should be addressed.

For some progressives, the problems of public economic life were seated in bad individuals, pure and simple. People could be either bad or good, and the bad ones spoiled the system as a whole. This was the simplistic view that journalist Ida Tarbell carried through life. For Tarbell, whose *History of the Standard Oil Company* was the first major piece of muckraking in the new century, the strong individual—the Napoleon, Rockefeller, or Ford—was at once the necessary and sufficient force for good or evil in society. "In walking through the world there is a choice for a man to make," Tarbell argued in her autobiography. "He can choose the fair and open path, the path which sound ethics, sound democracy, and the common law prescribe, or choose the secret way by which he can get the better of his fellow man."

When those selecting the latter path came to predominate, the standards of society suffered, "and bitterness and unhappiness and incalculable ethical deterioration for the country at large" resulted.[34]

This serpent-in-the-garden theory, by which Tarbell explained John D. Rockefeller's rise to dominance in the oil industry and the national ethical deterioration that she believed issued therefrom, was attractive to many Americans. It was moralistic, it focused attention on individuals, and its simplicity and lack of sophistication made it easy to understand. It also had the advantage of exonerating the capitalist system for economic evils. The removal of bad men would allow fundamentally good institutions to function as they should.

Others also focused on bad men, but their understanding of vice and virtue was more complex than Tarbell's. They argued that the problem of immoral behavior in the economy derived not from defective personalities but from privilege. When men enjoyed some special privilege—control of some essential good or service or dominance of some market—they behaved in an immoral and antisocial manner. "*Debasement of Human Nature* is a natural result of any arrangement by which a few selfish men are able to achieve industrial and political mastery over others," argued urban reformer Frank Parsons in 1901. "The monopolists . . . become arrogant, overbearing, undemocratic, disregardful of the rights of others, apt to look at men not as equals and brothers, but as so many *things* be used." [35]

Criticism of privilege had a long tradition in America, forming a vibrant strain in politics as early as the Jacksonian period and coloring such later movements as antimonopolism and Populism. It was also an analysis that suggested fairly clear and straightforward—if not always easily implemented—public solutions.

When privilege took the form of monopolistic control of essential services, it could be ended by government ownership and operation of the service in question. This was a particularly logical and attractive solution for the problem of privilege in municipalities, and during the progressive period dozens of towns and cities took over such essential services as water, gas and electricity, and public transportation.

The solution most often suggested by opponents of privilege to the problem of monopoly or oligopoly in industries that supplied nonessential goods and services was freer competition. A combination of tax, tariff, and antitrust policies, critics of privilege such as Robert LaFollette and William Jennings Bryan argued, would negate the unfair advantages enjoyed by monopolists and allow a return to equal and open competition. Robert LaFollette attempted to explain the reforms instituted in Wisconsin by his regime in these terms:

> Equality under the law was our guiding star. It is the special discriminations and unjust rates that are being corrected; the privileges, unfair advantages, and political corruption that have been abolished. . . . The honest investor, or business man, or farmer, or laborer, who simply wants equal opportunity with others and security for what he honestly earns, is protected and encouraged by the laws. The mere speculator, or monopolist, or promoter, who wants to take advantage of others under protection of law, is held down or driven out.[36]

The problem, for LaFollette as for Tarbell, was not systemic but personal. Capitalism was fine; it was special privilege enjoyed unfairly by individuals within the system that caused the problems. But for many other progressives the competitive system itself was the source of immoral economic behavior.

Few questions were more vigorously debated by Christian progressives than the question of the responsibility of competition for economic immorality. For some, it was the solution to the problem of unchristian economic behavior; for others it was the source of the problem. To its critics, the competitive system presented the antithesis to the Christian ethical standards that should inform public life. While the law of love should be inculcated in public life, argued a writer in the *Arena*, the competitive system upheld "the morality of medieval barbarism that made Might the basis of Right — the savage doctrine of the survival of the strongest." [37]

The materialism and selfishness encouraged by the competitive system threatened all that society held dear, according to some Christian progressives. "If it were proposed to invent some social system in which covetousness would be deliberately fostered and intensified in human nature, what system could be devised which would excel our own for this purpose?," asked Walter Rauschenbusch. "Competitive commerce exalts selfishness to the dignity of a moral principle." [38] The ethics of the competitive system were so powerful and so overbearing that they submerged the good intentions of businessmen. "Men are driven to dishonesty in business because of a vicious business system," argued a writer in the *Independent* in 1903. "That system, with its low ideal, its unmoral point of view and its loose distinctions, ties the hands of many a man of affairs, no matter how honest naturally he may be." [39]

Part of the divergence between the Tarbells, Bryans, and LaFollettes on one side of the competition question and people like Rauschenbusch on the other might be attributed to background. The former, with their small-town backgrounds, saw competition as a friends-and-neighbors enterprise in which one's behavior was restrained by his regard for the good opinion of the community. To them, the "bad" men and monopolists were outsiders effectively beyond community censure or control. The latter saw competition from a larger—even national—perspective. For them, competition without community was a vicious and antisocial phenomenon.

The rhetoric of progressives who abhorred competition often had a radical ring. "Religion," suggested the *Independent* in 1902, "might . . . condemn the entire structure of modern business as radically wrong and hostile to the true life of fellowship with divine perfection." [40] But moral criticism came more easily than practical solutions.

Part of the problem was that the competitive spirit was so pervasive. Everybody seemed to be animated by the desire to get ahead of others. As Florence Kelley of the National Consumers' League noted ruefully, "the pushcart peddlers and news vendors who have stands on city street corners are animated by precisely the same business motives as the gas trust, the surface car companies and all the large exploiters." [41] As Tarbell or LaFollette saw it, solving the problem was relatively easy—undertake an antitrust suit, municipalize a franchise, or lower a tariff. But if competition was the problem, nothing less than a systemic or ethical revolution would suffice. Some reformers saw signs of both in the cooperative impulse.

Christian progressives regularly expressed the hope that the spirit of cooperation would slowly replace that of competition. Certainly, apparent signs of growing cooperation were everywhere. Increasing social interdependence, industrial integration, the coordinated factory system, and even unionization were signs of more cooperative times to those who wanted to see them. "Our world is becoming more social, in the sense of being less individualistic," one Social Gospel writer believed. "Notwithstanding any attempts to put the clock back, there seems a reasonable hope of moving forward, out of the chaos of mere individualism with unrestrained competition and continual strife, into the more cosmic order of . . . combination and co-operation on a large scale." [42] Another writer went so far as to argue that "coöperation in industry is surely an application of this law [of love], and a beginning of the fullest realization of the Kingdom of God." [43]

The error that Christian progressives often made was in assuming that economic coordination or the formation of interest groups was actuated by motives higher than the desire for gain or group and individual self-interest. They were convincing themselves that the very things that their fathers had feared — industrial integration, increasing interdependence, the organization of capital and labor — were not only harmless but even beneficial developments that pointed the way toward a cooperative future. Competition and its antisocial products would melt away painlessly, through natural industrial evolution and the actions of moral people, without the necessity of disturbing the basic structure of capitalism, private property, or the distribution of wealth.

As people worked more closely together, as they became more dependent on one another, as they cooperated on enterprises of various sorts, Christian progressives believed a socially oriented individualism would emerge that would eclipse the narrow and selfish variety. The first step in this spiritual regeneration would be the development of a social conscience. When people learned of their divinely ordained social duties to one another, they would treat one another as brothers and sisters. Capitalists and laborers would realize their common brotherhood, and industrial strife would end. Businessmen would recognize their duties to investors, partners, consumers, and even competitors. And both employers and employees would see that their actions affected all of society and that it was their duty to serve all of society.

A new type of business demanded a new sort of businessman, as different from the old as night was different from day. "We need . . . men . . . who will go into the commercial life of to-day, as into a high and holy calling," Charles D. Williams believed, "men with a new ideal of trade, who will see in it . . . a God-given mission and ministry of social service, a part of God's great scheme for a redeemed universe, a Divine order of human society." [44]

Williams' remarks illustrate the fact that Christian progressives were working "for moral capitalism, for Christianized economics," in Robert Wiebe's phrase.[45] They did not see any necessary contradiction between a Christian industrial system on the one hand and private control of capital, private property, and even the unequal distribution of wealth on the other. Individual character was most important to them; institutions were secondary. And those, such as George Herron, who dared to suggest the incompatibility of Christianity and capitalism, rapidly lost influence among them.[46] They were idealists whose faith in people appears, in retrospect, to have transcended reason. They had so much faith in moral people that they believed good individuals could overcome an immoral environment. Their analysis of social ills and their recognition of the need for human regeneration might have been correct. Their belief that this regeneration could take place within the American capitalist system was wrong, and their inability to recognize this fact was one key to their failure.

The Christian progressives' attempt to impose the standards of private morality on the economic system was spirited. They emphasized personal responsibility, not simply of workers or capitalists but of everybody, and they saw the moralization of economic behavior as part of the regeneration of society in all its aspects. Their heavy reliance on public opinion as an instrument of change reflected their faith that people were basically good and that good people could change institutions. In the national community, they wanted public opinion to control behavior as it had controlled behavior in the pre-industrial village. If regard for the good opinion of his neighbors had prevented a man from cheating a friend or beating his wife, perhaps the arousal of indignant public opinion in the country could prevent corporations from poisoning consumers or from maintaining unsafe conditions for workers. In order for this to happen, a broader conception of what neighbors, communities, and duties were was necessary.

Much of the burden of arousing public opinion was assumed by the churches, which were developing a broad view of their social role. Churches took the leadership role in defining standards and in attempting to uphold them as well. In 1905, for example, Washington Gladden led a protest against church groups' accepting contributions from John D. Rockefeller on the grounds that the money had been earned in an immoral manner. In addition to helping rouse public consciousness regarding the history and methods of the Standard Oil Company, Gladden's action also contributed to healthy self-examination of church practices and of the degree to which churches were upholding the social imperatives of Christianity.

Exposés and investigations of immoral and illegal behavior were also means of raising public consciousness and sharpening public opinion. And Christian progressives sometimes sensed alterations in character as a result of public exposure. "From all sections comes the evidence that conscience has begun to speak again," announced the *Outlook* in the wake of the life insurance scandals of 1905 and 1906, "and that both in business and in public affairs there is coming a new sense of the moral elements involved, a new determination to enforce the moral law." [47]

Though an aroused public opinion might, in and of itself, induce some to alter their economic behavior, Christian progressives also believed it was the duty of the moral public to take steps to assure that alteration took place. It was the responsibility of moral men and women to band together to uphold and demand the enforcement of moral standards. And Christian progressives joined together in a wide variety of voluntary endeavors united by a sense of duty and responsibility.

A good example of this sort of organization was the National Consumers' League, headed by Florence Kelley. The League believed that consumers, because they were "interested in satisfying . . . wants as economically as possible," were responsible for the mistreatment of workers by manufacturers seeking competitive advantage. [48] Kelley hoped to use the universal guilt she believed existed as a spur to broad public action. If consumers, informed as to their social responsibilities, would demand that business behave morally and enforce their demand with economic pressure, mistreatment of workers would cease. "Consumers are entitled to a clear conscience if they act as conscientious people," Kelley explained. "They can, if they will, enforce a claim to have all that they buy free from the taint of cruelty." [49] Here, in microcosm, all of the characteristics of Christian progressivism can be seen

—the emphasis on public conscience and public opinion, social responsibility, voluntarism, moral regeneration, and the alteration of economic behavior.

Politicians recognized and attempted to exploit the heightened public moral consciousness represented and stimulated by Christian progressivism. This enterprise was fraught at once with promise and with peril. The promise lay in electoral success. The peril lay in attempting to devise policies that would please moralistic reformers and that would also satisfy the more traditional political demands of self-interested farmers, workers, businessmen, and ethnic groups.

Reforms designed to democratize and purify the political system were usually popular with Christian progressives, who had an optimistic view of the character of the average person. Such reforms were also usually, if not always, acceptable to farmers, workers, small businessmen, and others, even if political reforms in and of themselves did not touch the basic problems of these groups. In the case of North Dakota, for example, Charles Glaab notes that "the Progressive interlude had not altered the economic exigencies the farmer faced. . . . The reform program was primarily concerned with democratizing election practices and other political devices that would ensure honest government in the state."[50]

Devising satisfactory economic reforms was more difficult. Coalitions might hold together behind legislation to aid farmers, workers, small businessmen, or shippers, especially if it seemed the public interest or the cause of justice would be served thereby. But moralistic reformers always placed their greatest emphasis on individual self-regeneration, and they recoiled from "class" legislation, which seemed to reflect group selfishness. As long as progressive politicians could unite their followings under banners emblazoned with vague identifications such as "consumers" or "the people," they were all right, but specific policies and group demands always threatened to shatter the fragile and somewhat artificial unity of reform coalitions.

The most serious threats to progressive coalitions were social issues such as prohibition or woman suffrage, issues that drew sustenance from Christian progressivism but that were anathema to many of the other elements that supported reform politicians. Historians have often criticized progressive politicians—in particular, Theodore Roosevelt

—for their emphasis on moralistic rhetoric instead of substance, but it is small wonder that the successful ones so often made this choice. Moralistic rhetoric offended nobody in the reform coalitions and, indeed, for Christian progressives who focused on the need for moral regeneration, rhetoric was substance. Specific issues, whether pressed by farmers, workers, small businessmen, prohibitionists, or whomever, often threatened reform unity. For reform politicians, then, Christian progressivism provided a rhetorical style, certainly, and sometimes a tool of analysis, but it did not and could not provide a clear legislative direction.

The response of the business community to moral criticism by reformers was initially somewhat confused. Business could try to ignore the groundswell of public opinion, but only at its peril. Businessmen usually behaved in general conformity to the statute law and the standards of their peers. Rather suddenly, this seemed insufficient. Christian progressives were demanding that businessmen govern themselves, not by statute law or common business practice, but by the law of love. As one commentator noted in the *Atlantic Monthly*, "the new ethics of business proposes nothing less than to abolish a standard of right conduct by which the race has *lived*, and to put in its place an ideal of which a part of the race has often *dreamed*."[51] In vain did businessmen, accustomed to being celebrated as social heroes, argue that they acted legally, that they benefitted the community, or that they did only what everybody else did. Strictly legal behavior or social conformity does not impress a moralist.

The demands that were being placed on businessmen would have been severe, had they taken them seriously. Actuating the law of love in the home was one thing, but putting it into effect in the competitive economy was quite another. In his 1906 book *Moral Overstrain*, attorney George W. Alger suggested that the requirements being placed on businessmen by Christian progressives were too onerous. It was fine to suggest that people live by the Golden Rule, Alger argued, but businessmen must be given practical directions for doing so. "We have no more right to overload a man's morals than his back," Alger believed.[52]

One means of avoiding moral overstrain was by translating ethical standards into statute law, which all had to obey. Businessmen were sometimes willing to accept, and even support, statutory regulations and controls, particularly if by doing so they could standardize business practices and lift the odium of immorality from themselves. Beginning a generation ago, historians discovered the heavy involvement of businessmen in the development of legislation to regulate and control corporate behavior.[53] Because this legislation helped create a more stable environment for business, some scholars, of whom Gabriel Kolko was the most outspoken, concluded that regulation of business was not a reform at all, but was instead the creation of enthusiastic businessmen using the system for their selfish purposes.[54] The weaknesses of this interpretation are mainly that it imparts an almost divine prescience to businessmen and that it underestimates the fact that the instability in the economic environment came largely from the explosion of public indignation regarding business practices. The strength of the interpretation lies in its recognition of creativity and flexibility on the parts of American businessmen, traits that they exhibited throughout the progressive period.

Though their critique was a compelling and easily understandable one, and their analysis was powerful, the Christian progressives had difficulty devising concrete reforms for economic behavior. But they did not concern themselves only with national problems. They also operated in local communities, where they applied moral critiques, analyses, and solutions to municipal problems. In their towns and cities, Christian progressives were more successful in fashioning creative responses to the problem of immoral public behavior.

III

The Christian progressive impulse was felt initially in towns and cities during the crisis of the 1890's. In many ways, Christian progressivism was always most appropriate and successful on the municipal level.

For Christian progressives, the city was a microcosm of American society, illustrating all of the problems and prospects of the nation. In the cities, the narrow individualism, selfish materialism, hedonistic self-indulgence, and social disunity that suffused the country could be seen every day. In the cities, materialistic and impersonal, the stark contrast between standards of private behavior and those of public behavior was vivid. And in an urban environment of cruelty and brutality born of unbridled selfishness, the threat that the amorality of public life would pollute the institutions of private life was immediate.

But the city was a focus of hope as well as fear. It provided practical lessons in interdependence. Idealists conceived it as a unit small enough to allow the inculcation of selfless individualism and the creation of a true sense of community. In the city, it seemed to idealist Frederic Howe, "we are being drawn into an intimacy, a solidarity, which makes the welfare of one the welfare of all." [55]

The first step in municipal reform was always the replacement of the bad and selfish people of the machines with good and selfless people. The process of transferring control of city government from one group to another probably forms the most familiar image of progressive urban reform. It was an exciting and dramatic process that usually assumed the trappings of a morality play. The cast pitted the boss—usually a shadowy figure, corrupt and parasitic, with connections to privileged business and, worse, to organized vice—against the reformer—usually young, always idealistic, with an unshakeable commitment to the public interest; the drama of the campaign showed privilege and vice determined to uphold the machine through fair means or foul, while the reform forces depended on the good and selfless people exclusively. And at the climax—the election—the city redeemed itself by vanquishing vice and enthroning virtue. The scenes were played out in town after town, reported in newspaper after newspaper. Soon the process took on a stylized aspect, like the old Indian captivity narratives. Simply plug in different towns and different names; the basic script was usually the same.

The self-righteousness of these campaigns makes it difficult for modern people to take them seriously. But contemporaries took them seriously, in part because of the very moralism we find quaint. The Christian progressives were struggling for the soul of the city. They were stimulating popular guilt and inviting the public to participate in a process of civic regeneration. They were arguing that a public interest existed and bound the community and that it must be upheld relative to private individual or group interests. In most places their appeal was successful, at least for awhile. The machine coalitions, strained by the nineties, cracked apart, and reform coalitions, bridging numerous social divisions, triumphed.

For some reformers, getting rid of the bad men was sufficient evidence of redemption. But most took steps to develop the emerging sense of community and uphold the public interest. In many places, this entailed diminishing corporate privilege, especially through municipal ownership and operation of essential services. Municipal ownership was justified on grounds both of community self-determination and of a heightened moral tone. Not only would public ownership allow the community to master its own fate; it would also create an atmosphere of selflessness and service to supplant the selfish desire for profits exemplified by the corporations. *"Moral development . . .* is favored by public ownership," urban reformer Frank Parsons believed. "The change from profit to service as a motive and aim, is in itself a moral transformation of most vital moment." [56]

For private property that affected the community but on which the community did not depend, urban progressives usually favored increased regulation. Citywide planning, zoning and building codes, regulation of noise, smoke, and waste disposal, and standards for the treatment of workers and consumers were all facets of the attempt of communities to assert a public interest separate from and superior to the interests of private property owners.

Those who favored public ownership of some property and increased regulation of other property made some assumptions that most urban progressives shared. They agreed that the rights of society took precedence over the rights of individuals. They also believed that a public interest existed that could be defined for every issue and that was separate from the private interests of those involved. They were certain that public-spirited individuals could identify the public interest and that the public was rational and virtuous enough to accept that definition. And they believed that public power over private property, already reflecting a heightened degree of community consciousness, would help create an environment in which a true sense of neighborliness and brotherhood would thrive. In other words, public power, asserting a public interest, would alter behavior in the city as a whole, forcing it to conform more fully to a broadly Christian ethical standard.

Urban reformers were attuned to the possibilities of creating environments that would allow the more attractive aspects of the human character to dominate. Christian progressives did not discount individual character, but neither did these intelligent observers of urban life ignore the effect of environment in shaping human behavior. Jane Addams, for example, thought that there were both good and bad impulses within human beings, but that environmental factors helped determine which would be exercised.[57] Public ownership and regulation of private property were designed in part to create an environment more conducive to the development and exercise of community consciousness, neighborliness, and brotherhood, and Christian progressives worked to alter the urban environment on a number of other fronts as well.

Poverty was one problem with which urban reformers struggled. By the turn of the century, those concerned with the poor were well along the path, charted during the nineties, to an environmental explanation of poverty. Still, few were willing to deny that individual character was responsible for some economic hardship. Even Socialist Robert Hunter, in his touching and emotional classic *Poverty*, was quick to concede that some poverty derived from defective individual characters and that it was, therefore, deserved:

> The sins of men should bring their own punishment, and the poverty which punishes the vicious and the sinful is good and necessary. Social or industrial institutions that save men from the painful consequences of vice or folly are not productive of the greatest good. . . . It would be unwise to legislate out of existence, even if it were possible to do so, that poverty which penalizes the voluntarily idle and vicious.[58]

But Hunter differed from earlier observers in arguing that most poverty was "bred of miserable and unjust social conditions, which punish the good and the pure, the faithful and industrious, the slothful and vicious, all alike." It followed that because "men are brought into misery by the action of social and economic forces" and because "the wrongful action of such social and economic forces is a preventable thing," poverty could be best attacked by addressing environmental factors.[59]

- 103 -

Some of the environmental factors that caused poverty and dependency transcended the city. But others could be and were addressed there. Child labor, poor educational opportunities, substandard and unhealthy housing, and unsafe working conditions were all attacked by urban progressives hoping to create an environment that would improve character. The increasing environmentalism of those concerned with the poor was reflected in their particular attention to children. Only the most hard-hearted could possibly blame deprived children for the conditions in which they lived, and the apparent plasticity of juvenile characters provided support for those who emphasized the importance of environment.

Reforms that dealt particularly with children—the play movement, education reform, abolition of child labor, and the creation of a juvenile justice system, for example—attracted the most thoroughgoing environmentalists among urban progressives. One of the most famous of these was Ben B. Lindsey, the individual most responsible for the creation of the juvenile justice system in the United States.

As a judge in Denver, Colorado before the turn of the century, Lindsey puzzled over the causes for criminal behavior among the children who were brought into his court. Based on his investigation of individual cases, Lindsey became convinced that juvenile crime was environmentally caused. "I reached the basic conclusion that there were no 'bad kids,'" Lindsey recalled a generation later. "Instead, there were 'bad' conditions and environment which resulted in 'bad' conduct." "Down in every soul, notwithstanding the effects of bad environment and the defects of heredity," Lindsey argued, "there was what I then chose to call the Image of God and it was up to me to bring it out." [60] These conclusions led Lindsey in two directions. He turned to a long, bitter, and eventually unsuccessful crusade to create an environment in which "the Image of God" in every child could emerge. This effort entailed forays against corrupt politicians and economic privilege and involvement in a wide variety of controversial reforms. Eventually, Lindsey's multi-faceted activities led to his electoral defeat at the hands of the Ku Klux Klan, an organization that, ironically, drew sustenance from moralistic Christian progressives in Denver whose reformism had constricted and soured. More successful was Lindsey's creation of a juvenile court that attempted to guide and educate youthful offenders rather than punish them. The juvenile justice system, which spread throughout the country, was a clear institutional expression of Christian progressivism, carrying, as it did, an abounding faith in the goodness, rationality, and educability of people.

Urban progressives, accepting the notion that the environment facilitated the expression of particular character traits, attempted to create the sorts of surroundings in which community and brotherhood could be more easily expressed. The idea of environmental modification was not new. Good government enthusiasts, public ownership advocates, and vice and liquor reformers had long argued that their reforms, if implemented, would improve the moral tone of city life. After the turn of the century, however, there was increasing interest in shaping the urban environment to achieve positive goals rather than simply removing negative influences from it. "Positive environmentalism," as it is styled by Paul Boyer, could be seen in such reform movements as those for city beautification, civic centers, community pageants, public baths, and parks and playgrounds.[61]

In the minds of most Christian progressives, positive and negative environmentalism were complementary rather than competitive emphases. Both pointed toward improved individual characters and a heightened sense of community. Reformer Delos Wilcox argued that "the city must . . . be up and doing to so modify the conditions of life within its limits as to encourage virtue and discourage vice." To Wilcox, as to many others, that effort entailed abolishing "the gaudy allurements of license and . . . the intoxicating cup of vice," as well as encouraging "the right uses of leisure which naturally follow from the recognition of the meaning of brotherhood and social unity."[62]

Positive environmentalists believed they could create, or revive, a sense of community in the cities. When men and women recognized their commonality and interdependence, selfishness, alienation, and class, ethnic, and religious divisions would melt away, replaced by a community consciousness in which people treated one another like sisters or brothers. As Jean B. Quandt has pointed out, urban progressives were attempting to recreate the lost community of pre-industrial America, the community in which the ideal of human brotherhood was closer to reality, and in which people controlled their behavior because of their regard for the good opinion of their neighbors.[63] Institutional churches and social settlements, so popular at the turn of the century, attempted to foster a sense of neighborliness in working-class and immigrant areas. Those involved in these neighborhood movements hoped that the sense of community planted there would spread to the city as a whole and even beyond. Thus, the institutions of private life—the family and the neighborhood—governed by Christian ethical standards, would infuse public life and alter public behavior.

In recent years, historians have not viewed the efforts of Christian progressives to alter the urban environment with very much sympathy. Their emphasis on character and their relative disinterest in altering institutions has raised scholarly suspicions about their motives. It has become fashionable to highlight their fear and bigotry and to accuse them of endeavoring mainly to control workers, immigrants, and others. One scholar has even questioned the sincerity of their Christianity, seeing in it "little more than a commitment to convert the working class to middle-class values." [64]

Scholarly critics of urban progressives and their motives have added another dimension to what was once a rather flat picture. Unfortunately, we have sometimes allowed our own alienation and cynicism to prevent us from understanding fully the reformers and what they tried to do. As Don Kirschner pointed out in an important article in 1975, urban progressivism was a complex phenomenon. Bigotry, fear, and a desire to control others were there, but so too were idealism, altruism, and human compassion. [65]

At their most idealistic, urban reformers captured a vision of cities that were true communities in which people loved and cared for each other. When Frederic C. Howe looked forward to the day "when in addition to self-consciousness and family-consciousness there arises a city-consciousness, that instinct which is willingness to struggle for the common weal, and suffer for the common woe," he had clearly moved beyond a cramped and narrow conception of reform. [66] And when Brand Whitlock foresaw planned cities that "shall express the ideals of the people and work wonderful ameliorations in the human soul" and that would foster "a life that is fuller, more beautiful, more splendid and, above all, more human," he was expressing an inspiring vision, not obscuring sordid motives. [67] And when University of Chicago social scientist Edward Bemis compared the city to a church he did not mean that it should be an institution of restrictive moral control. He meant that the modern city glimpsed by reformers would educate, protect, and unify the people as the early church had. "The sense of brotherhood taught by the early Apostles is now best seen at . . . City Hall," he argued, innocently, perhaps, but not duplicitously.[68]

Social control, bigotry, terror of disorder, fear, even, of people — all of these played a part in Christian urban reform. But to emphasize these is to tell, at best, but half of the story. Whitlock and Howe, Addams, Lindsey, and all the others were shortsighted, certainly; their analyses were incomplete and their motives were mixed. But these were not their major problems. Their major shortcoming was that there were not enough of them, not enough "men of good hope" in Daniel Aaron's felicitous phrase, not enough people willing to commit themselves to a vision of true community based on neighborliness and love.[69] In retrospect, it seems less appropriate to attack their motives than to mourn their failure.

IV

As is clear from the name they took, progressives believed in the goodness and inevitability of progress. In this commitment, they were children of a Victorian age that had seen unparalleled material progress. Moral progress was less clear, for material advancement had been accompanied by threats to social unity, institutions and values, accepted standards of behavior, and society itself. The efforts undertaken by progressives were consequently based in fear as well as in hope, in anxiety as well as in optimism. Their fears and anxieties were reflected in the vehemence of their responses to suggestions that human progress was not taking place or, worse, that people were becoming less moral and less civilized over time.

Doubts about the direction of human development, prominent during the 1890's, did not disappear thereafter. In 1910, popular author Prestonia Martin published *Is Mankind Advancing?: The Most Important Question in the World*. In it, Martin argued that progress since the glory days of ancient Greece had been more material than moral, and she warned that the common people on whom the race depended for its future were deteriorating in quality.[70] Four years later, Guglielmo Ferrero, son-in-law of the great Italian social scientist Cesare Lombroso, published a comparison between ancient Rome and modern America in which he found progress in the latter to be "quantitative" rather than "qualitative."[71]

Neither Martin nor Ferrero is remembered now, and the quality of their thought does not justify a revival. The remarkable thing about their books was the amount of editorial comment each called forth. When Martin and Ferrero questioned the nature of American progress, they touched a sensitive nerve. In part they elicited a response because they were swimming against the current of the times. And they were also comparing America with Europe, which was a certain way to get attention. But they were also focusing on questions about which Americans themselves were worried—whether we were becoming too materialistic, whether we would lose our souls in the pursuit of things, whether our characters were becoming worse.

The Christian progressives, preoccupied with human behavior and the human character, had been troubled by these issues. Selfishness, materialism, cruelty, brutality, and inhumanity had disturbed them and had galvanized them into action. They had aimed at nothing short of a social revitalization through a regeneration of individual character. And the first years of the twentieth century seemed to indicate that their hopes for a regenerate civilization were on the threshold of realization. "The world is growing better," one reformer assured his readers. "No man can be a pessimist who realizes something of the spirit of the times."[72]

What was this "spirit of the times," and why did it make the Christian progressives so optimistic? What the Christian progressives thought they were seeing in their cities and towns, in popular behavior, and in the relationships among people was a social revitalization on the basis of Christian ethical principles. "The spirit of religion," Scott Nearing held in 1913, "dominates the American people."[73] Increasingly, it seemed, the basic moral truths of Christianity were guiding daily life. "Outside of the churches the social awakening is remarkable for the religious spirit which it creates in men who thought they were done with religion," noted Walter Rauschenbusch. "They are getting a faith once more. They show all the evidences of religion,—love, tenderness, longings mysterious to themselves, a glad willingness to sacrifice time and money for the salvation of their fellows."[74]

The vagueness and comprehensiveness of this regeneration was reflected in the descriptions of it. William Dean Howells believed that "the central principle" of the "genuine renascence of Christianity" was "human sympathy."[75] John Graham Brooks saw a growing sensitivity and circumspection in regard to once acceptable political and economic behavior.[76] Some perceived a greater sense of social responsibility and a new devotion to social justice. Optimists even twisted evidence that might show degeneration to support the case for moral progress. In 1903, the *Independent* bemoaned "lynchings in our Southern States, . . . primitive blood feuds and political lawlessness . . . in Kentucky; horrible massacres in Armenia and Bulgaria, and revolution by murder in Servia," but it argued that the shame and indignation stimulated by these events served as "the supreme proof of the reality of progress."[77] And J. Allen Smith assured the readers of *The Spirit of American Government* that they should not be concerned about the apparent "increase in crimes, misdemeanors, and acts which enlightened public opinion condemns. This is due . . . not to any decline in public morality, but to the fact that the ethical progress of society as a whole has been more rapid than that of the offending class."[78]

Even the normally skeptical were persuaded. The *World's Work*, a moderate and level-headed periodical, editorialized in 1911 that "any man who will study . . . the large forces now at work in the United States for the public welfare and their visible results will find reason for pride; for he will see evidences, of many kinds, of a moral awakening of the people."[79] And Thorstein Veblen, never known as a Pollyanna, cautiously predicted that "the Christian principle of brotherhood should logically continue to gain ground at the expense of the pecuniary morals of competitive business."[80] The regeneration of the American people and the redirection of public behavior, glimpsed in the nineties, seemed to be under way.

We are no better able than the reformers to prove or disprove that a change in character was taking place. We cannot determine motivation. We know that people joined groups and elected candidates and passed laws, but we cannot be sure why. Was there a moral awakening, or were people modernizing, integrating, showing status anxiety, or controlling? Did people build community centers because of love or fear? Did they throw the rascals out because of outraged morality or the desire for political advancement? Did they regulate business to protect the public or to shield the corporations? We know why they *said* they did things, and we know that they often spoke in moralistic terms, but what was the relationship between rhetoric and reality?

The moralism of Christian progressivism, the rhetoric of duty, character, and service, and the emphasis on ethical concepts provided its greatest strength. The Golden Rule, brotherhood, the law of love — these were concepts everybody understood and to which everybody was committed, theoretically at least. Everybody could understand the analysis of Christian progressivism, and most people could feel the guilt Christian progressives stimulated. No social scientist, interest group spokesman, efficiency engineer, or scientific socialist had a message as powerful, as legitimate, or as easily understood as that of the Christian progressive. The problem lay not in the message, but in putting it into effect.

The vagueness and comprehensiveness of the Christian progressive message was at once its main strength and main weakness. As Clyde Griffen concludes, "the very vagueness of the vision and rhetoric of a Christian democracy created a semblance of national unity of purpose, encouraging the progressive generation to minimize divisions between various kinds of reformers."[81] Only the vaguest constructs — the Golden Rule, brotherhood, the law of love — could begin to serve as comprehensive principles uniting an heterogeneous and pluralistic society. Only in an homogenous society, undivided by race, ethnicity, religion, class, or occupation, could these constructs serve as reliable guides for public policy.

The fact that most people accepted and, rhetorically at least, honored the truths of Christian progressivism, did not mean that they would or even could apply these truths in the same way. Christian progressivism "was effective only so long as it remained vague, so that each group could work for the Kingdom [of God] in its own way," notes historian Ferenc Szasz. "The introduction of specific points, however, proved its undoing."[82] In his post-mortem on American reform, written on the eve of World War II, Edgar Kemler noted that "the progressives could appeal to every right-minded man. They were campaigning for justice, brotherhood, peace and similar vague objectives." The problem was that specific issues had to be addressed, questions had to be answered that touched on the lives and fortunes of businessmen, workers, farmers, and consumers: "We found it necessary to bring our ideals down from the moral stratosphere. Who, we asked, would profit most in the realization of the progressive ideal? While everybody talked justice, some men obviously stood to gain by it and some to lose." In the process, the ideal was cheapened and those who believed in it were manipulated by the jugglers of rhetoric.

The problem of applying the ideals of Christian progressivism, as Kemler shrewdly noted, lay in the fact that "the battlefield was located, not in the economy, but in the recesses of the human soul."[83] "We are building our pyramid of civilization," William Allen White had said. "But it must rest upon its base or fall; and its base must be the practical Christian living of the people in their daily lives."[84] Christian progressives were concerned with the soul, which was, of course, the key problem. It was the foundation of the pyramid of civilization. But how could the quality of the soul be gauged, how could "practical Christian living" be measured? And how could the structure of the pyramid be built by men and women obsessed with its foundation? Christian progressivism remained a force that no one could ignore, but it did not impede the continuation of old-fashioned interest-group politics. Nor did it prevent the elaboration of other comprehensive principles that claimed to be guides both for life and for public policy. Nor, in the end, did it successfully redeem the American soul.

THE CHALLENGE OF
SCIENTIFIC PROGRESSIVISM

Each group of sciences will solve one or more of the
great problems which man has encountered in the
process of development. The physical sciences will
solve the problems of environment, the biological
sciences the problems of life, and the social sciences
the problems of society.

FREDERICK A. BUSHEE

I do not think anything will ever allay . . . unrest except democracy in industry. I don't know
just what that means, but I think it has to come
to pass some way; and I do not feel cocksure about
that — about anything, very much. I am very pragmatic.

MARY E. MCDOWELL

Christianity fueled the initial thrust of progressivism, providing reformers with a critique of society, a rhetorical style, a means of change,
and a social goal. The strength of Christian progressivism derived from
the fact that its ethical tenets were easily understood and readily accepted by most people and from its compelling sense that an improved
individual character was a necessary precondition for a reformed society. Its weakness lay in its vagueness and in its inconvertability into
clear public policies on which its adherents could agree.

Some contemporaries of the Christian progressives were disturbed
by their diagnoses, their prescriptions, and their moralistic tone. Politicians and businessmen attempting to respond to vague but comprehensive demands, interest-group leaders trying to craft durable coali-

tions, and reformers who wanted to chart a clear path for social change often found Christian progressivism excessively nebulous and vague. By 1910, some reformers were concluding that science, broadly conceived, provided a more usable means of explaining and solving social problems than did Christianity. By the early teens a "scientific progressivism" had emerged that analyzed social ills through empiricism rather than religious authority, that placed its faith in the expert rather than the goodness of the average citizen, and that yearned for an organized and efficient America rather than a morally regenerate one.

Scientific progressives agreed that Christianity, taken alone, did not effectively address the problems of modern society. They believed that the Golden Rule and the law of love, while admirable enough in the abstract, did not provide usable guides either for individual behavior or for social policy. Scientific progressives often agreed with their Christian counterparts regarding the nation's outstanding problems — materialism, social disunity, individual hedonism and selfishness — and they were usually quite moralistic in their own way, but they failed to see social salvation in the simple truths of homogenized Christianity. Consider, for example, the problem of making the Golden Rule a practical guide for living. In a textbook he co-authored with John Dewey, University of Chicago professor James Hayden Tufts pointed out some of the pitfalls of relying on the Golden Rule:

> We sometimes hear it stated . . . that the universal adoption of the Golden Rule would at once settle all industrial disputes and difficulties. But supposing that the principle were accepted in good faith by everybody; it would not at once tell everybody just what to do in all of the complexities of his relations to others. When individuals are still uncertain of what their real good may be, it does not finally decide matters to tell them to regard the good of others as they would their own. Nor does it mean that whatever in detail we want for ourselves we should strive to give to others. Because I am fond of classical music it does not follow that I should thrust as much of it as possible upon my neighbors.[1]

"Assume that you and he [your neighbor] are alike, and you can found morals on humanity," argued the young Walter Lippmann in 1913. "But experience has enlarged our knowledge of differences. We realize now that our neighbor is not always like ourselves." [2] A simple guide to behavior, fashioned for an homogenous (and pre-Freudian) people, simply was not sufficient for a modern, heterogeneous, dynamic, urban, and industrial society. Even the Christian progressives sometimes admitted that the answers might be harder than they had thought. "The conditions of an advanced civilization, instead of making righteousness more simple, complicate the problem," one of them conceded. "While living grows easier along material lines, it grows harder in the moral sphere." [3]

Scientific progressives affected a tone of realism and toughness to set themselves apart from their more moralistic and sentimental colleagues, but they, too, were quite innocent. Their faith in science was as complete and unquestioning as was the faith of others in basic Christian principles. They viewed science and progress as coincidental, and they believed that a functional and comprehensive science of society was being developed. The confident statement of Colorado College professor Frederick Bushee that social science would solve "the problems of society" reflected the attitude common among them. [4] Practicing reformers saw no necessary contradiction between the two systems, and devotees of science often exhibited the same moral intensity as the religious. As Charles Rosenberg has noted, "science, like religion, offered an ideal of selflessness, of truth, of the possibility of spiritual dedication — emotions which in their elevating purity could inspire and motivate." [5]

Rosenberg's insight provides a clue to understanding the fascination of reformers with science in the progressive era. It drew from the same Victorian wells of altruism and moralism that fed Christian progressivism. Young men and women with the compulsion to serve society could see in science a means to that end, just as others fastened on Christianity as a vehicle. One flowed into the other in a relatively smooth and subtle fashion. In practice, the break between scientific and Christian progressivism was not clear and sharp. [6]

In retrospect, though, we can see important differences between scientific and Christian progressives that were less clear at the time. Scientific progressives put their faith in professional expertise, not character. An efficient society, not a regenerate one, was their goal. Their means to the efficient society were diverse and, in some cases, ominous. Scientific administration and management, social engineering, eugenics, and behaviorist psychology were all seen as roads toward a society that was united, productive, abundant, and happy.

Scientific progressives embraced the pragmatic method as an empirical guide to individual action and the making of public policy. Pragmatism—the belief that decisions should be made on the basis of experience rather than in accordance with traditional secular or religious ideals—seemed a more utilizable guide to action than the Golden Rule. In time it became clear that pragmatism was an elitist guide to behavior, less useful to the average person than the easily comprehended, if imperfect, Golden Rule. Pragmatism effectively banished traditional, overarching values without putting much in their place save a vague utilitarianism and a devotion to efficiency. In the short run, scientific progressives were content to operate without the guidance of firm, traditional values. They wanted to modernize values *and* alter reality, while Christian progressives tried to make reality conform to traditional values. Still, the lack of firm guides led to confusion and unease among some who tried to embrace the new empiricism. "I do not feel cocksure . . . about anything, very much," social worker Mary McDowell revealed in her testimony before the United States Industrial Commission. "I am very pragmatic."[7]

Scientific progressives paralleled Christian progressives in their desire for social unity and their distaste for the unrestrained, selfish, materialistic, and hedonistic individual. They, too, believed there was a public interest, separate from and superior to the interests of selfish individuals and groups. For scientific progressives, though, self-restraint and social responsibility drawn from basic Christian principles was insufficient. They hoped to inculcate individual loyalty to society as society, to the state, or to the "race," or at least to make people behave in such a way as to serve those abstractions. Instead of hoping for a broad social regeneration, they placed their faith in intelligent, public-spirited experts who would move society in a desirable direction. They were less enamoured of voluntaristic solutions to social problems that depended on individual character than they were of statist solutions, which were often manipulative in nature.

Their self-conscious modernism and their self-proclaimed tough-mindedness makes the scientific progressives seem realistic. But, in the end, these characteristics did not make them any more effective than the Christian reformers they criticized. Their analysis of society's problems was, if anything, less compelling than that of the Christian progressives. Their solutions for these problems proved just as hard to put into effect. They, too, overestimated the potential for comprehensive change in a system that remained capitalistic. And they proved to be even more prone to manipulation than were the Christian progressives. In the end, scientific progressivism did not create a more attractive or viable alternative to Christian progressivism. Instead, the presence of this alternative served to divide, confuse, and demoralize the reform forces and to diminish their potential effectiveness.

I

Scientific progressives were products of the same Victorian age that shaped their Christian counterparts. As Victorians, they were preoccupied with the individual. The unrestrained individual, selfish, materialistic, hedonistic, and antisocial, was the primary threat to the community. The restrained and directed individual, the selfless devotee of the public interest and trained servant of the community, was society's hope. Scientific progressives grappled with the problem of developing the latter type of individual to control the former.

"The plain fact," lamented Herbert Croly in *The Promise of American Life*, "is that the individual in freely and energetically pursuing his own private purposes has not been the inevitable public benefactor." [8] Modern society had freed people from restraints in their public behavior without fashioning new external or internal checks on conduct. "If a man dare attempt to sum up the spiritual condition of his time, he might say of ours that it has lost authority and retained the need of it," Walter Lippman believed. "We are freer than we are strong. We have more responsibility than we have capacity." [9] As a result, E. A. Ross contended, "the community has become too often the prey of individuals. In the absence of prestige and reverence, social control, the control of the many over the one, has been pared down so far as to permit, too often, the counter aggression of the one upon the many." [10]

For scientific progressives the community—or society—was primary. It was more important than any individual, and it imparted definition and meaning to the lives of those within it. It was not an abstraction, but a palpable, organic essence. It was more than the sum of its individual parts; it encompassed them all, but it transcended them as well. For scientific progressives the Anglo-American political heritage, laissez-faire economics, Social Darwinism, and even Christianity were wrong insofar as they emphasized the importance of the individual—his rights, his powers, his free agency and self-determination—relative to society.

The scientific progressives' emphasis on the primacy of society reflected a strong counter-tendency in Western thought to Anglo-American individualism and a recognition of the unfortunate by-products of that individualism. American reformers who received academic training in Germany—or who were trained by academics who did—tended to adopt the German philosophical animus to unrestrained individualism and the German tendency to enthrone society and the state as the embodiment of society. To scientific progressives, the free and self-sufficient individual was an artificial creation that had little basis in reality. "A separate individual," intoned sociologist Charles Horton Cooley in a seminal work on the relationship between the individual and society, "is an abstraction unknown to experience." Cooley argued that "man has no existence apart from a social order, and can develop his personality only through the social order, and in the same degree that it is developed." [11]

The autonomous individual was an especially pernicious abstraction. Emphasis on the individual, Cooley believed, encouraged the expression of selfishness, fear, and anger. [12] E. A. Ross argued that the emphasis on individualism led people to behave in a beastly way toward society as a whole. His *Sin and Society* explored the impact of individualism on moral values. Ross highlighted an apparent contradiction that remains with us today—while those who sin against individuals, by mugging, robbing, or murdering them, face severe penalties, those who sin against society, by robbing consumers and taxpayers or poisoning the air and water, often receive social approval. Ross believed that this perversion of priorities derived from the tendency to exalt the individual over society. What Ross called the "criminaloids," or the "perpetrator[s] of new sins" against society, were celebrated because they conformed to individualistic social values. They "want nothing more than we all want,—money, power, consideration,—in a word, success." [13]

Scientific progressives hoped to nurture a higher degree of loyalty to society among individuals. Among some of them, this effort took on a sinister, authoritarian cast. Albion Small, for example, hoped to gain popular acceptance for the notion that "there are no rights, except rights of way in the performance of social functions." [14] Herbert Croly, on the other hand, looked forward to the development of a "conscious social ideal" that would impart definition and unity to American society without obliterating individual or group identities and differences. [15] All of them believed that something more substantial than Christian values was required to build loyalty to society of sufficient strength to overcome the individual's loyalty to himself. "The old regulative system is falling to pieces," argued Ross. "Few of the strong and ambitious have any longer the fear of God before their eyes. Hell is looked upon as a bogy for children. The Gospel ideas are thought unscientific. . . . So the question of the hour is, Can there be fashioned out of popular sentiment some sort of buckler for society?" [16]

Many of the scientific progressives believed that patriotism—loyalty to the nation—might be the sort of "buckler" Ross had in mind. In the past, when the nation was threatened, people had submerged their narrow and selfish concerns in the common interest, and they might be inspired to do so again. Scientific progressives saw the state as the political embodiment of society, and loyalty to the state as loyalty to society. "The state inspires . . . reverence because it is felt to express our best selves," Ross believed. "It embodies our reason, fair-mindedness, and humaneness." [17] For some scientific progressives, the state became the secular equivalent of God, compelling the loyalty of people and tying them to their fellow citizens. Small wonder that they imbued it with an aura that was almost religious. "The state is founded in the idea of reciprocity," Frank Vrooman believed. "So is the golden rule." [18] To its champions, nationalism promised to do what Christianity promised to do, to unite and inspire people and to call forth the altruistic elements of their nature. It would provide a middle ground between selfish individualism on the one hand and socialism on the other. When people committed themselves to the state, nationalists such as

Croly and Vrooman assured their readers, America could remain a liberal-democratic-capitalist society, with the same class and ethnic divisions, and still exhibit selflessness, sacrifice, service, and popular devotion to the public interest.

For some, loyalty to the nation was the first step on the road to a higher loyalty, usually defined as loyalty to the "race," identified vaguely and variously as Teutonic or Anglo-Saxon. "We look forward ultimately to something wider than Nationalism," Vrooman wrote, "racial federation." [19] But whether they hitched their wagon to the nation, to the "race," or both, scientific progressives were indicating that, in the modern age, the fatherhood of God and the brotherhood of man were too weak to unite and inspire people and were insufficient to overcome selfishness, materialism, and strife. Perhaps they were correct, but it is an indication of the poverty of twentieth-century liberal thought that they relied on such potentially vicious and divisive phenomena as racism and nationalism as alternatives. Christianity might not make people virtuous, but racism and nationalism, by their very nature, could never do so.

Scientific progressives did not believe that a thoroughgoing regeneration of character, in which all people devoted themselves to the society, the state, or the race, was necessary. For them, it was enough that an elite, strategically placed in industry and government, armed with the tools of empirical analysis and the power to use them, should be regenerate. This elite could manipulate the citizens in such a way that their behavior served society, regardless of their character. Thus, scientific progressives offered a shortcut to a united and efficient society.

II

Christian progressives evaluated an individual's character by determining the degree to which he or she treated others as brothers and sisters. Scientific progressives assessed the individual's character by measuring his or her efficiency. They equated efficiency with virtue and inefficiency with vice. The progressive fascination with efficiency was discovered by Samuel Hays, more than anybody else, and was explored first in detail by Samuel Haber.[20] Since the 1960's the progressive emphasis on efficiency has become an integral part of the modernization thesis, broadly defined, which holds that the progressives were concerned primarily with imparting organization, efficiency, and professional bureaucratic administration to many aspects of American life.

In recent years, historians have concentrated particular attention on scientific management, the movement to make industrial production more efficient. But the economy was only one area in which scientific progressives emphasized the need for greater efficiency. They also spoke of social, civic, and even moral efficiency.

Though they were not always clear on specifics, scientific progressives agreed on the general shape of the efficient society. The efficient society, like the efficient factory, would be composed of happy, productive people who would cooperate with one another harmoniously and would accept orders from and defer to an educated elite. This elite would be composed of experts who would make social policy in the interest of the public. Efficiency, at once the means to and the end of the model society, would be the guiding principle for the policies made.

At first glance, this model appears quite different from that which the Christian progressives had in mind. To many scientific progressives, however, the difference between a society based on efficiency and one based on brotherhood was less clear. Efficiency to them was a more scientific and thus surer means to a united, cooperative society in which people were animated by a regard for the public interest and a passion for service. In broad outline, the ideal society they projected was not so different from that foreseen by Christian progressives. Moreover, efficiency and morality often became mixed in their minds, resulting in a hybrid of pseudo-science and ethics. This was due in part to the fact that traditional values such as hard work, sobriety, and conscientiousness were important contributors to efficiency.[21]

They often equated efficiency with virtue. Stanford University president David Starr Jordan, for example, identified economic efficiency with morality and made both measures of virtuous citizenship:

No man is a good citizen until he can take care of himself and has something left over for the common welfare. If economically and morally alike he is a nonproducer, he is no fit member of a democracy. He is a public nuisance. If he earns no more than his keep, rich or poor, he is an economic nonentity. If he exerts no influence for good, he is a moral nonentity.[22]

The efficient person was moral because he served society, and society would become more moral as it became more efficient. Small wonder that some reformers saw in efficiency "a new religion, or a new ethics, —the service of all for all." [23] In retrospect, though, it is apparent that efficiency marked a retreat from the standard of Christian brotherhood rather than a positive refinement of it. Scientific progressives equated service with efficiency, but they usually did not care whether service was the motive for efficient behavior. "Habits are acquired that increase efficiency and inculcate sound principles of conduct," noted social scientist Simon Patten, who went on to admit that, despite the tendency to equate these habits with virtue, "personal advantage will always be the motive for their acquisition." [24]

To the devotees of efficiency, the behavior itself was primary, and the motivation for it was secondary. "Efficient service" was the key, explained Jordan. "Whether public or private service is a matter of minor importance. All efficient private service becomes sooner or later public." [25] Though garbed in the fetching new attire of science, this notion bore a strong resemblance to Adam Smith's invisible hand of the market theory, which had been used in the nineteenth century to excuse and even justify selfishness and greed. With all their failings, the Christian progressives at least emphasized motives, and they recognized that permanent changes in behavior must be grounded in an alteration of character. Though they often falsely equated character with behavior, the scientific progressives were much more obsessed with changes in the latter than in the former.

The self-consciously empirical scientific progressives concentrated on what could be observed, quantified, and measured. Human behavior was not exactly like the behavior of chemicals or physical objects, but it did lend itself to a certain quasi-scientific analysis. As social scientists emphasized the knowable and manipulable in society, empirical reform came to appear at once uniquely modern and especially promising. Reformers who concentrated on the unknowable human soul seemed increasingly old-fashioned and irrelevant. Their concentration on measurable behavior and their disinterest in human character contributed to a tendency on the part of scientific progressives to see human beings as objects to be manipulated rather than as possessors of unique individual personalities.

The tendency of scientific progressives to objectify people can be seen in their attraction to behaviorism. Scientific progressives were among those in the vanguard of a new view of human nature and human behavior that emerged after the turn of the twentieth century. As James Gilbert has noted, "the older theory that an individual acted according to an inner calling gave way before a theory that stressed the mechanical and behavioral elements of character." While the older theory saw permanent behavioral change resulting from regeneration or reformation of character, "the behavior model in social and psychological theory aimed to solicit desired action rather than instill Christian virtue." [26] People could be made to act in prescribed ways through a variety of means. Rewards and punishments, pleasures and pains could mold behavior. The institutional environment—schools, churches, factories, and government agencies, for example—could channel people in desirable directions.

Many Christian progressives also saw the importance of environment, but there was a world of difference between them and thoroughgoing behaviorists. For Christian progressives, an improved environment could facilitate the predomination of the altrustic side of the individual character, and different behavior would offer tangible proof of this character change. For behaviorists, a changed environment would alter behavior; any effect it had on character was inconsequential. Behaviorists showed a kind of idealism, but they discounted the integrity of the individual, and this was sometimes reflected in a cynical desire to manipulate and control people in order to bring forth desirable behavior. They tended to believe that an elite, which knew the way to efficient service for the society, should be given the power to shape the environment and thus human behavior. To cite one example, scientific progressives interested in agriculture hoped to create and control an institutional environment that would manipulate farmers to be more efficient producers of food. Presumably, this goal would benefit society as a whole, but the wishes of the agricultural population that was to be manipulated were never consulted.[27]

The eugenics movement, which also enjoyed a vogue after 1900, seemed to differ sharply from behaviorism. While behaviorists stressed the importance of environment, eugenicists hoped to improve human beings through heredity, which would be regulated by birth control, sterilization, and even selective breeding.[28] But the characteristics that they shared attracted scientific progressives to both. Eugenicists and behaviorists stressed the importance of society relative to the individual, both presented a "scientific" means of altering behavior, both discounted the importance or integrity of individual character, both were manipulative and elitist, and both promised the achievement of an efficient society.

Behaviorism and eugenics promised a revolutionalized society, and they thus commanded the respectful attention of scientific progressives. But in the short run each was practiced on a small scale only, with special and limited populations, and existed most vitally as theory. In scientific management, which promised an efficient economy and, by implication, an efficient society, theory and practice were joined.

Scientific management involved the efforts of trained industrial experts—usually professional engineers—to study industrial processes scientifically and to attempt to alter these processes in the interest of economic efficiency. Beginning rather modestly in Frederick Winslow Taylor's time-motion studies of workers' tasks, scientific management blossomed during the progressive era into a comprehensive system of industrial management that had important implications for public policy.

The leaders of the scientific management movement shared certain characteristics that attracted scientific progressives to them. Their goal was the same goal scientific progressives set for society as a whole—efficiency—and they were experts who seemed to possess the technical means to realize that goal. Reflecting a similar tendency among scientific progressives, the engineers saw efficiency in idealistic terms, as service to society and thus as an ethical imperative. Industrial efficiency for them encompassed both material and moral aspects. As one student of scientific management has noted, "Taylor saw science as a moral system taking the place of a dying Christianity in the new industrial order." [29]

Engineers enamoured of the utopian facets of scientific management believed they were selfless, public-spirited experts serving society. They saw themselves as "stewards of technology, . . . agents of social progress," whose role it was to defend the public interest "in the factory against the narrow vision and vested interests of worker and employer." [30] Whatever self-serving individuals and groups might want, efficiency served society. The engineers were servants of the public because they were professionals whose training shifted their devotion from their selfish interests to science, and thus to the public interest.

The faith scientific progressives expressed in the professional was similar to that expressed by Christian reformers in the regenerate individual. Indeed, scientific progressives believed that professional training—of engineers, businessmen, public servants, what have you —transformed individuals in the same way spiritual regeneration transformed them. They believed that professional training lifted trainees above their petty concerns, giving them an elevated view of themselves and their social role, making them selfless, and directing their energies toward social service.

Louis Brandeis was one scientific progressive who placed his faith in the professional. He defined a profession as more than "an occupation for which the necessary preliminary training is intellectual in character." He saw it as "an occupation which is pursued largely for others and not merely for one's self" and one "in which the amount of financial return is not the accepted measure of success." The accepted measure of success for a profession, he concluded, was "excellence of performance in the broadest sense," including "service to the community." [31]

Their faith in the professional indicates how minimal the divergence often was between scientific progressives and their Christian counterparts. They, too, placed their faith in people rather than measures, in the regeneration of character rather than institutional reformation. They simply saw a secular road—a couple of years in a professional school and membership in a professional society—to the regenerate individual.

Still, there was the difference that while Christian progressives believed regeneration was possible for anybody, scientific reformers confined it to those whose intelligence, luck, or wealth allowed them to receive professional training. This elitism was one unattractive by-product of faith in the professional. Others were the tendency automatically to equate expertise with virtue and to perceive professional experts' opponents as invariably selfish. All of these tendencies could be seen in the way scientific management was viewed by the engineers and progressives.

The picture of the industrial future painted by the champions of scientific management was an appealing one to scientific progressives. Instead of an industrial scene in which selfish capital and selfish labor battled, with little regard for the public interest, scientific management promised an efficient and cooperative industrial world, run by selfless professionals devoted to serving society as a whole. By creating an industrial system of high productive efficiency, engineers would serve society's material needs cheaply and abundantly. Best of all, this could be done without changing fundamentally the economic system or the positions of capital and labor within it. The engineers would not own the system or overturn its internal relationships; they would merely manage it in the public interest. George Morison, an early tribune of scientific management, assured his readers that "the owners and the workers both have rights; the managers have principally responsibilities." [32] Owners' and workers' "rights"—which in the progressive lexicon was virtually a synonym for selfishness—would endure, but scientific managers would be given the opportunity to fulfill their responsibilities to society.

In practice, it was difficult for scientific managers to gain the power they needed to carry out their responsibilities. Both labor and management were more or less resistant to control of the work place by engineers. This resistance derived not from a selfish disregard for the public interest but from a fear that the existing positions of owners and workers would deteriorate. In theory and often in practice, scientific management threatened both employees and employers.

The more serious threat seemed to be to workers. Workers were particularly reluctant to embrace scientific management, and organized labor was its most vociferous foe. Workers complained that the engineers, with their stop watches and time-motion studies, threatened to make all industrial tasks simple, repetitive, routine, and mundane, that most jobs would become unskilled or semi-skilled, that jobs would be lost as workers became more efficient, that piece-work rates would be imposed, that slower, older, and less efficient workers would be dismissed, and that, generally, workers would lose control over the nature of the work they did and the pace at which they did it.

Managers saw promise in many of the same aspects of scientific management that workers feared. To them, the engineers offered a tool for getting control of the productive process away from the workers.[33] In practice, though, they often found the increasing autonomy of the engineers and the apparent superfluity of traditional managers disturbing. Autonomy, of course, was what the engineers wanted and needed if they were to serve society adequately. "The management more and more under scientific management of an establishment is getting away from the man who owns the business," boasted Taylor disciple Morris Llewellyn Cooke to the United States Industrial Commission. "I can give you any number of cases where the man who owns the business can not go into his shop and have done what he wants done in there."[34] This development was promising to scientific progressives but it horrified owners and traditional managers, who desired to run their businesses as well as own them. When scientific managers were dismissed from companies, it was usually due to disputes over control between them and the existing managers.

When they attempted to overcome the resistance of workers and owners, scientific managers did not appeal to their public interest or their instinct to serve society. After all, as non-professionals, workers and owners would have little devotion to or even sense of the public interest. Scientific managers promised them more material rewards — wages for workers and profits for owners. More efficient production meant something for everybody — more money for workers, greater returns for owners, and cheaper, more abundant, and better goods for consumers. Everybody would benefit materially, and nobody would be harmed. This was a seductive vision, but one that had serious implications for Christian progressivism. For the scientific managers and their followers, materialism was the solution to society's ills rather than part of the problem. Their solution demanded no soul-searching, self-sacrifice, self-restraint, or other character reformation on the part of the individual. Taylor never altered his assumption that "men pursue their self-interest and attempt to maximize their prosperity." [35] Indeed, he counted on their doing so. The scientific managers were retreating to the amoral capitalistic conception of human nature that each man pursued his own selfish interests and that society was advanced by that pursuit. They showed no interest in altering this fact; they merely suggested means by which people could pursue their selfish interests more effectively.

It did not take scientific managers very long to add human engineering to the technical engineering on which they concentrated originally. Industrial production involved machines and techniques, but it concerned people as well. Hence, scientific managers embraced a broadly conceived "human engineering . . . to control the human element of production at the individual and group level through the study and manipulation of human behavior." [36] The application of science to human behavior would complement the application of science to industrial techniques, with a more efficient factory and society resulting.

As David F. Noble has noted in *America by Design*, human engineering differed little from technical engineering: "It similarly consisted in the prediction of behavior based upon careful observation, and the determination and creation of the conditions necessary to produce a desired end" of more efficient production. [37] The means to that end included scientific personnel work to identify efficient workers, industrial education to teach efficiency, health and safety improvements to minimize absenteeism, alterations in the plant environment, and a variety of innovations, covered under the general heading of "welfare work," that were designed to make workers more contented and thus, presumably, more efficient.

Some of these things had been suggested by reformers—including Christian progressives—for some time, but there was a dramatic contrast between a Christian employer such as Golden Rule Jones and a scientific one such as Henry Ford. The Christian employer displayed a regenerate character when he treated his employees as brothers. The scientific employer saw his workers merely as a means of production. His character was unregenerate. He was still selfish, materialistic, and concerned primarily with profits. He had simply learned a more functional behavior to achieve the things he wanted. Scientific progressives, with their self-conscious "hard-headedness" and "tough-mindedness," showed more interest in tangible, empirically measurable results than in motives. "The discovery of manufacturers that degradation spoils industrial efficiency must not be cast aside by the radical because the motive is larger profits," argued young Walter Lippmann, who enjoyed the opportunity to be tough-minded for most of this century. "The discovery, whatever the motive, will inevitably humanize industry a good deal. For it happens that in this case the interests of capitalism and of humanity coincide." [38]

The reformers who embraced scientific management believed they had discovered a way out of the problem that deviled Christian progressives and such scientific progressives as E. A. Ross. They had found a way to improve society that depended on neither individual regeneration nor the broad inculcation of loyalty to the state or the race or some other social entity. This is not to say that they held low motives or that they did not admire the professional experts who upheld the public interest. But they did believe it was unnecessary for most people to be publicly interested in order for social avancement to take place. It was not a long step from believing low motives irrelevant to seeing them as beneficial when they contributed to efficiency. The Christian progressives recognized low motives, but they never considered them irrelevant. For this they were accused of hypocrisy and a lack of realism. These charges are not without foundation, but at least Christian progressives had the decency to urge people to be virtuous and the faith that they could be virtuous. The scientific progressives assumed most people were—and always would be—vicious, and by so assuming they encouraged people to be vicious.

By promising widespread material benefits with little sacrifice, the champions of economic efficiency were painting an attractive picture. Through much of human history, people had struggled with the problem of scarcity, and modern industry seemed to hold the key to its solution. Louis D. Brandeis told the Industrial Commission that increasing productivity would offer Americans a second chance, a new frontier, a reopening of opportunity. Colonel Edward House believed that efficiency would usher in a society in which "there would be none who were not sufficiently clothed and fed" and in which would be removed "the inequalities in opportunity and the consequent wide difference between the few and the many."[39] George Morison reminded his readers that "devices . . . of a . . . material character . . . gave opportunities for mental and moral improvement." And Walter Weyl saw abundance as the salvation of democracy: "It is the increasing wealth of America, not the growing poverty of any class, upon which the hope of a full democracy must be based. It is this wealth which makes democracy possible and solvent, for democracy, like civilization, costs money."[40]

There were those who wondered whether greater wealth would necessarily benefit society. The increasing wealth of the late nineteenth century had not noticeably diminished selfishness, materialism, or class conflict, nor had it improved moral character in any permanent way. By the early years of the new century, it was possible to discern a "consumer culture," spawned by material abundance, that stressed individual fulfillment through material things.[41] Reasonable people could be excused for wondering whether the material fruits of improved efficiency would solve America's moral problems.

There were those willing to grapple with the relationship between materialism and morality in a systematic way, and none did so more thoughtfully than social scientist Simon Patten. Patten was part of that first generation of German-trained scholars who professionalized American academic disciplines and provided intellectual leadership for scientific progressivism. Patten believed that the world was moving from an "age of deficit" characterized by "disease, oppression, irregular work, premature old age, and race hatreds" to an "age of surplus" marked by "plenty of food, shelter, capital, security, and mobility of men and goods."[42] Patten believed this shift was desirable, because with the banishment of want would come not only material comfort but an alteration of human character as well. In an age of abundance, he reasoned, fear, hatred, selfishness, and class divisions, all appropriate to the age of scarcity, would be replaced by altruism, selflessness, and social unity. In the meantime it was necessary, as one of Patten's interpreters has noted, to address "the problem of cultural lag: the survival, in a period of potential abundance, of behavior appropriate to an age of scarcity."[43]

Patten believed that the continuing problems of selfishness, hedonism, and social disunity could be addressed in three ways. First, he thought natural selection would operate to diminish the number of people exhibiting inappropriate character traits. The selfish, the hedonistic, and the antisocial would not thrive in an age of abundance, which emphasized opposite character traits. They would die out and would leave fewer offspring than those exhibiting social values appropriate to the new age.[44] Later, he emphasized conscious efforts to change behavior. He urged the church to emphasize man's duty to love and serve others—behavior appropriate to an age of surplus—instead of concentrating on fear, mortality, and narrow, self-centered faith.[45] And he emphasized the role of education, broadly conceived, to make men social. As Daniel Fox puts it, he believed "psychology could be used to educate men to prefer the pleasures of . . . altruism—to develop habits suitable for an age of plenty."[46]

Patten could see pitfalls in the abundant future, but like most scientific progressives he saw mainly promise there. Reformers excited about the material horizon were unable to view the pathbreakers to that future with much objectivity. Thus scientific progressives lionized Frederick Winslow Taylor and approached his theories with reverence. Henry Ford, the personification of productive efficiency and abundance, the friend and protector of the workingman, and the benefactor of the consumer, became a hero to them in the years before his crank theories, anti-Semitism, and labor-busting thugs sent them reeling away in disillusionment. They were drawn to "technician-philosopher" Herbert Hoover, the public-spirited engineer and prophet of the permanent plateau of prosperity.[47] Logically, some of them concluded that, because the engineers could work such wonders with the economy, the engineers should be given control over other areas of society as well.

Some of the engineers also yearned for the opportunity to make public policy. They believed they could solve a variety of human problems because "the laws of nature governed man and society. Thus, engineering could be assumed to include politics and economics as part of its subject matter." Edwin Layton adds that "overlapping this idea was a second: that the important thing was the nature of the method and the qualities of mind employed rather than the specific subject matter." [48] Implicit in this idea was the extremely elitist and undemocratic notion that social policy decisions should be made by technical experts rather than by the public. Such elitism was not particularly disturbing to scientific progressives. They saw most problems as technical problems, the solution of which by professionals would necessarily be in the interest of the public. The experts' means might be scientific, but their ends would be democratic, in the sense that they would benefit society as a whole.

However attractive this model was in theory, it never applied very accurately to engineers working in industry. Despite the tendency of leading scientific managers such as Taylor, Cooke, and H. L. Gantt to stress their devotion to the public interest, working engineers in industry did not behave much differently from other white-collar workers. As Noble has indicated, the vaunted professionalism of the engineers did not prevent them from identifying their interests with those of their employers rather than with that of the public. In the end, according to Noble, their efforts strengthened corporate capitalism and the people who dominated it, increasing their hold over the economy, society, and the political system. [49]

Despite contrary assumptions, science was not value-free. It benefitted some groups and individuals and harmed others, and it seldom worked any ill on the people who dominated society. In agricultural research, for example, this phenomenon can be discerned clearly. Science supposedly served the public, but it ended up "helping the richer farmers, the owners, and the growers . . . to become even more prosperous . . . [while it operated] to drive the smaller, less efficient, poorly capitalized ones out of business." [50] Scientific progressives never did believe there was a necessary contradiction between a scientific and a capitalistic society. But most of them failed to foresee that the development of the former would operate inevitably to strengthen existing relationships in the latter, regardless of what the "public interest" might be.

III

In government, scientific management found its analogue in professional public administration, which promised to make government operate efficiently and thus serve the public.

Criticism of government on the grounds of inefficiency was not new in this country, and reformers had been around for some time who suggested more efficient government structures or administration by experts. Businessmen, for example, had long criticized government for its high cost and inefficiency. And the civil service movement, one of the reforms that made the passage from the Gilded age to the progressive era, upheld the idea of professional administration of the public's business. But those who criticized government for its inefficiency had seldom been much more than junior partners of those who criticized it for its immorality. With the rise of scientific progressivism, however, those who looked for solutions to public problems that transcended Christianity seemed to gain strength and confidence, and they moved beyond favoring simple professional administration to championing policy making by experts. Their general attitude toward reform is well expressed by Dwight Waldo's characterization of New York's Bureau of Municipal Research:

> They were tired of the simple moralism of the nineteenth century.
> . . . They were sensitive to the appeals and promises of science,
> and put a simple trust in discovery of facts as the way of science
> and as a sufficient mode for solution of human problems. They
> accepted—they urged—the new positive conception of govern-
> ment, and verged upon the idea of a planned and managed society.
> They hated "bad" business, but found in business organization
> and procedure an acceptable prototype for public business.[51]

Scientific progressives presented an array of proposals to make government operate more efficiently. For municipalities they suggested civil service, the creation of an expert bureaucracy to do the public's business, the commission system, whereby elected officials became experts in particular municipal functions, and the city manager system, in which a professional was hired to run the city. All of these reforms illustrated the tendency among scientific progressives to take the business corporation as their model. Scientific progressives correctly perceived that American business corporations were in the forefront of modern bureaucratic development and innovation, and they sought to replicate business structures and techniques in municipalities. They assumed that "economy and efficiency" were the "watchwords" of corporations, and they believed cities would achieve these ends when they developed modern business structures.[52] They believed, as one historian of the commission system has noted, "that good government would necessarily flow from efficient machinery."[53] But their attraction to corporate models reflected more than a simple commitment to efficient structures. It also reflected the support structural reformers often received from businessmen, who saw the city's many problems melting away if only municipalities were operated as businesses.[54]

One problem with the corporation model was that the reformers attracted to it failed to see clearly the purposes for which it was created. The purposes of corporate bureaucracies were not so much economy and efficiency as profits and power. Bureaucratic structures were designed to make profits larger and more secure, which meant, among other things, helping those who dominated the corporations to control them, their employees, and the economy in which they operated more perfectly. Administrative structures and techniques that were designed to manipulate and control the many in the interests of the few were not necessarily appropriate means of doing the public's business in a democracy.

Moreover, efficiency and service to the people of the society were not always or necessarily compatible. John R. Commons noted of the Socialist administration of Milwaukee that "their goal was Efficiency coupled with Service to the poor and the working classes."[55] But that linkage existed not because of the *structure* of the government, but because of the *intent* of those doing the governing. Christian progressive Newton Hall complained that scientific reformers ignored character:

The right management and government and development of a city is not simply a business proposition. That is where many reformers are making a mistake. They seem to think that all the gross evils of American municipal government will be overcome if only we can place the city on a strictly business basis. They forget that business as well as politics may become corrupt. The government of a city is essentially a problem in righteousness.[56]

Talk of character embarrassed scientific progressives, and they saw broad public regeneration as both impossible and irrelevant. They believed that public servants operating in more efficient structures would serve the public because they were professionals, whose training had lifted them above petty and selfish concerns. If economic problems would be solved by scientific management, then urban problems would be solved by professional administration. Nor was this solution appropriate only for municipalities. Professional supervisors would solve the problems of education, county agents would solve the problems of agriculture, and trained social workers would solve the problems of the poor. Nonpartisan experts would regulate railroads, insurance companies, commerce, corporate activities, tariffs, and a variety of other matters on the state and federal levels. Because they were scientific these people would make the best possible decisions, and because they were professionals these decisions would inevitably serve the public interest rather than the interests of private groups or individuals.

Policy making by expert administrators was an attractive idea to some Americans. Public policy, particularly as it related to the economy, was becoming increasingly complex as the United States became an advanced industrial nation. Louis Filler argues that, by 1908, "the public had had enough of trying to follow tortuous arguments in a dozen important fields. It longed for competent people of executive ability and social vision who would make decisions for it and see that they were carried out."[57] This is an overstatement, but there is no question that people used to relatively clear and simple issues such as the tariff or territorial expansion might feel bewildered when confronted with some of the many-faceted political-economic issues the nation faced. Politicians, so sure of themselves on the stump, were less clear on how to resolve issues when they reached legislative chambers or executive mansions. For them, expert administrators and regulators were as much a means of removing troubling problems from their own shoulders as they were of really solving those problems.

Government by expert received a boost in 1911 with the Eastern Rate Case, in which Louis Brandeis showed the Supreme Court that shipping rate increases demanded by several Eastern railroads, with labor support, were unjustified. Brandeis argued successfully that the savings obtained through increased efficiency would obviate the necessity of higher rates. Here was the expert in the most favorable light—a professional, dedicated to efficiency and thus the public interest, which he held above the interests of selfish individuals or groups.[58]

By the time the Eastern Rate Case was heard, experts were making inroads elsewhere as well. Educators were becoming imbued with the notions of such leaders in the field as John Dewey, George Herbert Mead, and Ellwood Cubberly, who saw teachers and supervisors as experts who should shape the child in a comprehensive way for his or her future. The better colleges and universities accepted enthusiastically the notion that they were preparing trained experts to make public policy.

In state after state, commissions and boards of experts regulated particular and often esoteric areas in which government had involved itself, such as corporate behavior, railroads, insurance, public utilities, banking, purity of food and drug products, and industrial safety. The public had demanded that something be done to protect its interest from private misbehavior in these areas, and ongoing regulation by experts often seemed to be the best thing to do. It was an appropriate response because, as William Graebner notes of coal-mining safety, "the problems to be solved required sophisticated analysis and . . . the temptations to view . . . [the problems] in moralistic terms were so great."[59]

Regulation was an attractive solution for many of those concerned. Politicians liked it because it removed from them the necessity of responding to the moralistic outcries of rage from those savaged by private interests. The experts liked it because it gave them power and importance. And the corporations liked it because it imparted an element of predictability, control, and stability to their relationship with the political system, even while it potentially placed some limitations on their freedom of action.

Scientific progressives believed the expert could better serve the public if his power extended far beyond the outposts he held. Some foresaw the day when the entire economy would be directly or indirectly controlled by government professionals, who would plan, regulate, and coordinate in the public interest. "The industrial goal of the democracy is the socialization of industry," argued Walter Weyl. "It is the attainment by the people . . . of the largest possible industrial dividend." Despite the ominous sound of "socialization," Weyl did not believe that public ownership of industry was necessary to make it serve society. The Christian progressives believed capitalism could be consistent with Christianity, and their scientific cohorts believed it could be compatible with an efficient economic system that served the public. "What the democracy desires . . . is not government ownership for itself," Weyl explained, "but merely enough government ownership, regulation, or control as may be necessary to a true socialization of industry." [60]

Scientific progressives were working for a directed society, in which conscious and intelligent choices were substituted for wishful thinking and the operation of capricious social and economic forces. Walter Lippmann argued that society could and should embrace "mastery" in place of "drift." He defined mastery as being "the substitution of conscious intention for unconscious striving. Civilization, it seems to me, is just this constant effort to introduce plan where there has been clash, and purpose into the jungles of disordered growth." Lippmann differed sharply from the Christian progressives, with their Victorian notion that advancing civilization was measured by improvements in the behavior of individuals. To Lippmann, secular knowledge rather than ethical behavior was the way to a better world. "To shape the world nearer to the heart's desire requires a knowledge of the heart's desire and of the world. You cannot throw yourself blindly against unknown facts and trust to luck that the result will be satisfactory." [61] The state, through laws and the regulatory and directive operations of powerful and active experts, would bring social progress regardless of the character of individuals. Indeed, to scientific progressives, individual character as Christian progressives had defined it meant very little. "How vain," snorted E. A. Ross, "to expect to better conditions simply by adding to the number of good men!"[62]

There were those who believed that the advanced, activist state might create an environment in which character could be reformed. "Democracy must stand or fall on a platform of possible human perfectibility," Herbert Croly wrote. "If human nature cannot be improved by institutions, democracy is at best a more than usually safe form of political organization."[63] And Frank Vrooman, whose Christian background prevented him ever from totally discounting the importance of character, emphasized the reformative possibilities of the activist state:

> The new democracy of nationalism claims for itself that it offers the forms of a rational association in a sphere of the state, enlarged and moralized, which will constitute a political environment where everything in the individual that is best and worth preserving will be encouraged instead of thwarted, and where the kindlier impulses of the human heart, the most of which are being choked in the maelstrom of individualism, shall have at least even chances for existence.[64]

For Croly and Vrooman, improvements in human nature might result from institutional progress, but progress was not dependent on changes in character. For Lippmann, who was enamoured of the Freudian analysis of human behavior, character was always the same. Whether character was manifested in "good" or "bad" actions depended not on the individual's self-control, but on the direction imposed on him or her by society. "Much the same energies produce crime and civilization, art, vice, insanity, love, lust, and religion," Lippmann extracted from the theories of Sigmund Freud. "Training and opportunity decide in the main how men's lust shall emerge. Left to themselves, or ignorantly tabooed, they break forth in some barbaric or morbid form. Only by supplying our passions with civilized interests can we escape their destructive force."[65]

Scientific progressives were as fearful of the unrestrained individual as were the Christian progressives, but their view of his or her possibilities was much different. Christian progressives believed individuals could and should shape themselves, could and should restrain their antisocial impulses, could and should choose to benefit society. Without self-direction and choice, there was no morality or immorality, no sin or salvation. Scientific progressives tended to see the individual as, by definition, a threat who had to be controlled and directed in such a way as to benefit society. Freedom for the individual, they believed, had always to be subordinated to social need. As Herbert Croly noted, "individual freedom is important, but more important still is the freedom of a whole people to dispose of its own destiny." [66]

Their anti-individualism, their depreciation of the importance of character, their stress on social rather than self control, their fascination with expertise, and their statism eventually led some scientific progressives into illiberalism, elitism, and a tendency to view people as things to be manipulated. This was not, however, the destination they had in mind, and, despite their pose of hard-boiled tough-mindedness, they were as idealistic in their own way as were the Christian progressives. Their devotion to the interest of society as a whole could be inspiring. They foresaw a future not unlike that glimpsed by Christian progressives, a future in which social unity ruled and people served others. They recognized that individualism, as it was often manifested in America, was a destructive force, and that liberty was not praiseworthy when it excused those who harmed society. But they did not believe that the regeneration of individual character was the way to achieve the future they saw. It was enough, they thought, if professional experts, devoted to the public interest, dominated society. The character of the average person might not—perhaps could not— change, but if his or her behavior could be altered that was sufficient. It was not necessary, they thought, that businessmen, workers, or farmers be made to love their fellows. As long as laws, commissions, or boards forced them to act differently toward them, that was enough.

The achievement of what the scientific progressives called "democracy," a united society in which people served one another and the state efficiently, demanded a new mode of thinking, new standards of truth, and new ways of making decisions. Instead of determining policies on the basis of traditional and supposedly immutable principles— such as liberty, private property, the Constitution, or the Golden Rule

—scientific progressives searched for flexible, empirical means both for evaluating principles and for making policies.

The search for new methods of determining what was true and of guiding action had started in the years after the Civil War. In an age of rapid social and economic development, in which a theory of continual change—evolution—reigned in the scientific world, the given and immutable principles no longer seemed sure guides to action. The standards of religious truth were less satisfying in an increasingly complex and secular world. And the traditional canons of American political and economic life—as such people as Lloyd, Bellamy, and George so clearly showed—seemed productive more of misery than of human happiness.

For some the problem lay not in flawed values and institutions but in the unwillingness of people to live their lives in conformity to traditional standards. Christian reformers believed the Golden Rule was sufficient as a guide to action and the law of love was an imperative that, if strictly followed, would bring social harmony and happiness. Others questioned the validity of religious values in a secular and scientific age. Lester Frank Ward, the self-trained father of American sociology, believed that evolution must apply to human ideas and society and that people must have the ability to direct social change. Other scholars engaged in what Morton White has called a "revolt against formalism," which questioned long-accepted dicta in politics, economics, and law.[67] Oliver Wendell Holmes Jr., Thorstein Veblen, J. Allen Smith, and Charles Beard, among others, worked to demythologize such formalistic constructs as the common law, the capitalistic economy, and the Constitution, showing that each was an evolutionary product appropriate to particular circumstances rather than a transcendent and immutable set of principles. And pragmatic philosophers, such as William James and John Dewey, argued that men could and should test the truth of ideas and determine their courses of action on the basis of their experience.

The concept of an empirical test for ideas was understandably attractive to scientific progressives, who chafed under the saddle of inherited values and traditions that they thought inappropriate and restrictive in the modern age. It also seemed immediately useful to experts eager to alter society. "If the inevitability of change were to be successfully faced by society as a whole," David Hollinger notes, "a philosophy of limited scope was surely needed by the class of managers and bureaucrats assigned the task of supervising American public affairs." [68]

In traditional societies, values could be static and individuals could be inner-directive. In modern societies, in which material realities were rapidly changing, people and values had to adapt to social demands. "The static man . . . is of the past. His days are numbered," concluded Franklin Giddings. "The future belongs to the adaptable man, the man who can continue indefinitely to change, to be whatever the conditions of his age and his land shall demand of him." [69] Values and institutions from an earlier time were not appropriate in the modern day. "We cannot expect to meet our problems with a few inherited ideas, uncriticized assumptions, a foggy vocabulary, and a machine philosophy," Walter Lippmann warned readers of *A Preface to Politics.* "Our primary care must be to keep the habits of the mind flexible and adapted to the movement of real life." [70] Ideas, Lippmann argued, must be analyzed by the standard of how well they worked to maximize human happiness.

> Justice, harmony, power [and] democracy are simply empirical suggestions which may produce the good life. If the practice of them does not produce it then we are under no obligation to follow them . . . . Every abstraction, every rule of conduct, every constitution, every law and social arrangement, is an instrument that has no value in itself. Whatever credit it receives, whatever reverence we give it, is derived from its utility. [71]

Utility was the only reliable test of truth for Lippmann: "A theory by itself is neither moral nor immoral, its value is conditioned by the purpose it serves." [72] Values, institutions, and traditions, regardless of how ancient, sacred, or widely accepted they were, should be viewed as nothing more than hypotheses, always to be tested and challenged in the light of changing realities. For society to advance, it had to recognize this fact. "Reflective morality is a mark of a progressive society, just as customary morality is of a stationary society," James Hayden Tufts wrote. "Reflection on values is the method of their modification." [73]

For serious pragmatists, this was an ongoing process, similar to evolution, which would never end in the discovery of immutable principles. Some scientific progressives recognized this fact. "We say that the truth will make us free. Yes, but that truth is a thousand truths which grow and change," argued Lippmann, who understood the implications of pragmatism. "Nor," he continued, "do I see a final state of blessedness. The world's end will surely find us still engaged in answering riddles." [74]

For those who understood pragmatism as Lippmann did, it was a liberating attitude that promised to free people from the past and all of its traditions, values, and institutions. As such, it appealed to modernists in an age of change. The danger was that a thoroughgoing moral relativism would emerge in which nothing—American or Christian values, institutions, the family, even the sanctity of human life itself—would be accepted as universal and immutable. Even the decent and humane values concealed beneath the reformers' empiricism could be, and were, threatened. This result was not foreseen by most scientific progressives. As a number of scholars have shown, the reformers saw the application of empirical tests to institutions and values as a means of freeing society from the dead hand of the past and of assuring social progress toward a utopia in which harmony, efficiency, and happiness reigned.[75] That this was not, and perhaps could not, be attained through their chosen method should not obscure the admirable quality of the scientific progressives' goal.

The pragmatic method was a tool for policymakers, just as the stopwatch was a tool for scientific managers. It would help experts determine what was true, and thus what social policy should be. And when social policy was determined scientifically, who could disagree with it? As Walter Lippmann assured the readers of *Drift and Mastery*, "the discipline of science is the only one which gives any assurance that from the same set of facts men will come approximately to the same conclusion." [76] Scientific progressives who hoped to apply their expertise to public policy questions tended to emphasize the empirical analysis of single issues. As Benjamin Parke DeWitt, the first historian of progressivism, said of the movement for efficient public administration, "it is . . . a protest against generalizations and definitions, standing [as it does] for the specific duty and solution of particular problems." [77] However, as Steven Diner implies in his study of University of Chicago professors who involved themselves in urban reform, scientific progressives saw themselves addressing distinct problems far into the future:

> Professors and their reform colleagues envisioned in the future a continuing series of responses to new problems based upon popular determination to do what was just and efficient and upon the expertise to analyze problems and find workable solutions. Thus they envisioned a future society that would call upon them continuously for assistance and would demand the knowledge and skills that they imparted to their students.[78]

For scientific progressives, then, reform was a process that had value in and of itself. It was valuable because experts would control it, elevating their own status while they served society. In place of decision making by powerful, but selfish and ignorant, individuals and groups, they proposed policy determination by selfless experts motivated by a desire to serve society. They were not willing to promise the public a future society in which perfect harmony, happiness, efficiency, and service reigned. But they did believe the making of public policy by experts would make society more harmonious, happier, more efficient, and more service-oriented than it was.

Despite their pose of mental toughness, the scientific progressives were as optimistic in their own way as were the Christian progressives. They had tremendous and, as it turned out, unjustified faith both in the experts and in the public the experts served. Because they were professionals, commanding the "facts" and "science," the experts were expected to act in such a way as automatically to serve the public. More surprising was the expectation that a rational public would accept the leadership of the experts and would dutifully support their policies. Considering their elitism and their oft-expressed fear of and contempt for the people, this was a remarkable supposition, but one that scientific progressives were compelled to make. They recognized that, in a democratic society, public policy cannot be made without at least the consent of the populace or of socially significant segments thereof.

In practice, the experts did not always, or even usually, prove to be public-spirited paragons of scientific virtue. Like the scientific managers, they too could become self-centered, materialistic, and status-conscious. They also had a tendency to erect bureaucratic empires, as removed as possible from the public, which they saw as valuable in and of themselves. Soon regulatory boards, planning commissions, and other agencies controlled by experts became sluggish bureaucracies that confused the public interest with their own perpetuation. Moreover, the experts often became the captives of powerful interest groups. They had dreamed of freedom of action, but that was seldom realized. As Martin Schiesl has noted, "extensive reform . . . could not permanently insulate civic management from partisan influence and informal networks of power within city politics."[79]

The scientific progressives never saw a capitalist society marked by inequalities of wealth as a bar to social control by experts. This proved to be a serious error, because those who controlled the economy and dominated the political system had no intention of surrendering that control or dominance to earnest young public-spirited experts. Public administrators who ignored the realities of power found themselves forced from their positions, but most made their peace with the country's masters. Soon they were serving those who dominated industry and finance, helping them achieve their goals for rationalizing and stabilizing society and the economy, facilitating their realization of large and sure profits, and deflecting public anger from them. The experts had been correct in believing their expertise was valuable, but they had erred in assuming it would necessarily benefit the public.

Sometimes they came under pressure from other, less powerful, interest groups as well. In scientific progressive theory, the public was supposed to recognize the superior intelligence and virtue of the professionals, to whom it was expected to surrender a degree of decision-making power. Some hoped that the public would look to the experts for identification of social problems and the proposal of solutions for them. Others, such as Herbert Croly, who was deeply interested in the relationship between expertise and democracy, believed the public should set general policy directions but should then withdraw from the process, giving the experts wide latitude to put policies into operation.[80] In either case, it was essential that the public, considered as a corporate entity, voluntarily defer to the experts at some point. Voluntarism, the tribute paid by elitism to democracy, did not work as scientific progressives hoped it would. The experts came under the same political pressures that touched elected officials.

One problem was that the social or economic "facts" on which experts depended to convince the public of the correctness of policies were not accepted in the way, say, gravitation was accepted when natural scientists explained why things fell down rather than up. As Benjamin Parke DeWitt explained, "the great problems of . . . government . . . are questions of policy, questions on which men disagree even when they know the facts and, in a sense, because they know the facts." [81] Knowledge of facts, even when people could agree what the facts were, was no more useful as a guide to public policy than the Golden Rule had been, because facts must be organized by people, who manipulate them to fit their own pre-existing ideas and interests.

But the larger problem was that the experts found themselves hamstrung by the very traditions, institutions, and values they sought to change. Rather than alter the realities of a capitalist economy and a democratic political system, the experts were dominated by those realities. People, whatever their expertise, could not change or ignore deeply rooted institutions and behaviors. This is not to say that experts contributed nothing. Their bureaucratic expertise benefitted a modern society, which needed data and which depended on experts to carry out policies. They could, ironically, help politicians avoid sensitive decisions when appointed to "blue-ribbon" panels to study this or that controversial issue. And they could be used to support political positions already held. No substantial union, business organization, farm group, or political party in our day is without its stable of economic "experts" who are trotted out periodically to support some particular, self-interested version of capitalist economics. And the fact that we are all so careful to cite or appeal to our favorite expert giving our preferred version of the "facts" shows that the scientific progressives had some impact on us. What they did not and could not do was to change the institutional realities of American society. Self-consciously empirical and thus fitted to the modern age, the scientific progressives proved no better able to analyze or solve the problems of American society than were the Christian progressives, with their Victorian sentimentality, their vague ethical principles, and their hopes for individual regeneration.

IV

The practical weaknesses of scientific progressivism were not immediately apparent. For a time, it seemed to point in a new and hopeful direction, away from the vagueness and moralism of Christian reform. It carried the promise and authority of science, which was more comforting to many modern people than the old verities of faith. And it promised a progress that was not dependent on individual regeneration.

Their self-conscious empiricism—and thus modernism—gave the scientific progressives a sense of superiority over reformers who found their inspiration in Christ. They tended to see themselves as technicians contributing expertise to the solution of social problems, and they were reluctant to associate themselves with the enthusiasm, idealism, or sentimentality that they believed characterized the older reform tradition. The *New Republic* even went so far as to mock those whose reform efforts rose from ethical concerns:

> To be a reformer is not to have cast your skin and to have been seized by a grace which transforms. What is called public spirit is nothing but an occasional phase of people's lives. It does not descend with enveloping solemnity upon a few individuals and distinguish them from the rest of mankind. Men are worried into reform, driven into it, lured into it, earn their living by it, gain fame in it, make a habit of it, and through it release their ambitions. . . . The reformer does not differ in motive or character from the men who suspect him. His actions do not arise from a different source; they are merely pointed sometimes to a different end. His selfishness, his hobbies, and his desires happen now and then to produce effects larger than himself; not always, not even most of the time.[82]

It was unfortunate that the *New Republic* felt compelled to prove the tough-mindedness of scientific progressives by attacking reformers' motives. It was also wrong. It was wrong because it denied the high-mindedness and idealism of the scientific progressives themselves. It was also wrong because those who think of and work for others *are* superior to those concerned only with themselves, by any decent standard of civilized society. And it was wrong because it gave aid and comfort to those outside reform who attacked reformers' motives by projecting their own less elevated impulses on them. The *New Republic* was anticipating the cynical tendency of the modern day to degrade and debase every decent human impulse by connecting it with self-centered desires and drives, an attitude reflected in the comment to me by a junior executive in a public utility that "idealism is just selfishness for someone else instead of yourself." By denigrating the tender-hearted people of good will and by cheapening their motives, the editors were breaking paths for a new and unfortunate attitude within reform and without.

The great differences between scientific and Christian progressivism that the editors of the *New Republic* liked to emphasize and that are so clear to us today were less readily apparent to reformers themselves. As James Nuechterlein has noted, we have "focused on a fundamental tension in progressive thought: the conflict between a liberalism centered in humanitarian and moral passion and one based in an ethos of scientific analysis." However, Nuechterlein continues, "among the progressives themselves, the distinction was never absolute."[83] In fact, Christian and scientific reform concepts were mixed rather promiscuously by all sorts of progressives.

Among some, "exposure to, even training in, the new inductive techniques of the social sciences did not immediately overcome the older evangelical propensity for moralizing issues" or for using moralistic rhetoric.[84] Leading social scientists, such as Ely, Ross, and Patten, continued to reflect the Christian ethical concerns of their Victorian childhoods, and the profession of social work grew out of the older settlement houses without completely jettisoning the Christian humanitarianism that had motivated the unprofessional settlers.

Social Gospelers, such as Graham Taylor and Washington Gladden, integrated concepts of empiricism and efficiency into their messages with little difficulty, and a writer in the *Outlook* in 1911 argued, with no apparent sense of contradiction, that "scientific management is a definite and practical statement of ethics in that it recognizes the total moral law."[85] The prohibitionists, reformers whose Christian moral pedigree could be traced into the early nineteenth century, quickly and easily applied scientific techniques and findings in their assault on liquor. And Theodore Roosevelt, who personified progressivism and the many currents thereof, combined moralism, nationalism, a call for service, and a commitment to efficiency in his political message, which appealed to a spectrum including strict Christian moralists as well as *New Republic* intellectuals.

The ability of Christian and scientific progressivism to conjoin derived in part from the fuzzy-mindedness of the reformers, who strove to minimize differences and emphasize similarities, and in part from their optimism that scientific and moral progress were helpmates. But it was also true that there were real affinities between the two branches of progressivism. Both saw individualism and disunity as social problems, and both pointed to a future in which the unfortunate manifestations of the first would be curbed and the second would be ended. Both thought change was possible without altering fundamentally the economic or political systems. Both had a great faith in people or, at least, in some people. Apparently sharing so much, progressives could understandably de-emphasize their differences.

But practical cooperation and wishful thinking could not bridge the wide intellectual gulf between Christian and scientific progressivism. The reformers differed regarding the nature of people and their possibilities, the means of solving the problems of society, and the shape of the good society. Christian progressives believed that antisocial individualism, hedonism, materialism, and disunity would be overcome primarily by regeneration of the individual character. As people determined to live their lives in closer conformity to the Golden Rule, as they recognized that the universal fatherhood of God made all of them brothers and sisters, their behavior toward one another would change. Alterations in character, reflected in changes in behavior, would result in a virtuous society, united and selfless, living the law of love.

Scientific progressives perceived hedonism, selfishness, and disunity to be dangerous only because they contributed to social and economic inefficiency. For them an efficient society could be achieved when people behaved socially and economically in such a way as to serve society. And the means to this end was control of the economy, government, and society by professionals whose expertise and devotion to public service would result in social progress.

The scientific progressives were interested in human behavior rather than human character. They were concerned with measurable results, not with motives. People who were efficient, for whatever reason, served society and were good. People who were inefficient, even if virtuous by some non-scientific standard, harmed society and were bad. One reformer, impatient with Christian standards of virtue, stated the case clearly:

> Outside of reform politics . . . we are primarily interested in goodness only as it may have a bearing on efficiency. . . . Our photographer must know how to take pictures; our dressmaker or tailor must know how to fit clothes; we do not forgive a blundering dentist because he is of irreproachable character. We measure the caterer's viands, not his morals. A gardener must grow beautiful plants, not good intentions.[86]

The scientific reformism for which this writer argued offered a radical redefinition of virtue, objectifying it and instrumentalizing it in the process. For scientific progressives, virtue was indicated by specific, functional behaviors that were defined as efficient. Efficiency could be achieved without any alteration of individual character.

In the process of redefining virtue, scientific progressives severely constricted the range of individual volition. Some people could make themselves efficient, others could be trained or manipulated to behave efficiently, and some could not be efficient — and therefore could not be virtuous — regardless of their efforts. Small wonder that perceptive reformers were concerned about the shift in direction. Scientific progressivism paralleled modern industrial development in that "the higher moral values, judgment, wisdom, character, sympathy, humility, self-control, are unjustly depressed, while skill and knowledge — values lower in rank — are abnormally exalted." Moreover, continued this author in the *Atlantic Monthly*, "the scale of efficiency inverts . . . the ethical scale; the moral waste is great, and the premium on character is lowered."[87]

The scientific progressives were people with good intentions. They hoped to see a united, humane, just, and abundant society in which people served one another. They simply believed that, in the modern, industrial world, Christian ethical principles were insufficient, either as guides to action or as models for society's future. Science, to them, promised a surer, truer guide to action and held out the possibility of a better future. One of the problems with their pseudo-scientific concepts lay in the fact that they were much less easy to understand for the average person than were the ethical concepts Christian progressives advanced. The Golden Rule might have seemed anachronistic in a complex society that was discovering Sigmund Freud, but the average person could understand and apply it much more easily than he or she could understand and apply the pragmatic test. And, though the law of love might create an inefficient society and a weak state, it remained an attractive concept to many people. Despite his apparent irrelevance to the modern age, Jesus Christ remained more popular in society as a whole than Frederick Winslow Taylor.

The scientific progressives might have been fashioning a more modern type of reform, but in the process they were making it an occupation that would, perforce, be elitist in nature. As reformers became more attracted to empiricism, they necessarily became alienated from substantial segments of the public. Their elitism, their arrogance, and their felt need to derogate Christian progressives were some of their minor shortcomings. Their blind faith that the experts would serve the public interest and their belief that their goals could be attained without substantial modification of economic or political institutions were major shortcomings. Most important, in their haste to devise empirical reform they ignored or slighted the real insights that the Christian progressives had—that the nation's problems were, in the broad sense, at least partially moral and that any permanent solution to these problems demanded a regeneration of individual character. In slighting ethical concerns and the importance of character, the scientific progressives modernized reform and made it more utilitarian, but they also cheapened it and made it less compelling.

LOSING THE WAY

The valuable features of modern progress may be summed up briefly by saying that there is a greater amount of constructive thought in the world at the present time than there ever was before. Problems of all kinds, social, political and economic, which before were barely touched on, are now handled with breadth and thoroughness.

EDITORIAL, *Scientific American*

Slip slidin' away,
Slip slidin' away,
You know the nearer your destination
The more you're slip slidin' away.

PAUL SIMON

American progressivism reached its zenith in the early and mid-teens. Progressive values seemed to sweep all others before them. Never were selfishness, hedonism, and materialism so universally denigrated. Never were selflessness, sacrifice, service, altruism, brotherly love, and devotion to the public interest more widely celebrated. The spirit of human betterment was a palpable presence in the land. New York social worker Mary Kingsbury Simkhovitch was one of many who saw a fundamental change in the character of the nation: "The passion that has hitherto so largely gone into commerce and all forms of material enterprise is beginning to manifest itself in other fields. The last decade has witnessed not only a revival of spiritual forces but really a new epoch in American life."[1] Los Angeles reformer Dana Bartlett added that "for the past ten years a moral wave has been sweeping over the land. The people are growing in a sense of spiritual values, and the purely material conception of life is losing its hold. Men everywhere are being moved by a 'religion of democratic aspiration.' " [2]

Tangible proof supported the optimism of reformers. Business was getting better—more efficient, more professional, more cognizant of its responsibilities to workers, consumers, and society as a whole. Government was getting better—more honest, more efficient, and more responsive to the public interest. In neither case had major structural or institutional changes been necessary. More moral and/or efficient people appeared really to be more important than institutions.

Developments on the national level contributed to progressive optimism during the teens. The election of 1912 featured a presidential contest between the two men who, correctly, came to symbolize progressive reform. Theodore Roosevelt personified progressivism, and his complexities—his moralism, sense of duty, preoccupation with character, devotion to efficiency, and nationalism—mirrored those of contemporary reform. His opponent, Woodrow Wilson, was an only slightly less perfect embodiment of progressivism. Serious, altruistic, moralistic, and devoted to the public interest, Wilson lay somewhat closer to the Christian than to the scientific reform impulse. But his deep ethical convictions did not blind him to the importance of science, efficiency, or national power, nor did they prevent him from functioning adroitly as a democratic politician. His years in office saw the achievement of a wide variety of progressive goals—economic regulation, social justice legislation, prohibition, and woman suffrage.

The apparent trend of the times nurtured the optimistic faith in progress held by Christian and scientific progressives alike. Both saw abundant evidence that human and social progress were occurring and that moral and material development paralleled and supplemented one another. "There is a greater amount of constructive thought in the world at the present time than there ever was before," the *Scientific American* assured its readers. "Problems of all kinds, social, political and economic, which before were barely touched on, are now handled with breadth and thoroughness." [3] And the direction of progress was also clear. The world was becoming more civilized, human character was improving, and society was becoming more harmonious. "The darkness still lingers, but it visibly retreats before the coming of the light; and the spiritual civilization of the race, retarded from time to time, moves forward," the *Outlook* assured its readers in an editorial greeting for the new year of 1914. "No other outcome of history is possible, because the fortunes of humanity are in the hands, not of the devil, but of God. In Him history began; in Him history will end."[4]

Still, some thoughtful progressives believed that the progress of the teens was more apparent than real. On inspection, some apparent successes seemed tainted. Business seemed to become moral, but the appearance of change masked a stubborn consistency of motivation. Political reforms were achieved, but the vitality of self-interested social and economic groups cast doubts on whether the people were really becoming more selfless and more devoted to the public interest. Ironically, while public behavior became more elevated, individualism and materialism corroded the family, the church, and the other institutions of private life.

Christian progressives had the most cause for concern. They faced the implicit challenge of scientific progressivism as well as a rising tide of dissent within the churches. The Social Gospel was challenged by fundamentalists on one side and by those who totally demystified Christ on the other. Socially oriented Christianity failed to reclaim middle-class skeptics for the churches, and this failure contributed to a split in Social Gospel ranks between those emphasizing character and those stressing the importance of environment. Christian progressives also faced intellectual challenges to their most fundamental beliefs regarding the nature of human beings, the character of morality, the roles of the sexes, and the sanctity of the family.

For those progressives who thought in "scientific" terms and who suggested an empiricist path to progress, the challenges seemed less serious, but they were evident. Scientific progressives believed the most troubling aspect of the American scene lay in the general unwillingness of the public to embrace empirical reform. Despite the successes of scientific progressivism the people showed little inclination to turn the making of policy over to professionals, nor was there any pronounced public tendency to follow the leadership the experts offered. The experts' ability to discover the "facts" and prove their "truth" neither diminished the power and activity of self-interested individuals and groups nor bent the public to particular courses of action. Public stubbornness indicated ignorance or selfishness to scientific progressives. Their own shortcomings—arrogant elitism, a tendency to serve the interests of wealth and power, and a willingness to use expertise for illiberal and antisocial purposes—remained obscure to them.

Reformers of both stripes remained optimistic, and they found more reasons to be hopeful than not. Generally, "it was a good time for liberals," as one historian has pointed out. "Things were humming."[5] But it is clear in retrospect that Paul Simon's comment on the tragedy of life applies to reformers and their goals during the teens. The nearer Christian and scientific progressives approached their destination, the more it was slip slidin' away.

I

Of the developments of the teens, none were at once more perplexing and more promising to progressives than the changes in business practices, behavior, and organization evident in industry. These alterations, which included such varied innovations as more circumspect behavior toward competitors and consumers, industrial cooperation, acceptance of government regulation, attention to public relations, welfare work with employees, bureaucratic restructuring and professionalization, and scientific management, were made in response both to the realities of an increasingly complex modern economy and to public pressures articulated by progressives. By 1920 American industry had moved far beyond its position of 1900 in a number of areas, and this movement indicated that progressive reform was real and vital. Somewhat paradoxically, however, the changes in American industry also showed that the impact of reform pressure on the essential character of economic institutions was limited. In the end, it became apparent that American business was more adept at responding to public demands and shaping these to its own benefit than progressives were at making business truly serve the public interest.

The period between 1890 and 1920 appears to have been one of the most difficult in the history of American business. Intense foreign and domestic competition existed for both internal and external markets.

Deflation, followed by inflation, added to the uncertainties in a period marked by a severe depression, two sharp recessions, and two wars. An heterogeneous, uncertain, and sometimes restive labor supply, and rapid changes in technology and in consumer tastes contributed further elements of risk. Small wonder that businessmen sought order, stability, predictability, and control in this environment.

Businessmen also faced increasing public criticism, a development that must have been discomforting to people used to public praise. Some of the criticism was specific and pointed, referring to embarrassingly frequent instances of corporate misbehavior — mistreatment of workers and consumers during the Depression of 1893, the misdeeds of the trusts, the corruption of government, the Northern Securities affair, the coal strike, the food and drug exposés, insurance scandals, the armor plate scandal, and so forth. Muckraking journalists exposed and highlighted examples of corporate misbehavior, helping in the process to create an impression of universal corruption in the national business community.

More disturbing were the vague, but telling, criticisms that focused on the immorality and/or inefficiency of business as it was practiced. Christian progressives became increasingly vehement during the early years of the century in their criticism of business immorality. They believed that common business practices provided the most glaring examples of the incongruence between public behavior and private values. The recognition that private and public values diverged was not new. What was new was the decreasing tolerance for that divergence. As minister and author Gerald Stanley Lee noted in 1908, when he reflected on the anthracite coal strike, a substantial segment of the public seemed unwilling any longer to accept the continuation of accepted business methods and standards:

President [George F.] Baer had been doing nothing new that winter [of 1902]. He had been merely proceeding upon the old common business ethics of always getting all one can. . . . [But] he made us begin to suspect our whole business ethics. . . . The coal strike caught us hoping and wondering and making up our minds about business. We made up our minds that business should not be any longer a specially marked-off barbarian country, a fighting-place or cock-pit where a man can go out and crowd and bully and strike below the belt and steal for his family, and then come back into the house and put on his coat and coo to the baby and be a beautiful character until ten the next morning.[6]

Christian progressives demanded a regeneration of business behavior that would bring it into closer conformity with the values of private life. "In the very heart of the marketplace we have come face to face with our souls," the *Outlook* concluded in 1911; "now, for the first time in any clear way and on any great scale, we are striving to make the marketplace as clean as the church." [7]

Criticisms of corporate ethics disturbed businessmen in part because they saw themselves as moral from a traditional standpoint. They tended to see wealth and success, if not as direct rewards for superior morality, at least as just compensation for their exhibition of divinely sanctioned character traits. Suddenly, these men of high character, who believed they were serving the community through action and example, found themselves accused of corruption, selfishness, and hypocrisy.

Criticism of business methods and the unfavorable contrast drawn between corporate ethics and private morality struck business commentators as wrongheaded, ignorant, and narrow. Businessmen complained that, in their zeal to rectify abuses, reformers often attacked practices that were perfectly legal. One writer in the *Atlantic Monthly* bemoaned "the tendency to extend . . . condemnation, which has been properly called forth by certain flagrantly dishonest practices, to methods of competition that until lately have never been questioned." [8] Businessmen believed that not only were most of their practices legal, but that "the great majority of transactions have been, and are, just and equitable, and according to all reasonable standards of right conduct." [9] Moreover, despite the scandals that punctuated American life during the progressive era, businessmen had the impression that their practices were generally more ethical than those of their predecessors. In this assumption they were probably correct. Saul Engelbourg argues that there was a general improvement of business ethics in the late nineteenth century in the areas of "conflict of interest, restraint of trade, competitive tactics, stock watering, and financial reporting." [10]

But neither the realities of business life nor the corporate perception of those realities had much relevance in the face of rapidly shifting public attitudes. The fact of the matter was that public opinion was changing, and obedience to the law, to commercial ethics, or to traditional social standards on the part of the business community was no longer sufficient in the eyes of a growing segment of the populace.

In a lecture entitled "The Morals of Trade in the Making," delivered in 1908 at Yale University, New York merchant and good government reformer Edward D. Page pointed out that "morality in its essence is the conduct-standard . . . established by the general opinion of the community as to the point at which self-interest should be subordinated to the interest of that society of which the individual forms a part." This morality, as was becoming clear, "is by no means fixed in form, but is subject to an evolution corresponding in some measure to the evolution of our . . . civilization." Because it was upheld by public opinion, morality was stronger than the ethics of a particular group and even stronger than the law. Hence, it was useless for businessmen to expect legal protection when they offended the moral sense of the community. "The Law always lags behind and never forestalls the moral consciousness of the community—it is generally impossible to punish . . . social wrongdoers . . . by the Law." [11] At a time when consumers refused to buy products produced in a manner that they deemed immoral, and when churches turned away donations on the grounds that the money had been acquired unethically, this was a point businessmen could easily understand.

What businessmen had to develop was a response to the inchoate but potentially dangerous criticisms leveled by Christian progressives. How, businessmen must have wondered, could the Golden Rule and the law of love be reconciled with a system that put a premium on selfishness, that celebrated competition over cooperation, and that elevated private property over the public interest? It was not a minor question, attractive only to idle speculators. It was, instead, a major problem, and the continuing social dominance of the business community might depend on its successful resolution. For it was unlikely that the public would allow behavior to thrive that blatantly violated its values.

The criticisms of corporate behavior leveled by scientific progressives were less threatening to the businessman's self-image and were more easily integrated into his movement toward a more ordered, predictable industrial environment than were those of Christian progressives. The scientific progressives' emphasis on industrial efficiency in general, as reflected in scientific management, improved administrative methods, and professional personnel practices, did not in itself threaten businessmen. However, they were threatened by suggestions that they should surrender control to engineers, that they should welcome government regulation and planning, or that they should take advanced steps in behalf of workers, consumers, or the community. The utopian goal of scientific progressives, that business should function primarily to serve the public interest, was also threatening, in part because it implied that business was not serving the public interest already and in part because it potentially imperiled profits and the profit motive.

Most scientific progressives found the profit motive distasteful and unworthy. "In science, art, politics, religion, the home, love, education,—the pure economic motive, profiteering, the incentive of business enterprise is treated as a public peril. Wherever civilization is seen to be in question, the Economic Man of commercial theorists is in disrepute." Moreover, Walter Lippman continued in *Drift and Mastery*, "there is in everyday life a widespread rebellion against the profit motive. That rebellion is not an attack on the creation of wealth. It is, on the contrary, a discovery that private commercialism is an antiquated, feeble, mean, and unimaginative way of dealing with the possibilities of modern industry." [12]

Scientific progressives saw in professionalization the path away from the profit motive. And they saw professionalization as an inevitable by-product of increasing industrial complexity. Louis Brandeis grasped the trend of the times in 1914:

The field of knowledge requisite to the more successful conduct of business has been greatly widened by the application to industry not only of chemical, mechanical and electrical science, but also the new science of management; by the increasing difficulties involved in adjusting the relations of labor to capital; by the necessary intertwining of social with industrial problems; by the ever extending scope of state and federal regulation of business. Indeed, mere size and territorial expansion have compelled the business man to enter upon new and broader fields of knowledge in order to match his achievements with his opportunities.[13]

Brandeis' recognition that complexity would further professionalization was correct. But he and other scientific progressives were on much less firm ground when they argued that professional businessmen —like engineers or public administrators—would automatically serve the public interest. "When business careers are made professional, new motives enter into the situation," argued Walter Lippmann; "it will make a world of difference if the leadership of industry is in the hands of men interested in production as a creative art instead of as a brute exploitation." When professionalization occurs, Lippman continued, "economic conflicts are at once raised to a plane of research, experiment and honest deliberation."[14]

This innocent faith in professionalism was questioned at the time, in part because the professionals whose behavior was to provide a model for businessmen were often touched by narrow self-interest. Reflecting on lawyers, Brandeis himself admitted that they had "allowed themselves to become adjuncts of great corporations and have neglected the obligation to use their powers for the protection of the people."[15] And publisher Henry Holt, one of the lecturers in Yale's "Morals in Modern Business" series, argued that "our terrible American commercialism, and love of ostentation and luxury . . . , have been doing much to send professional ethics to the dogs."[16]

Scientific progressives liked to think that the process of professional education and the development of professional self-consciousness— the taking of courses and the adoption of professional techniques and attitudes—would somehow create people who were devoted to the public interest. Holt saw the situation more clearly. To him, character was more important than training in the creation of an attractive society. The decline in professional ethics, he argued, was due less to "the mere spirit of competition" than it was to "the moral breakdown that has followed the weakening of the old religious sanctions."[17] Holt was unlikely to accept the delusion that physicians are devoted to the public interest simply because medical schools do not offer classes on tax shelters.

Their faith in professionals demonstrated a good deal of wishful thinking on the part of scientific progressives. Unsatisfied with the old religious standards, devoted to science, and unwilling to suggest an end to capitalism, they grasped professionalization as one of the only available paths to an industry that served the public interest. For them, professionalization became a secular means of regeneration, reforming the normally selfish individual into a public servant. Their faith in education was such that they believed a college course could succeed where God had failed, transforming values and behavior and creating a person who served the public.

Christian and scientific progressivism added instability to the environment in which business had to function, and both critiques potentially threatened business as it was practiced. Reformers of both types were demanding that businessmen behave differently and that they embrace ideals that had little relation to traditional corporate goals. The vagueness of some of the criticisms and the reformers' own divisions in regard to industrial problems and solutions contributed an element of uncertainty to the corporate response. But the economic and political penalties that might be imposed on those unwilling to respond to public opinion decreed that some positive response was necessary.

The great advantage the business community enjoyed was that it had the opportunity to adjust to the altered public environment. Generally satisfied with the capitalist system, committed to private property, and comfortable with an hierarchical social and economic structure, progressives were eager to give business the opportunity to criticize and reform itself. The demands of the public were potentially great, but business would have the chance to meet them, reshaping and manipulating them in the process.

In his book *Inspired Millionaires*, Gerald Stanley Lee noted that Americans wanted businessmen who behaved according to the Golden Rule and served the public, who were at once efficient and altruistic, who yoked together the positive essences of both science and religion. The people believed businessmen could be all of these things, Lee argued, because of the faith they had in the character of the individual. "What the American people is really believing to-day is . . . that men may be deliberately true and enviable and generous, and that society may be based from the bottom to the top on the capability of men for noble, voluntary, individual social development." Moreover, he continued, "we have believed in America that noble individualism can produce a noble society. This is our American vision."[18]

The public was willing to give business the opportunity to meet its expectations, however inflated these might be. But failure to meet them—or, more accurately, to convince the public that they were being met—presented potential dangers to business. "We are about to choose between the socialized millionaire and socialism," warned Lee in an extreme statement, but one characteristic of progressive critics of business.[19] It was up to business to determine how to "socialize" itself.

Though a public-be-damned attitude continued in some segments of the business community, many businessmen responded to the implicit pressures of public opinion, and virtually all of the largest and most vulnerable corporations reacted in some positive way to progressive criticism. Early on, commentators professed to see alterations in business behavior and a higher standard of corporate morality as a result of public pressure and muckraking. The *Century Magazine* contended in 1905 that the exposés of business misbehavior would have "a highly wholesome effect upon the conduct of all business" and recounted the opinion of a "captain of industry" that "the rising generation would find a higher standard of business ethics established."[20] In 1906 the *World's Work* revealed the results of a poll of 2,000 business leaders and other men of public affairs. Three out of four of the respondents saw "indications of an uplift in business morals, methods, and tendencies."[21] Businessmen who stood convicted of violating the law, or even of offending the moral sense of the community, accepted guilt. Within the business community there appeared a new emphasis on community service and ethical conduct. And organizations such as chambers of commerce and advertising clubs on the local level, and the National Civic Federation on the national level, emphasized the eagerness of businessmen to be good, moral, public-spirited citizens.

Even though behavior of this sort was a direct response to public criticism, it was not necessarily dishonest or hypocritical. Businessmen were products of the same culture that produced the progressives, and some of them were no doubt themselves eager to see the inculcation of higher ethical standards in economic behavior. "Multitudes of business men are swayed to some extent by . . . moral impulse," argued John Graham Brooks.[22] For these men, progressive criticism was as much an opportunity as a threat. Certainly, internal critics of corporate behavior such as George Perkins of the House of Morgan and Elbert Gary of United States Steel enjoyed a good deal of respect in the business community and with the public at large during the progressive period. Both Gary and Perkins were "business leaders with strong religious [and] humanitarian . . . orientations," which could be exercised and strengthened in the more morally sensitive corporate environment.[23]

But Gary, Perkins, and the other farsighted industrial leaders of the era were complex men. Their interests transcended business ethics, and they did not see the reformation of corporate behavior as an end in itself. They sincerely believed corporations could be more ethical, but they were also attempting to defend business against its critics. They attempted to strengthen business politically and regain the favor of public opinion. They hoped to buttress the capitalist system in general, retain their dominance of the American economy and political system, and increase their profits. And they hoped to order the economy, imparting a greater degree of rationality, predictability, and control to labor, production, and markets. Though some of these goals were at least implicitly contradictory, American business managed to achieve them to a remarkable degree.

The progressive period was a time of transition in America to a less competitive capitalistic order, as were the periods before and after it. Major corporations grew in power and strength, developing markets throughout the nation and the world, controlling numerous subsidiaries, and employing tens of thousands of people across their empires. Their dominance of markets, the development of brand names advertised nationally, and the searchlight turned on their behavior by politicians and muckraking journalists made them increasingly visible to the public. In this atmosphere, the stereotypical nineteenth-century corporation czar—secretive, competitive, selfish, distrustful of government, contemptuous of consumers, and disregardful of labor—was anachronistic, and his continuing existence presented a threat to business. Cognizant both of the temper of the times and the increasing interdependence of the economy, insightful corporate leaders urged the development of a new economic order, which would be highlighted by cooperation, openness, and business responsibility to the community. In this new order, the major corporations and their dominance of the economy would be more secure against internal and external threats.

The spirit of cooperation spread throughout the business world during the progressive era. National organizations, the best example of which was the National Civic Federation, were formed to promote cooperation and understanding among business, labor, and the public. National trade associations and manufacturing and commercial groups stressed cooperation within industries and spoke to the public with a unified voice. On the state and local levels, as well, business groups stressed cooperation within the business community and between it and the society at large. In the major corporations could be seen "a new generation of business executives who sought co-operation rather than competition in industry."[24] Spokesmen for the new cooperative spirit saw many good things coming from it. In a less competitive environment, businessmen would not feel compelled to mistreat one another and misserve the public. The odious things they did to gain competitive advantage would become extinct. In a cooperative environment, the altruistic side of the employer would come to dominate. "I do not believe that competition is any longer the life of trade. I have long believed that cooperation is the life of trade," George W. Perkins told the Industrial Commission. "I believe this because it is clear the competition, driven to its logical end, gave us the sweatshop, child labor, long hours of labor, insanitary labor conditions, and bred strife and discord between employer and employee."[25]

The largest corporations were most attracted to increased cooperation, because it fit their self-image, it would facilitate their attempts to maintain and extend their dominance of the economy, and it would help protect them from internal challenges and public wrath. Large corporations, confusing interdependence with cooperation, believed their size and complexity already proved the value of working together rather than competing. When it was extended to industry as a whole, cooperation could decrease uncertainty and insecurity, advancing the goals of order, predictability, and control. If cooperation took the form of agreements to set wages, limit production, divide markets, and determine prices, it would result in larger and more secure profits. And when the antisocial by-products of fierce competition were minimized, unfavorable public opinion, and the political and economic threats it carried, would diminish.

The bitter fruits that might be harvested under a continuation of competitive business as usual were already on the vine. In part because of outrage over corporate abuses, state and federal regulation of industry had increased dramatically in the early years of the century. Despite their early fears, businessmen had usually found that they could work with regulatory bodies and that these agencies had even helped them achieve some of their purposes and had diminished public hostility toward them. Some farsighted industrial statesmen even came to welcome regulation, for it put government behind their efforts to curb "irresponsible business conduct and to assure stability in marketing and financial affairs."[26] Still, at best regulation symbolized the failures of business, and it did introduce a new and potentially unstable element into corporate affairs. At worst, it indicated the determination of the public to assert its interest in business behavior, and it carried the threat of more severe measures. Prudence dictated corporate acceptance of regulation and attention to its implications.

Thus, for the business community, the impulse to cooperate was a response to more than one factor. It reflected industrial realities and needs in a modern world in which order, stability, and control were at once possible and desirable, and it was a response to public pressure for more moral and responsible corporate behavior. A heightened degree of cooperation would satisfy public demands and, in part because of that fact, enhance the security and stability of the system. In cooperation businessmen saw the opportunity both to have and to eat their cake. They could appear altruistic and public-spirited without altering the essentially selfish profit orientation of the system. Perkins combined these two implicitly contradictory goals into an attractive package:

I believe that with the awakening of the business conscience is coming what might be called an enlightened selfishness—by which I mean a realization that for one's own best pecuniary interests the methods of the past cannot be the methods of the future; that as we are living in a "get together" age we must do business on a "live and let live" basis, and that one's own selfish interest makes the doing of business on a coöperative basis more profitable in the long run than on the basis of ruthless competition.[27]

The new emphasis on cooperation and "enlightened selfishness" can be seen with clarity in labor relations during the progressive era. At the turn of the century, the varied experiments in labor policy that came under the broad headings of "welfare work" or "welfare capitalism" were generally discredited. Genuinely democratic experiments in labor policy, such as those of Nelson Olson Nelson and Golden Rule Jones, were stigmatized as radical and visionary. More narrow and self-interested innovations, such as those of George Pullman and John Patterson of the National Cash Register Company, were widely seen as un-American because of their paternalism and anti-individualism and as unsuccessful because they did not produce a more quiescent labor force. Though some businessmen continued to countenance a degree of welfare work, they generally believed that workers should be as individualistic and competitive as employers were.

With the growing criticism of corporate behavior and the new emphasis on social responsibility and cooperation, businessmen turned to a reconsideration of welfare work. Education and safety programs were developed for workers. Grounds and plants were beautified, lunchrooms were provided, and company outings, picnics, concerts, and sporting events were instituted. Company health and welfare plans took shape, and profit-sharing and stock-option programs appeared.

One leading scholar of welfare capitalism includes in it "any service provided for the comfort or improvement of employees which was neither a necessity of the industry nor required by law."[28] In the strictest sense, this definition applies to the welfare work of the progressive era. But welfare capitalism, like the other corporate innovations of the period, did not take place in a vacuum. Instead, it was a response to public opinion—sometimes expressed in law—and to the imperatives of the modern industrial order. For example, education and safety programs were undertaken at least in part because of the implicit demands employer liability laws placed on corporations. Inno-

vations to meet workers' needs served to gain favorable public attention and to forestall laws forcing employers to care for workers better.
One student of employee welfare programs at U.S. Steel has concluded
that most labor reforms there "were hurried responses to threatened
governmental investigations or muckraking exposés of conditions in
the plants.[29]

Employee-benefit programs also improved the atmosphere in the
factories, making workers happier, more efficient, productive, and
pliable. Its champions saw welfare work not as a one-sided benefit to
workers, but "as a means of bringing harmony between labor and
management — on the company's terms. It was hoped that a loyal and
happy work force would increase productivity, improve the quality
of the product, and reduce the cost of manufacture."[30] Like the scientific management to which it was related, welfare work was originally
feared by business but came to be accepted as a means of responding
to public demands and of achieving a more modern industrial order.

Public contrition, self-examination, commitment to higher standards of morality, cooperation, welfare work, and scientific management in the business community led to a more favorable public attitude
toward business after 1910. "A new conscience is appearing in our
business world," a subscriber informed the *Outlook* in 1911. "The old
conscience was commercial. It conducted business wholly for the
money there was in it. The new conscience is philanthropic. It con-
ducts business for the service it can render to the community. The old
corporation had no soul, the new one is distinctly human."[31] Incoming
Secretary of Commerce William C. Redfield argued in 1913 that the
reform efforts of the previous decade had borne fruit. He perceived
"outward and visible signs of an inward moral growth" in the business
community.[32] Redfield was no more insightful than the average commerce secretary, he was simply echoing an increasingly prominent
public attitude, and one shared by many progressives.

Christian progressives exhibited a more favorable attitude toward
business, seeing the operation of the law of love in the new emphases
on cooperation and welfare work. Graham Taylor was happy to report
in 1911 that "American business men are squaring themselves and
their methods to the new demands of the ethics of the group," and

Gerald Stanley Lee concluded in 1913 that "the Golden Rule at last [was being viewed] as a plain business proposition."[33] Within a few years, articles were again appearing in popular periodicals that celebrated business as a training ground for character and businessmen as paragons of moral virtue.[34]

Cooperation, welfare work, scientific management, and professionalization in industry heartened scientific progressives. "The real news about business," Walter Lippmann informed the readers of *Drift and Mastery*, "is that it is being administered by men who are not profiteers." The new corporate managers, he continued, were motivated by "the instincts of workmanship, of control over brute things, the desire for order, the satisfaction of services rendered and uses created."[35] Muckrakers Lincoln Steffens and Ida Tarbell showed their fascination for the new industrial order in extravagant praise for such leaders as Ford, Taylor, and General Electric's Owen D. Young. In her autobiography, Tarbell recounted her belief that Ford and Taylor were leading the country to an industrial economy based on the Golden Rule.[36]

Those progressives who explained changes in industry in idealistic terms were overly optimistic, but they were not deluding themselves completely. Saul Engelbourg has argued that "the code of business morality was quite different by 1914 from what had been sanctioned in 1900, and by common consent, the difference constituted an improvement."[37] Businessmen, at the very least, were engaged in a degree of self-examination and self-analysis. They were, perhaps, more cognizant of their responsibilities to others in society, including workers and consumers. At its best, the business environment was characterized by more humane or at least more circumspect behavior, there was more attention to public opinion, and workers and local communities were, perhaps, treated a bit better and with more respect.

The progressives had stimulated the expression of a degree of business altruism. Businessmen, a Chicago printing plant owner told the Industrial Commission, "have a very acute sense of their responsibility to the community. . . . You know employers do a great many things for their employees, just because they want to be men, and they want to have sympathy with them."[38] Commissioner John B. Hibbard of the National Metal Trades Association argued that businessmen wanted to learn, grow, and progress with the rest of the community:

I do not believe . . . that proper credit is given at the present time to the . . . employer who to-day realizes he has been taught . . . as we all have been taught, that . . . conditions as they used to exist were not proper, and he is just as good a citizen, he is just as humane an individual, and just as much interested in the improvement of conditions as are any of the rest of us.[39]

The fact that progressives freed generous impulses in the business community did not mean that they had transformed businessmen into practicing idealists overnight. The pure altruist could not survive in a competitive, capitalistic economic system. As one witness before the Industrial Commission candidly put it, "if I gave my altruistic spirit full rein I would be broke in a month."[40] Nor, despite the beliefs of some progressives, were businessmen motivated by humanitarianism solely or even primarily when they made changes. Altruism was but one of several motives for corporate actions. As Mansel Blackford notes in his study of welfare work at the Buckeye Steel Castings Company of Columbus, Ohio, the company's officers sponsored worker-benefit programs for a variety of reasons:

Many had a genuine desire to improve the working and living conditions of their employees for humanitarian reasons. . . . However, Buckeye's management also viewed welfare work as good business. In particular, they hoped that improved working and living conditions would lessen the turnover rate at their steel plant and, thus, decrease the costs of production. . . . Finally, . . . Buckeye officials believed they had a duty to insure that their employees would be loyal, patriotic Americans imbued with middle-class citizenship values.[41]

Buckeye was by no means unique in pursuing several goals at once when undertaking industrial innovations, and greater profits and enhanced corporate security were always among these. Christian progressives had nothing against profits, as long as they were not the primary motivation for behavior. Scientific progressives were interested more in results than in motives. They believed, of course, that professionalization would somehow transmute businessmen into conscious public servants, but they always focused on behavior rather than on the reasons for it. Indeed, they implicitly encouraged changes on the grounds not that they would benefit society, but that they would profit businessmen. For example, Louis Brandeis praised the Filenes, department store operators in Boston, not simply because they "accepted and applied the principles of industrial democracy and of social justice" in their employee welfare program but because "they have demonstrated that the introduction of industrial democracy and of social justice is at least consistent with marked financial success. They assert that the greater efficiency of their employees shows industrial democracy and social justice to be money-makers." The confusion and lack of direction of scientific progressivism was illustrated in Brandeis' next paragraph, in which he transmuted the shrewd self-interest of the Filenes into high industrial statesmanship. When businessmen followed the Filene's lead, he argued, " 'big business' will . . . mean business big not in bulk or power, but great in service and grand in manner. 'Big business' will mean professionalized business, as distinguished from the occupation of petty trafficking or mere money-making." [42]

In Brandeis' formulation, we can see a key problem of scientific progressivism. Supposedly realistic students of human nature, contemptuous of the sentimental and unempirical attitudes of Christian reformers, scientific progressives refused to ignore or to denigrate what the Victorian age had stigmatized as low motives. Yet they remained idealists—in a sense more wildly idealistic than Christian progressives —devoted to inspiring social goals. In assuming that society would advance because of the individual expression of selfish motives, they were unwittingly refurbishing and legitimizing the old argument for capitalism that all benefitted from the selfishness of each. And, implicitly at least, they were also encouraging those in the business community who favored innovation for profit mainly and discouraging those who favored it primarily because they were altruistic. People have many motives for the actions they take. But the values and the expectations of others can encourage them to act on some motives more than they act on others. The scientific progressives were encouraging people to act on selfish motives—thus validating and legitimizing them—because they thought people would do so anyway and they expected a socially beneficial result to obtain. Their first assumption might have been correct. Their second could not be.

Perhaps it was not completely coincidental that businessmen became less reticent about emphasizing the "selfishness" in their "enlightened selfishness." Edward Filene and Henry Ford, both of whom were widely praised for employee-welfare work, emphasized that what they did for employees was motivated primarily by their own self-interest. Of course, the promise of profits might cause businessmen to do things that benefitted workers or society as a whole. The problem lay in the fact that the desirable activities would continue only as long as they were profitable. With no higher motivation underlying them, they were never secure. Within a few years the same Henry Ford celebrated by scientific progressives cut wages, laid workers off, filled his plants with goons to beat labor organizers, and protected his properties with machine guns. But the times, not the man, had changed. Ford remained devoted to the pursuit of profit; he simply found it necessary to alter his means.

During the progressive period, external critics of businessmen commonly compared them to medieval barons, pre-revolutionary French aristocrats, and other groups known for inflexibility, myopia, and self-destructive conservatism.[43] In retrospect, though, it is clear that the American business community was flexible rather than inflexible, that it was regardful of public opinion, and that it was quite willing to respond to the demands of the age.

Unlike the French aristocracy, American businessmen were not really separate from the community. In general, they shared the values that predominated within the American middle class, and they responded to the pressures of mainstream opinion. As Saul Engelbourg has noted, in order to enjoy success in a democratic capitalistic society, "businessmen must ultimately internalize the views and values of the community."[44] Their self-examination and criticism, their concern with business morality, their emphasis on cooperation, welfare work, and efficiency were all indications that businessmen were attempting to respond to a wave of criticism from a public that previously had generally admired them.

In addition to responding to public opinion with real and symbolic changes, businessmen began the process of shaping public opinion in order to make it more favorable to them. As Richard Tedlow has argued, "conservative businessmen in the twentieth century never doubted that the locus of power lay with public opinion. What is more, they accepted this situation as right and proper. If the public turned against them, as . . . it was tending to during the Progressive era . . . , it was up to them to set it right through mass communication." [45] This effort involved, in part, the sort of economic pressure that eventually choked off muckraking. But it also involved a positive effort to develop a more favorable public image through the use of professional public relations experts.

The use by business of public relations practitioners was at once "a harbinger of a changed attitude and approach by the business community to its social responsibilities" and "a defense for the beleaguered businessman." [46] Businessmen saw organized public relations as a means of counteracting what they believed to be false attitudes, and early public relations experts, reflecting the professional ideal, saw themselves as community servants whose devotion to the truth served their employers and society.

Soon, however, businessmen came to see public relations as just another device—such as welfare work and scientific personnel management—for human engineering. It became a tool for manipulating public opinion in favor of business and against labor, government, and other threats, and the "truth" in which progressives had such faith got lost in the shuffle. Public relations professionals in many firms discovered that serving their employers—by misrepresenting or hiding their actions and by controlling damage when egregious behavior was exposed—necessarily meant misserving the public. The most conscientious quit or were fired, and the rest followed the path trod by engineers and professional managers, becoming timeservers devoted primarily to corporate profits. Once again, corporate America had adopted the technique the professionals offered and had left the ideal of professionalism behind.

During the progressive period the American business community showed an adaptability and a willingness to adjust that provided it with great strength and that assured not only that it would survive but indeed that it would thrive. Facing a myriad of criticisms from a newly aroused public, businessmen adjusted their behavior, their attitudes, and the ways in which they did business. They developed devices that responded to public demands, strengthening themselves in the process. At the same time, they were able to use cooperation, regulation, welfare capitalism, professional management, and other devices to impart a higher level of stability, order, predictability, control, and security to the American economic environment. They were following the advice of George Perkins, pursuing the "enlightened selfishness" he had recommended.

Historians who have focused on the result of this process have sometimes assumed, understandably, that it was the goal of progressivism to modernize corporate capitalism and increase its wealth, power, and security. This is not correct. Progressive reformers, whether they spoke in Christian or in scientific terms, were genuinely committed to the achievement of a better society, in which people would serve one another and in which harmony would reign. Their basic error was in their assumption that this kind of society could be achieved without fundamental alterations in the capitalist economic system. They gave those who dominated that system the opportunity to change, and these men did so. The changes addressed the criticisms of progressives in some superficial ways, and they humanized industry to a limited extent. At the same time, the changes facilitated the development of a more modern form of industrial capitalism without doing anything to alter the essential nature of the system. Changes were made that propitiated an adverse public opinion and that satisfied many progressives. But the main motivation of businessmen remained economic gain, and as long as that was true, business could never truly be characterized by a devotion either to the law of love or to the public interest.

II

The ability of business to respond to progressive criticism without really meeting it was one of the developments that lent an air of ambiguity to the teens. The emergence of interest-group-based politics was another. As in the case of changing business behavior, alterations in politics and political behavior resulted in part from progressive criticism of the system and progressive measures to reform it. And yet the interest-group politics of the teens prsented a stark contrast to the moral, publicly interested political system the progressives had foreseen and championed.

Few historical problems have been investigated more creatively and fruitfully in recent years than that of the nature and alteration of politics in the late nineteenth and early twentieth centuries. Though they differ on some specifics, Paul Kleppner, Richard Jensen, Samuel McSeveney, Robert Cherny, and Richard L. McCormick, among others, have provided us with a relatively clear picture of political development.[47] From the end of the Civil War until the 1890's the party system was relatively stable. On the state level, the parties were strong and tightly organized. Party loyalties were intense, deriving their strength from ethno-religious identifications and from the tight bonds forged during the Civil War. Party functionaries, dependent on the spoils system for their livelihoods, were devoted to partisan success. Elective and appointive positions were bestowed on deserving partisans, and they used their positions further to benefit their parties. In power, the parties were concerned primarily with patronage and the distribution of favors—often symbolic in nature—to constituent groups. Because government had relatively few functions that affected him, the average voter was little interested in most of its operations. As a consequence, groups and individuals—such as railroads, public service corporations, and public contractors—that made tangible demands on government enjoyed a relatively open field. Voters exercised the franchise in record numbers, but they perceived politics more as a recreation or a means of symbolic validation of ethnic and religious identification than as an arena for economic interest-group combat.

The shape of politics did not change completely, and it did not change overnight, but the existing system and its practices came under increasing stress during the nineties and after. Faced with the economic and social pressures attendant on commercialization, increasing interdependence, industrialization, and urbanization, farmers coalesced into new groups—the most famous of which was the Populist party—that made economic demands on government. Feeling control of their work and their lives slipping away in an economy dominated increasingly by large-scale industry, workers also became more politically active, demanding protection and favors from government. Businessmen became more appreciative of what government could do for them and fearful of what it might do to them, and they, too, developed a new interest in politics. In each of these cases, the group involved was based on economic self-interest rather than on ethnic or religious identification. As such, it enjoyed more flexibility and could shift from party to party or even from candidate to candidate with relative ease. Economic interest groups were not new, either in American history or in the Gilded Age. What was new, as Richard L. McCormick notes in his study of New York politics, was that "to a greater degree than at any time previously, the diverse producer groups in society became conscious of their distinct economic positions and began organizing intensely to influence politics and government in their own interests."[48]

In addition to feeling new pressures and demands from self-interested economic groups, the parties also faced broad public discontent arising especially from the depression experience of the 1890's. During the depression, state and city government and the parties that controlled them were perceived as corrupt by a growing segment of the public. Government generally was unwilling or unable to cope with the problems of economic collapse. Moreover, city and state bosses proved unsympathetic to citizens—whether white- or blue-collar workers, farmers, small businessmen, or professionals—ravaged by favored businesses such as railroads and public service companies. Bosses also showed an arrogant disregard for the law in their open support for organized vice and crime in a number of cities. Citizens responded by demanding clean and honest state and city governments that would serve the public interest rather than private interests and that would enforce the law. This impulse, in which progressivism was rooted, was accompanied by a general hostility to parties. Many reformers believed the parties were little more than organized expressions of the selfishness and materialism that was too characteristic of American society.

It might seem that the newly mobilized economic groups and the reformers galvanized by the depression had little in common. Both were discontented, but while the first represented organized selfishness, the second favored a political order in which the selfless devotion to the public interest would reign. However, the selfish and the selfless were often able to coalesce in vague groupings, as "citizens," "taxpayers," and "consumers," under banners emblazoned with "reform."

In practice, this coupling was not as odd as it was in theory. Producer groups and reformers were both victimized by big business of various kinds, and both demanded a measure of public control over corporate behavior. Both believed that government was unresponsive or, perhaps, that it was responsive to the wrong people. Reformers often sympathized with groups, such as farmers, workers, and small businessmen, that had suffered at the hands of industrial capitalists and their political minions, and producer groups felt little kinship with the urban criminals despised by moral reformers.

What David Thelen calls "insurgent progressivism" was embodied in the demands of this coalition of self-interested groups and public-spirited individuals.[49] In the years after 1900, insurgents were able to force the adoption of a variety of municipal and state reforms. Political reforms, such as nonpartisan elections, the Australian ballot, and the direct primary, reflected the anti-party spirit of the times. Each weakened the parties and their discipline and facilitated the expression of either the public interest or the interests of organized groups outside the party structures. The insurgents demanded and received increased government regulation of business behavior, regulation that benefitted the public interest as well as the interests of economic groups that previously did not enjoy government's favor. And legislation to protect consumers, investors, and workers was fashioned that particularly aided certain groups but that also served the public interest.

The assaults by producer groups and reformers resulted in significant alterations in the way politics was conducted and in the nature of the parties. Politicians who were able to adjust to or even capitalize on the changes thrived, while others struggled. Politics became more complicated for politicians. It was no longer sufficient mainly to be a loyal partisan; now officeholders had to be sensitive both to group demands and to broad public opinion. Moreover, politics became more issue-oriented as interest groups and public opinion shifted depending on the particular public question being addressed. Those who were sensitive to these new factors, such as Robert LaFollette of Wisconsin, used the electoral reforms to transcend the parties and create personal followings. With the parties weakening and loyalty to them declining, a premium was placed on charismatic candidates who could galvanize public opinion through their personalities or their ability to define and dramatize issues. Candidates with voter appeal could become independent of parties for all intents and purposes. Now parties depended on candidates more than candidates depended on parties. Shrewd executives used the new spirit to gain greater independence from legislative bodies as they turned their popular appeal into grants of power for administrators. Politicians recognized the potential gulf between self-interested insurgents and public-interested ones, and they bridged it as best they could. The most successful politicians of the era—LaFollette, Bryan, Roosevelt, and Wilson all come to mind—were genuinely devoted to the public interest as they saw it, but were also willing to recognize the legitimacy of group demands.

The survival of the insurgent coalition depended on a number of implicit agreements. It was necessary, first, for the producer groups to support policies that did not affect them directly. It was also necessary for the components of the coalition to define and justify policies in the same way. For this purpose, vague groupings such as "taxpayers," "citizens," and "consumers" were useful, as were broad and amorphous concepts such as "the public interest" and "justice." The fact that so many diverse groups and policies could fit under these labels seriously diminished their descriptive utility, but broad terms helped unite an heterogeneous and potentially unstable coalition.

Most important, the maintenance of the coalition depended on the ability of public-spirited reformers to convince themselves that policies that aided producer groups were just, and were thus in the larger public interest. They were reluctant to support class legislation of any kind —that is, legislation that benefitted one particular group at the expense of others. When they supported legislation that benefitted workers, farmers, or small businessmen, they did so not to help these groups reach a selfish goal but to redress social wrongs and correct systemic imbalances, to achieve greater justice and thus to serve the public interest. George Mowry argued that the typical California progressive "pictured himself as a complete individual wholly divorced from particular economic as well as class interests. Ready to do justice in the name of morality and the common good, he was, in his own estimation, something akin to Plato's guardians, above and beyond the reach of corrupting material forces."[50] Most other reformers had a similar self-image.

Not only did progressives see themselves as apart from selfish individuals and groups; they also believed this separation gave them a superior ability to determine what best served the interests of the public as a whole. Nor did they doubt that policies that served the whole public could be devised. McGeorge Bundy said of Henry Stimson that "he believed . . . that there was always a policy which was best for all the people, and not good merely for one group as against another." [51] What was true of Stimson was true of Roosevelt, Wilson, and the other giants of the period as well.

The self-conscious independence and devotion to the public interest of the progressives meant that their producer-group allies could depend on them only as long as the former could see that policies benefitting the latter also served the public interest. When the producer groups appeared selfish or unjust, the public-spirited reformers' support for them declined. From the perspective of the twenties, Social Gospel minister William Rainsford expressed the progressive position of neutrality and devotion to the public interest, while at the same time illustrating why reformers were undependable political allies:

> For more than thirty years the struggle between capitalists and their labour has profoundly disturbed our land. . . . At first capitalists had their way, and often the things they did were indefensible, unjust, and tyrannous in the extreme. The wrong they were guilty of in their day of power was not a wrong done to their employees alone. It was a wrong done to every man, woman, and child in the nation. Now Labour is steadily gaining power, and still more power; and it aims to do, and sometimes has already done, things just as unjust, just as harmful to the whole land, as the offending capitalists were guilty of. [52]

By the first years of Woodrow Wilson's administration, the hidden stresses in the insurgent coalition were being exposed. Organized producers were becoming more aggressive and demanding, asking for government favors simply on the grounds that the requesting group had political clout, regardless of any public interest. Apparently tiring of playing second fiddle to public-interest-oriented progressives and of receiving favors from them, workers and farmers showed a new willingness to demand self-serving measures that were clearly class legislation. Part of this shift resulted from the new prominence of "bread-and-butter issues" deriving from the recession of 1914.[53] But it also reflected the growing unity, strength, and self-confidence of producer groups and a new willingness on their parts to assert themselves politically.

The weakening of the party system had created greater opportunities for organized groups to influence politics, and they were quick to take advantage of these. Successful politicians recognized the change, and their appeals became more class-oriented in nature. As David Thelen has noted, "during the Wilson years . . . old appeals to the united community of consumers and taxpayers gave way to narrower appeals to interest groups based on people's jobs."[54] As so often happened, progressives' actions had unintended consequences. Instead of leading to a broader commitment to the public interest, progressive efforts on behalf of producer groups had merely whetted appetites for more narrowly based class legislation. Political reforms weakened the parties, but this merely increased the ability of self-serving groups to influence the system, regardless of the public interest.

The progressives themselves deserve some blame for the heightened group selfishness that was evident in the teens. Not only had their reforms contributed, albeit inadvertently, to this unfortunate outcome, but they themselves had formed groups to pressure politicians for particular reforms. They believed that their organizations served the public interest, and perhaps they were correct, but there is no question that they added to the number of groups struggling in the political arena. "The progressives' refusal to accept the concept of conflicting and competing groups and classes was ironic, since they helped construct some of the most effective pressure groups," John Whiteclay Chambers II has pointed out. "In their search for a larger public interest, progressives inadvertently contributed to the growth of the interest-group democracy they bemoaned."[55] Moreover, as they involved themselves in interest-group politics, with its compromises and short-term considerations, progressives sometimes lost sight of the transcendent, selfless goals they once had. What William O'Neill has said of woman suffragists applies in some degree to virtually every progressive group. "The more suffragists behaved as simply another interest group, trading a principle there for an advantage here, the less capable they became of preserving what had brought them into politics to begin with. In a sense, suffragists were depleting their moral capital."[56]

The increasing tendency of American political life to be characterized by competition among selfish interest groups was not the only threat to the insurgent coalition. Social issues such as prohibition and woman suffrage became increasingly devisive. And changes in corporate behavior tended to woo some reformers away from reform or, at least, away from their producer-group allies. But the increasingly pluralistic nature of politics did signal the failure of the progressives to fashion a broad and unifying commitment to the public interest, however expressed. With the war thus lost, the outcome of individual battles did not mean much.

Progressives responded to the emerging pluralistic order in a variety of ways. Some made their peace with it, participating in it with varying degrees of enthusiasm. Others "could never be in accord with a policy which saw reform primarily in terms of the parceling out of material favors to clamoring groups." In part for this reason, as Otis Graham has noted, many progressives could not support the avowedly pluralistic New Deal.[57]

Scientific progressives generally adjusted to the situation more easily than did their Christian counterparts. Their self-conscious realism led them to accept the fact of human selfishness. They even tended to believe that pluralism made the public-spirited expert more important, both because it made it more imperative that key areas of social and economic policy and administration be removed from the political arena and because the expert was particularly suited to mediate among competing groups. Albion Small took note in 1914 of a "selfish tug-of-war between interests," but he also professed to see a public demand "for an arbiter between and over the interests, that shall be above and beyond complicity with either of them in preference to the rest."[58]

As Small's remark implies, their apparent acceptance of interest-group politics did not mean that scientific progressives had abandoned their belief in the existence of a public interest that could be defined and served by selfless professionals. Nor did the emerging organization of politics into an arena for interest-group competition lead them to alter their vision of a transcendent society. "Society is not merely a result of the harmony or the conflict of individual interest or wills,"

Croly wrote in 1914. "It is an end in itself."[59] Their realistic pose obscured the idealistic conception of society and of the professional that continued to inform the scientific progressives' thought.

Events during the teens seemed to vindicate those whose social and economic diagnoses and prescriptions were scientific rather than Christian in nature. The tough-minded seemed better able than the tender-hearted to integrate social and economic realities with their ideals. In business, scientific management of plant and personnel and professional administration seemed to have caught hold. In municipal and state government scientific administration and advisement and regulation by expert commissions had come to be widely accepted and applied. Science even seemed to point the way toward the solution of such seemingly intractable problems as poverty and ignorance. Social surveys in urban and rural locales, inspired by Paul U. Kellogg's ambitious Pittsburgh Survey, provided the facts that reformers believed pointed inexorably toward specific ameliorative social changes.[60] Leading scientific progressives such as Herbert Croly, Louis Brandeis, and Walter Lippmann developed national followings and achieved a degree of political influence. First Theodore Roosevelt, then Woodrow Wilson appeared to come over to the cause, and the administration of the latter seemed to promise fulfillment of the scientific progressives' dreams. The buzz words of scientific progressivism—"efficiency," "professionalization," "management," and "expertise," for example —were tossed about by most commentators on public affairs, who often mixed them more or less promiscuously with more traditional ethical concepts.

Many Christian progressives adopted the language of their scientific counterparts, and some, like minister and Wilson Administration official Charles Ferguson, went over completely. In 1900, Ferguson had published *The Religion of Democracy*, a weird, Social Gospelesque tract that lambasted American society in general and business in particular for failing to obey the laws of God.[61] By 1915 he had become a committed scientific reformer. In *The Great News* he called for control over finance, politics, commerce, and industry by engineers. For him, social problems were now technical rather than moral. "The political problem in a democracy is a problem in engineering," he argued.[62]

Ferguson did not forget God, but he certainly altered him. Instead of a divine figure to be obeyed without question (in *The Religion of Democracy* Ferguson had held that "if there is any cosmical ordinance that you do not like, then there is something wrong with you"[63]), God became a super-engineer, the father of scientific management as much as the father of humanity. Ferguson saw Christ as one of the "authentic experts and specialists in knowledge of the nature of men." He was the "prime instigator of the modern spirit" who "did not sacrifice his body to his principles, but to his project," which was "the inauguration of a society in which the credits should be administered . . . by the creators thereof."[64] Ferguson was an extreme case, but he exemplifies the fact that "science" was replacing Christianity in reform, just as it was in socialism and just as it had in the explanation of natural phenomena. God still had a place, perhaps, but if it was to be secured he had to become subject to natural selection. He had to adjust and adapt in order to survive in the hearts of twentieth-century people.

III

Scientific and Christian progressives alike saw mainly hope in the economic and political developments of the early and mid-teens. Many promising things were going on, and most reformers placed an optimistic interpretation on ambiguous phenomena. On the other hand, there were developments within reform itself and within basic social institutions that gave progressives pause. The scientific had to contend with those who took their values in an inhumane direction. And the Christian faced a rising crisis in the home and the church.

In these heady prewar years that gave scientific progressives so many reasons for optimism, neither the basic flaws in their thinking nor the problems of translating their concept into action were readily apparent to them. They believed that forward-looking businessmen were accepting their goals and assumptions along with their techniques. They assumed that politicians supporting administration and regulation by experts were interested solely in advancing efficiency and thus serving the public interest. They thought science showed the way to a society in which human well-being, happiness, and unity could be achieved without broad alterations in individual character. There were already indications, however, that science ungrounded in ethics was potentially destructive, vicious, and inhumane, and nowhere were these indications stronger than in eugenics.

Eugenicists were "scientific," and they vigorously proclaimed their devotion to the public interest, and for these reasons they enjoyed a following that included many progressives. But they also showed how "science," bereft of ethics, could subvert the most basic ideals of Western civilization. The eugenicists' classification of human beings on the basis of physical and intellectual attributes, and their support for selective breeding and sterilization of the "unfit," contradicted traditional Christian values of individual goodness and integrity and human equality. "Humanitarian ideals, democratic principles, Christian beliefs and medical practices, are unalterably opposed to the ruthless extinction of the unfit," admitted Smith College sociologist F. Stuart Chapin in 1915. "Yet," he continued, science decreed that "our *mores* need to have injected into them the idea that abiding human progress can come only through the improvement of the stock of the people." [65]

In 1916, Madison Grant showed the potential of a science uninformed by ethics in *The Passing of the Great Race*. Grant was a popularizer who yoked eugenics together with the "sciences" of heredity, history, archeology, anthropology, physiology, and linguistics to "prove" the inferiority of "non-Nordic" peoples and to argue that America's self-preservation demanded an end to their immigration. In the process, Grant subjected such basic beliefs as democracy and equality to empirical analysis—finding them untrue on the basis of his scientific facts—and he derided America's "altruistic ideals" and its "maudlin sentimentalism." [66] It was a disturbing performance, but one that held lessons for those with the courage to learn. Grant had used all of the devices of the scientific progressives. Tough-mindedness was there, as was the denigration of sentimentality. Grant had used science in support of social policy, and he subjected values and institutions to empirical analysis. All the while he trumpeted his devotion to the public interest. But he also showed that an amoral, unethical science was not necessarily the path to human happiness. In the hands of people like Grant, the tools used by scientific progressives could lead to a vicious inhumanity worthy of the most debased barbarians. Character did make a difference, after all.

Another potential difficulty for scientific progressivism that had appeared by the mid-teens was that experts had trouble putting their theories into practice in public policy. The only power experts had lay in the informal authority their technical expertise gave them. However, they assumed that those who held power would allow the experts to formulate policy without interfering in the process. And they also assumed that the people, in mass or in interest groups, would accept the policies formulated voluntarily because of their rationality, their recognition that their self-interests and the public interest were compatible, or their willingness to defer to the public interest. Reality intruded on both assumptions.

Rather than leaving policy formation to experts, powerful interests involved themselves in the process at every stage, selecting experts, shaping their decisions, and determining whether or not policies should be put into effect. And interest groups resisted policies, even when these were supposedly in the groups' interests. A good example of this phenomenon can be seen in rural life reform. Scientific progressives formulated a comprehensive set of policies designed to alter rural social institutions and economic practices. The purpose of this alteration was the more efficient production of food, and, in theory, it would benefit farmers by uplifting their occupations, increasing their incomes, and improving their lives, and it would serve the public interest by decreasing food prices. The problem was that farmers failed to play the part assigned to them by voluntarily accepting the policies. They did not see how the suggested changes would benefit them, and they suspected that their self-interest was not perfectly congenial with the larger public interest as the scientific progressives defined it.[67]

Lacking autonomous power and functioning in a democratic society, scientific progressives were stymied when voluntarism failed. Reflecting their elitism and their frustration, some scientific progressives were longing for modifications in democracy by the mid-teens, modifications that would give independent power to the experts. This was a minority sentiment in a period in which scientific progressives remained optimistic regarding their own potential and popular responsiveness as well, but it was also a hint that even in their golden days scientific reformers were finding that life refused always to imitate theory.

Most Christian progressives remained optimistic during the mid-teens, finding abundant evidence that public behavior was conforming more closely to the Golden Rule and the law of love. "The social power of the Church of Christ has been particularly shown in its capacity to put new spirit into institutions that possessed the capacity for being reformed," Shailer Mathews contended in 1914. "When one recalls that it is less than a quarter of a century since the social interpretation began to be given the message of Christianity, the extent of this new social enthusiasm is fairly amazing." [68] Positive developments in public behavior in business and politics indicated that Christian progressives were achieving their goals. On the other hand, the deterioration of the institutions of private life, and of the family in particular, continued and even accelerated.

The importance of the home to Christian reformers cannot be overemphasized. They defined it as the basic institution of civilization and the repository of humanity's finest values. They hoped to protect the integrity of the home and family by obliterating encroaching threats from public life — specific ones such as alcohol, prostitution, pornography, and mistreatment of women and children, as well as the general selfishness, materialism, and hedonism reflected in these particular phenomena. The package of reforms developed to protect the home was broad and, from the point of view of our modern political configurations, contradictory. The same reformers who were "opposed to divorce, prostitution, erotic literature, and unwed motherhood" could also be found supporting such things as "unemployment insurance" and "the Social Gospel." [69] Reforms designed to defend the home were mixed together with others meant to generalize its influence in society in a compound that was perfectly sensible to Christian progressives.

Women were the key people in the home, and as such they were the central figures of Christian reform. Christian progressives believed women were intrinsically different from and, in important ways, superior to men. Women were the maintainers and advancers of civilization, nurturing its values in the families for which they were responsible. They were the mothers on whose strength and character the future of the human race depended. They were more sentimental, peace-loving, moral, kind, and tender than men. Because of all of these characteristics, Christian progressives agreed, women should be protected *and* their influence should be extended further into society.

A substantial number of middle-class women agreed. During the late nineteenth and early twentieth centuries tens of thousands of women —more educated, more inspired by Victorian values, and possessed of more leisure than their sisters of earlier generations—threw themselves into reform activities. In those areas that male and female progressives agreed were particularly appropriate for the attention of women because of their special character—areas such as health, education, social welfare, protection of children, antiprostitution, and prohibition—women dominated in numbers if not in leadership.[70] Moreover, woman suffrage became a popular progressive reform in large measure because Christian progressives believed the franchise would allow women better to protect the home and to extend its influence into public life.

The progressive effort to protect the home and to extend its values into the larger sphere had a good effect on American society, both in the tangible reforms it facilitated and in the more decent and less vicious public mood to which it contributed. By the mid-teens, however, it was evident that the glorious design of Christian progressivism was not being realized. The home seemed weaker rather than stronger. There were more single people in society and divorce was becoming increasingly common. Moreover, it appeared that greater opportunities for women outside of marriage and their rising expectations from marriage were largely responsible for this trend. Prostitution seemed to be in retreat, but a recent student of the subject argues that "this decline was attributable in part to the increase of sexual activity unrelated to prostitution, which was one of the results of the demise of civilized morality."[71] Christian progressives had hoped to expel prostitution from society by extending the morality of self-restraint from the private to the public sphere, not by abandoning that morality. Nor was sexual behavior the only area in which the decline of the morality of self-restraint was apparent. Materialism and selfishness seemed increasingly to inform family dynamics. Consumption of material goods was becoming a major family function, and it centered increasingly on women. The ideal woman was evolving from a selfless civilizer to a selfish consumer.[72] Progressives did not take this as progress.

In the face of rising challenges to the home, some reformers became increasingly shrill and protective, attacking divorce and redoubling their efforts to extirpate promiscuity, hedonism, and their manifestations. Retreating into a defensive posture, they laid the groundwork for today's "pro-family" conservatives, whom we do not normally think of as reformers. Others attempted to understand the new realities in more modern terms, but understanding did not often lead to acceptance, much less enthusiasm.

It was difficult to ignore the fact that increasing numbers of people were willing to question the goodness of traditional marriage and to wonder whether dissolving matrimonial unions was necessarily bad. A sign of the times was William Carson's *Marriage Revolt*, a careful and insightful exploration of modern marriage and divorce. Carson argued that the causes of divorce rather than the act itself should be deplored and that the rising divorce rate might actually be a good sign, "proving, as it does, that people have become less tolerant of evils which were once endured and for which divorce is the only remedy." Carson noted that the expectations people brought to marriage and their standards for it had changed and that narrow religious authority was less widely respected than previously. He believed it was appropriate to analyze marriage and question it. The criticism of conventional marriage, he said, "is typical of the restlessness and dissatisfaction with which we approach the moral questions of our time. There is nothing that we do not analyze, examine and criticize." [73]

Carson concluded that marriage as it was might pass away, but he assured his readers it would be replaced by a more appropriate arrangement. "Be assured that conventional institutions can only disappear with the advent of other institutions," he wrote optimistically, "which, while preserving all the good that is in the old, will bring through the new an enhancement of existence far beyond anything at present achieved." [74] Marriage might be improved, and the pragmatic test could be applied to it as well as to anything else, but the alteration of so basic and important an institution was not—and could not be—taken as lightly by Christian progressives as it was by Carson.

Carson observed that women's expectations regarding marriage had changed much more radically than had men's and that wives were more inclined than previously to stress their individual rights and liberties. The tendency of women to alter their view of themselves, their place in society, and their relationship to men could be seen in other areas as well. By the mid-teens more women were defining themselves as equals of men rather than as their superiors in one sphere and inferiors in another, and they were increasingly likely to stress their rights rather than their duties to others. Victorian women had generally looked to protecting their sphere and extending its values. By the mid-teens some women were eager to invade the male sphere, accepting the values they found there.

As is the case with most attitudinal shifts in history, this one was neither totally new nor sweeping. There had long been those who had argued that women should enjoy economic opportunities comparable to those of men, and at the turn of the century Charlotte Perkins Gilman and Olive Schreiner had advanced this argument elegantly in important books.[75] And people who argued for free love (or, as was often the case, freedom *from* love for women) had existed in American society for some time and had been objects at once of fear and of fascination. During the progressive period, for example, Swedish feminist Ellen Key generated a good deal of interest with her championship of free sexual unions and procreation outside of marriage.[76] But as American society became more modern, as urbanization and industrialization advanced, as the economy became more complex and technically oriented, opportunities opened for women that, for all practical purposes, had not existed before.

As desirable economic opportunities beyond the home appeared, women increasingly embraced a new self-image. Rather than superior beings who guarded the private sphere and who hoped to civilize the public one, they strove to be equals who were escaping the former to participate in the latter. They were willing to trade the duties and responsibilities of Victorian womanhood for the greater apparent independence that accompanied participation in modern industrial society. Modern science conspired with economic reality in the movement for female equality. Psychoanalytic theory seemed to indicate that there were no intrinsic differences between men and women and that females were driven by the same basic (or base) compulsions and impulses as males (though, as David Kennedy has noted, Sigmund Freud still saw fit to place women in a subordinate position by attributing penis envy to them).[77]

The struggle between those fighting to keep women on a pedestal and those women trying to scramble off was central to the whole shift from the Victorian to the modern world view, and it was joined in earnest during the twenties. But it could already be seen in some issues before World War I. Suffragists, for example, split between those who emphasized that the franchise would allow them to reform public life and those who believed they could use the vote to benefit themselves. The former saw women as superior bearers of civilization, while the latter saw them as an interest group in need of greater influence. As time went on, the latter came to predominate, and during the war they acted as the other selfish interest groups acted, threatening, compromising, wheeling, dealing, and practicing the art of the possible, while loudly proclaiming their devotion to the public interest. In the process they unwittingly provided support for their argument that they were no different from men. More's the pity.

The accelerating crisis of private life was one indication that reality was not conforming to the Christian progressive vision. Another was ferment in the churches. The churches had been the institutional bastion of Christian progressivism since its beginnings in the late nineteenth century, and the Social Gospel had provided it with a broad analysis of social ills and a Christian solution for those ills. In general terms, the Social Gospel movement had attempted to do two things — to socialize Christianity and to Christianize society. By the early teens it seemed well on the way to achieving both goals.

The Social Gospel seemed to have captured most of the seminaries of the mainline Protestant denominations, and few ministers any longer ignored the social duties of their churches or of their parishioners. The ecumenical spirit of the Social Gospel—institutionally represented in the Federal Council of Churches—had gained strength, as had the complementary tendency to emphasize the broad ethical principles all Christians shared. Likewise, the liberal Protestant tendency to Christocentrism, to emphasizing the New rather than the Old Testament, and to humanizing and modernizing Christ, which most in the Social Gospel movement adopted, had become prominent in the churches. A more Christian society seemed to be accompanying a more social Christianity. "The spirit of religion . . . has grown far beyond its pale. The world is full of religious feeling, of brotherly kindness, of ethical conduct," observed Social Gospeler Paul Moore Strayer in 1915. "A moral awakening has swept over the country and is setting new standards for politics and business and personal life; the public conscience was never so sensitive and alert as it is to-day; modern life is aflame with social feeling." [78]

The fathers of the Social Gospel were concerned primarily with how it would benefit society, and they were generally gratified by the apparent social trend. They had also hoped that, by making Christianity more immediately relevant to the life and work of the people, the Social Gospel would strengthen the church as an institution. In the late nineteenth century American Protestantism had confronted a growing crisis of religious indifference, reflected in an apparent decline in church membership and attendance among all classes. Social Gospelers hoped that a de-emphasis on individual salvation and narrow doctrinal points would allow the churches to reclaim lapsed members and return to a position of social leadership. It was clear by the midteens that this was not occurring.

Apparently, people could become more ethical, even more Christian in the broad sense, without feeling a need for formal institutional affiliation or participation, or without even believing in God in the traditional sense. A 1916 study of college professors and students— mainstays of middle-class Protestantism in the Victorian age—showed that rising moral standards were actually paralleled by a weakening belief in God and immortality and a declining identification with religious institutions. [79] In their vain attempt to reclaim this segment of the population for the churches, Social Gospelers had done no little social good, upholding the principles Americans, whether Christians or not, honored in the breach as much as in the observance. Ironically, though, the Social Gospel might have become part of the problem it was supposed to solve. By associating religion closely with secular society, Social Gospelers tended to demystify it, unconsciously diminishing its "miraculous and transcendent quality." And, in their attempt to appeal to those outside the churches, they slighted the needs of those within, who, presumably, continued to be concerned with immortality, individual salvation, and the doctrinal paths to those destinations.[80]

The Social Gospel movement failed to reverse the apparent decline in American Protestantism. Moreover, some liberal Protestant doctrines seemed to lead in directions that Social Gospelers had failed to foresee and that they abhorred. The tendency to humanize and personalize Christ, for example, and to make him more clearly relevant to social problems, did not always have the result Social Gospelers hoped to see. A more human and less mystical Christ could, in the hands of Charles Ferguson, become a pioneer of scientific management. In 1914, Bruce Barton turned him into something of a star of the youth culture and an all-around good fellow who advocated important and enduring, but moderate, social reforms. Somehow, the divinity of the figure did not shine through.[81]

A more human and personal Christ could even contribute to the sort of self-centered individualism against which the Social Gospel movement reacted. For example, the Emmanuel Movement, a sort of mind-cure fad combining psychology, sociology, physiology, and hypnosis, tried to harness the power of Christ in an effort to have victims of nervous disorders cure themselves. Elwood Worcester, the founder of the Emmanuel Movement, talked like a Social Gospeler. He celebrated the "tendency to dispense with the tedious processes of criticism and dogma and return to the Christ of the Gospels," and he deplored the "inability [of the church] to come into close relations with real life."[82] He also believed that the church would be revived when it developed a more relevant message. But while Social Gospelers moved from the same premises to a more socially oriented and socially active theology, Worcester developed a self-centered and even narcissistic one.

A more human Christ was more usable for all kinds of people with all kinds of purposes; instead of uniting society, as the Social Gospelers had hoped, he was used further to fracture it. A more human Christ was also less divine. As he was enlisted to serve more secular—sometimes transient—purposes, he became more of a psychologist, engineer, hail-fellow-well-met, or whatever. William Rainsford was one of several commentators willing to strip him of all divinity:

> It may be hard to give up our fancies and dreams about Jesus, but do it we must. By so much as Jesus is pronounced to be supernatural, by His birth, or death, or rising from the dead, by so much are we robbed of our elder Brother, robbed of a real son of man who is a real practical guide and example; one we can follow and imitate down here on earth.[83]

The next logical step was a broad, areligious humanism. Only the "genuinely religious attitude distinguished the social gospel from humanism," Shailer Mathews noted. "Indeed, humanism . . . might almost be described as the social gospel minus reliance upon God."[84] Though most liberal Protestants did not take this step, it is clear that our contemporary Christian right is not fantasizing when it sees a connection between modern theology and the "secular humanism" it deplores.

By the mid-teens there was a growing reaction in the churches against liberal Protestantism and the Social Gospel. Conservatives argued that liberal Protestantism conceded too much to the forces of science and secularism it had meant to counter and that the Social Gospel deflected the churches too much from the problems of individual sin and salvation. For many, it seemed that the churches faced a choice. Either they could become more secular, more socially oriented, more favorable to science, and more oriented to the modern world, or they could return to traditional doctrine and traditional concentration on individual sin, salvation, and immortality. As the new and striking popularity of fundamentalist revivalism, so clearly personified by the flamboyant Billy Sunday, indicated, many ministers and laymen were choosing the second path.[85]

Through much of the late nineteenth and early twentieth centuries there was no necessary contradiction between Protestant fundamentalism and social reform.[86] Indeed, the early Social Gospel movement included theological conservatives and liberals as well, and both branches were rooted in nineteenth-century evangelical Protestantism. The former emphasized the primacy of individual regeneration, while the latter were stronger believers in the reformatory possibilities of institutions, but they submerged their differences in the common effort. By the mid-teens events had rendered this continuing alliance less feasible.

As the alliance pulled apart, each of the two major components lost something. The conservatives excised the impurity of theological modernism, but in the process they ignored real social problems. They felt compelled to attack the Social Gospel along with liberal theology, thereby aiding and comforting the real enemies of the spirit of Christ in the United States. From the teens forward, the fundamentalists ceased to be positive factors in American reform, and they sometimes allowed themselves to be catspaws for the political and economic right.

For their parts, the liberals moved further in the directions of science, secularism, and environmental determinism, embracing the transient and the trivial in the process. They lost the fundamentalists' understanding of the importance of religion in the life of the individual, slighting the reality of sin and the importance of character in the process. Increasingly, they embraced a sort of vague, happy-face, I'm-O.K.-You're-O.K. humanism that showed good intentions without deep understanding.

It was perhaps inevitable that Protestant unity would be a casualty of modernization, but it was a shame nonetheless. The Christian progressives had the goal of uniting society under a banner emblazoned with the Golden Rule and the law of love. By the mid-teens the achievement of their goal seemed closer, but remained distant, and the institutional expression of their values was crumbling.

The early and mid-teens was a time of ambivalence for both Christian and scientific progressives. On the surface, public life seemed to be conforming more closely to their conceptions of how it should operate. And yet there were suggestions that changes were ephemeral and that their own values were sometimes being twisted into grotesque shapes by those who understood them differently. They should have been pleased, and they usually were, but the apparent approach of their destination did not make it less elusive. At least they could hold on to their faith in human progress. But then World War I came along and took care of that, too.

THE LEAP OF FAITH

It can never be doubted that this was a high and altruistic motive and the mere fact that a nation had acted
upon it marked the beginning of a new era. . . . Here
then was a great moral triumph; even the nations
upon which America must make war acknowledged
the purity of its motives.

CHARLES EDWARD RUSSELL

The world stumbled into this Great War and the
period of great fear settled like a fog upon the human
race—to last, perhaps, for generations.

HERBERT HOOVER

World War I was the central event in the lives of most of the progressives. When it began they were stunned, because it cast doubt on
their most basic assumptions regarding the nature and destination of
human beings and society. But progressives were resilient. They came
to see virtue in necessity and opportunity in catastrophe. In time they
accepted the war, and even embraced it with enthusiasm. This was the
last great leap of faith for people accustomed to leaping.

The progressives convinced themselves that American entry into
the conflict would be good for the United States and the world. At
home we could achieve unity and brotherhood and efficiency and all
of the other goals that remained so elusive even in the hopeful prewar
years. And we could regenerate the world as well. President Wilson
made it easy for those who wanted to believe that a country that could
not reform itself could reform the world. When he defined our war
aims he chose not to mention our interests or even our rights. It was
ignoble to go to war for the Morgan loans, or even for American security. We were going to war to end war and to "make the world safe for

democracy." "Here then was a great moral triumph," pro-war Socialist Charles Edward Russell argued in 1919; "even the nations upon which America must make war acknowledged the purity of its motives." [1]

"The war was a pivotal event because liberals *made* it a pivotal event," Stuart Rochester has noted.[2] They expected it to solve all of the problems of the country and the world that peace could not solve. "Our actions were sound when we went into the first World War," reflected Lewis Mumford as the country contemplated entrance into another world war; "but our dreams were vain ones; for they were founded on the belief that one single high act would enable us to live happily ever afterward." [3] It was also pivotal because it occurred at a crucial time, when progressives' values were coming into question and when their goals were sliding out of reach. The progressives "attached to it an epic significance, because it became for them an intensely personal affair which placed them squarely at the crossroads between an uncertain past and a summoning future," Rochester argues. "They counted on the war to resolve certain critical questions—about themselves, about society, about the course of human history." [4]

It did not—could not—work as it was supposed to. Russell wrongly identified the triumph of moralism with moral triumph. The war witnessed plenty of the former; it could not result in the latter. When the progressives realized this, the depth of their disillusionment was proportional to the extravagance of their hopes. The war crippled American reform and the values that underlay it. It validated illiberalism and legitimized racial, ethnic, and class prejudices. It facilitated the realization of some reforms, but its intolerant and conservative spirit suffocated many others. Rather than inspiring true social unity, the war loosened social bonds, weakened reform coalitions, and encouraged individual and group selfishness, demanding only the hypocrisy of a rhetorical devotion to the nation. And it encouraged a cynical hedonism and materialism that was antithetical to everything for which the progressives stood. The weaknesses of both Christian and scientific progressive formulations, glimpsed before 1917, were glaring by 1919.

But the war was more than a temporary setback to American reform. It was more, even, than the death of 20 million people or the collapse of the European order. It initiated the rapid decline of Western civilization, and it cast doubt on the values in which the men and women living in the ultimate epoch of that civilization believed. The goodness and dignity of the individual, the goodness, unity, and inevitability of progress, the increasing civilization of people and of society, the beneficence of God and of science—all of these were casualties. The issuance from the war of bolshevism and fascism, of Stalin and Hitler, and of other ideologies and figures contemptuous of Western values clearly indicated the new weakness of that value system.

The progressives came to realize what had happened, slowly, reluctantly, and sometimes sullenly. They did not always admit their realization, because to do so was to question the legitimacy of their own lives, but they could not ignore reality. As an old man, reflecting on his life thirty years after the war, Herbert Hoover remarked that "the world stumbled into the Great War and the period of Great Fear settled like a fog upon the human race—to last, perhaps, for generations." [5] The West had lost its way, never to find it again.

I

Few historical actors are able accurately to gauge the importance of the events of their lives when those events are happening. Normally, the progressives had no deeper understanding or greater prescience than most of the people preceding or succeeding them. But many of them did recognize immediately the importance of the First World War, and they saw, with remarkable accuracy, the implications of the conflict for their reforms and for the ideology that underlay those reforms. In time they learned to ignore their own insights and submerge their doubts. But their initial flash of understanding was correct.

The outbreak of fighting in Europe in the summer of 1914 was a shock to thinking Americans, in part because it was so sudden and unexpected, but more because they shared the general belief of people in the West that war among civilized peoples was passing away permanently. Victorians believed that as the world grew closer together, forming itself into an interdependent intellectual and economic community, war became less likely. Nations were too closely connected to and dependent on one another, the argument went, to go to war again. Victorians also considered war a survival of barbarism, inappropriate to an age in which human sensitivity and broad social consciousness seemed to be displacing viciousness, selfishness, envy, avarice, and other low, conflict-inducing motives. They assured themselves that war, like infanticide, slavery, bear-baiting, prize-fighting, and other relics of barbarism, was fading from the scene. Material, scientific, and moral progress, benevolent and inevitable, doomed it.

Most of those in the progressive generation agreed that war was passing away. A few, such as Theodore Roosevelt, who was obsessed with Teutonic virility and vitality, worried about this fact. Those in the active and vibrant peace movement celebrated it and worked to bring it about more rapidly. But few, before the summer of 1914, believed that war would again play a major role in human affairs in the West.

The outbreak of war immediately challenged the core beliefs of the Victorians—that the individual was basically good and enjoyed dignity, that people and society were progressing materially and morally, and that higher and higher levels of civilization were being attained. The whole idea that people were civilized came into serious doubt, and only the thoughtlessly optimistic still argued that human beings were progressing. As Henry May has noted, the early months of the war "seemed to challenge not only the progressive view of history, but an assumption still more deeply rooted in dominant American ideology, the fundamental decency of modern, civilized human nature."[6]

There were those who took a perverse satisfaction in the degradation of human character that the war revealed. Franklin Giddings, for example, assured the readers of the *Survey* a few weeks after the war broke out that "the passions of primitive man survive in us all and easily break through the inhibitions that civilization has with infinite difficulty provided."[7] And Rear Admiral Bradley Fiske, whose military position presumably gave him something of a vested interest in recrudescences of barbarism, assured the country in 1915 that "civilized nations" had only a "veneer of courtesy" and that they were "fully as jealous of each other as the most savage tribes."[8] But most found only peril in this sudden intrusion of savagery and barbarism in human behavior. "The problem before us" reflected Missouri University professor Charles Ellwood in January of 1915, "is . . . how to avoid the decay and disintegration of civilization itself."[9]

Those who believed society was conforming more closely to Christian ethical standards were stunned by the outbreak of war. Some openly wondered whether Christianity had had much impact at all on human behavior. Fiske reminded his readers that, despite the greatness and power of Christianity, "the nations now warring are Christian nations, in the very foremost rank of Christendom; that never in history has there been so much bloodshed in such widespread areas and so much hate, and that we see no signs that Christianity is employing any influence that she has not been employing for nearly two thousand years."[10] "We must wait for dispassionate history to weigh in its balance the causes of this savage bloodshed and carnage, but on one point all are agreed," Paul Moore Strayer noted in a classic understatement in 1915. "Christianity has made less impression on our Western civilization than we thought."[11]

The war could be explained with traditional Christian concepts. Washington Gladden saw the conflict as a divine punishment visited on the nations of Europe for their violation of the law of love:

> With one accord the nations of the earth have set this law at defiance. They have refused to base international relationships on good will; they have insisted on founding them on suspicion and fear and enmity. They would not obey the law, but they cannot escape its penalty. Hell is the penalty of the disobedience of God's law and war is hell. Can any one conceive a pit more nearly bottomless than the nations of Europe have digged for themselves, or hotter flames than those into which they are now plunging?[12]

This conclusion was a realistic and appropriate one for a sincere Christian to draw. But it was an especially courageous for Gladden, who had previously shown great faith in the nature and direction of the individual character and of society.

Those who saw progress in Christian terms could at least advance a consistent explanation for the war, however painful that process might be. The notion that science provided a sure road to progress suffered much more serious damage in anguished analyses of the war. The heretical suggestion of such earlier questioners of progress as popular authors Prestonia Martin and Guglielmo Ferrero that the material advances of Western civilization had not been paralleled by moral improvement became a commonplace observation. Suddenly, the imbalance between material and moral progress seemed self-evident and dangerous. "The present war is the *débâcle* of materialistic civilization," argued philosopher Joseph Alexander Leighton in the *Forum* in 1915. "It reveals in the most vivid light the futility of placing utter faith in the all-redeeming power of applied science." [13]

Others expanded on the same theme, exploring the pitfalls of an amoral materialism. Professor Ellwood argued that Western civilization had taken a dangerous path in the nineteenth century and that war had resulted:

> We have supposed that we could rear a secure social structure upon the basis of an egoistic and materialistic social philosophy. We have permitted a rebarbarization of the individual's moral standards without imagining that these would actually express themselves in the life of nations. We have thought that somehow, out of a program of self-interest, material satisfactions, and brute force followed by men and nations, a settled and harmonious order would result. . . . The egoistic, socially negative doctrines, which got such a hold of western civilization in the nineteenth century, both in theory and in practice, are the sources of present disorder. [14]

In their indictment of science, Ellwood and others were implicitly criticizing scientific reform as well. Too often, scientific progressives had accepted selfishness and materialism, emphasizing that technique was more important than character and that efficiency was the only important human value. They had glimpsed a model society, characterized by efficiency, unity, and abundance, and they has seen science as a means of bringing it to reality. Now Europeans exhibited unity in highly mobilized and tightly regimented societies, efficiency in slaughter, and an abundance that permitted the slaughter to go on indefinitely. Technique without character, science without ethics, threatened the survival of civilization. The facile assumption that science would more or less automatically have good results was discredited by events, and, in the process, the optimistic notion that science and Christianity were partners in progress suffered as well.

Indeed, the very fact of war, regardless of its grisly specifics, had dealt a severe blow to the whole idea of progress. Now there were new and serious doubts whether society had advanced and whether the supposed vehicles of progress were really what they seemed. The comfortable assumption that progress was inevitable, it appeared, could no longer be held by thoughtful people. And even the notion that progress was good was questioned by those who pointed to new and destructive weapons as products of material advancement. Faith in progress was central to the belief system of the West in 1914, and nobody embraced it more fervently than did American progressives. The widely held sense "that progress is . . . *the law of humanity*; that human beings as such tend to perfect themselves; . . . that they are better now than they were in the past, and will be better tomorrow than they are today" provided society with reassurance and direction.[15] There had always been some who did not share this faith, and now reality seemed to prove them correct. "The war has destroyed not only men, money or goods . . . but ideas," journalist Robert Duffus pointed out in 1917. "A faith has withered, a faith that the Victorian held as firmly as he held that two and two made four. The Victorian worshipped before the shrine of a secular deity of progress." Duffus believed that, in a mere three years, "the rising tides of the new age have swept away nearly all of the Victorians. Those who survive . . . are the most pathetic of men." The world, he concluded, had come to realize the lesson of the war: "Ten million men have perished to prove that progress is not automatic, not comfortable and not in any way a law of nature; even more, that there are dark forces that tear at the fabric of civilization as fast as it is woven."[16]

Duffus was a young man in 1917, and a perceptive one. He saw the serious challenge presented by the war to the faith in progress, but it was easier for him to abandon it than it was for his elders. Indeed, even in the depressing early months of the war, when its implications for the Western faith in progress seemed so ominous to so many, some refused to abandon their optimistic beliefs. In June of 1915, for example, the *Nation* confronted the gloomy Gusses editorially:

> When peace returns, we shall be thinking of this war as, indeed, a monstrous evil, a frightful calamity, but we shall not be thinking of it all the time; we shall be engaged, in the main, with the same kind of interests and strivings which have occupied our attention

hitherto. And if anybody then denies that there has been progress, we shall ask him—just as we might have asked him a year
ago—at what previous time in the world's history there had been
as much effort bestowed upon the succor of the unfortunate, as
little of religious persecution, as wide a sense of the claims of all
persons to decent conditions of living.[17]

Others rose to defend science. Astronomer W. W. Campbell, writing
in August of 1915, explained that "the prostitution of science to the
killing and crippling of men is indeed an ugly fact, but its results are
negligible in comparison with the daily ministrations of science to the
people's needs." Campbell went on to compare the scientific method
with the Golden Rule and to argue that science would ultimately cure
international conflicts: "The greatest need of the times is in the science
of international relationships, to the end that truth and reason may
replace deception and brute force." [18] Other defenders of the faith also
argued for more, rather than less, science. Harvard biologist Robert
Yerkes, for example, contended that a redirected science would again
promote human progress: "Surely this war clearly indicates that the
study of instinct, and the use of our knowledge for the control of
human relations, is incalculably more important for the welfare of
mankind than is the discovery of new and ever more powerful explo-
sives or the building of increasingly terrible engines of destruction." [19]

To argue that the war did not disprove progress was one thing, but
some intrepid commentators even advanced the notion that the conflict would be a vehicle for human advancement: "The war has been
a bitter dose to swallow," a contributor to the *American Journal of
Sociology* admitted in July of 1915. "We must revise a good many
particular opinions, but we shall find ere long that even the terrible
war has not seriously shaken the profound belief in progress. For are
not thoughtful men and women already saying that the war itself may
become a potent instrument for progress?" This, the author implicitly
admitted, was less a rational appraisal than a leap of faith: "Out of evil
good may come—nay *must* come. Human nature, derided and condemned by many, will attend to that operation." [20]

Before long, optimism began to reassert itself among reformers.
First came the belief that war was not as devastating to reform and the

values that underlay it as had been thought; then came the assertion that the conflict might actually be good. As one speaker put it in an address to social workers at the National Conference of Charities and Corrections in 1915, "after we have recovered from the first shock we take for granted not only that something can be saved out of the ruin of civilization, but that there is a forward step."[21] Once the second assumption was accepted, American entry into the war came to be hoped for rather than feared.

II

Progressives of every hue came around, sometimes slowly and reluctantly, to the notion that the war represented opportunity rather than calamity. Those concerned with social justice, who feared initially that American participation would trigger domestic reaction, convinced themselves the war would provide a laboratory for social engineering and would increase public sympathy for the disadvantaged. Scientific progressives, abhorring social and economic inefficiency and the failure of voluntarism as a means to change, welcomed war because it put a premium on efficiency and statism. And progressives supporting specific reforms, such as prohibition, woman suffrage, and immigration restriction, believed the war presented them with extraordinary opportunities for success.

Reformers came to see great possibilities in the war because they believed it could help them overcome stubborn impediments to change. Group and individual selfishness, materialism, disunity, and hedonism would all be submerged in the war effort. A true sense of unity and loyalty to the community would arise because of the social recognition of interdependence—even oneness—that the wartime emergency would bring. Discipline, sacrifice, and service to the community would become honored values. People would forget their petty desires and their self-centered concerns and would devote themselves to public service. And when people saw how well a united, efficient, service-oriented society operated, they would be unwilling to resume their selfish ways after the war. Entry into the war, in short, would give the reformers a second chance. Their peacetime efforts to unite and inspire America had failed; perhaps war would allow them to succeed. As Rochester notes, "with the domestic malaise deepening, the war acquired a growing significance as a solution to progressivism's problems."[22]

Hopeful progressives came to see as many benefits for the world in the war as they saw for the United States. The narrow nationalism, economic rivalries, and territorial ambitions that produced the conflict were nothing more than selfishness on a large scale. The war would force the people of the world to see that these things were wrong and would lead them to a more united and interdependent international order based on universal justice and sympathy. Even the challenge to Western beliefs was good, because only antisocial values would be permanently destroyed, allowing the unimpeded dominance of the good ones. Out of the horrors of war a resurrection would take place. Civilization would be purged of its evils and would emerge on a higher order.

The notion that something wonderful would emerge from something horrible was self-deceptive. Expecting justice, compassion, selflessness, and respect for the individual to arise from the brutal carnage of World War I was rather like expecting that an increased supply of liquor would lead an alcoholic to sobriety. There were those who recognized this. The antiwar movement was based on the beliefs that American entry would contaminate the nation, violate its ideals, and lead to repression and reaction at home. Others cautioned that unthinking optimism was inappropriate. Professor Ellwood, who agreed that "Western civilization needs a great social and spiritual awakening" in which the "rotten stones . . . laid in the foundations" would "be removed," warned that war did not assure such an outcome: "The decay of higher social values may . . . go on in times of peace through the undermining of the sense of social obligation and social responsibility by materialism and individualism . . . , but in periods of international war . . . the process of social disintegration and of relapse toward barbarism may be indefinitely accelerated." The uncertainty inherent in a fluid situation forced Ellwood to conclude that "there is no assurance that when the institutions and values of a civilization are destroyed they will be replaced by better ones."[23]

Progressive expectations for the outcome of the war reflected a misunderstanding of the nature of the conflict and also of the factors that drew America toward participation in it. Realities, not ideals, dictated the decision of the United States. American security and prosperity, national and international political and economic interests — not messianic fantasies of regeneration — informed the thinking on Wall Street and Pennsylvania Avenue. These motives were not necessarily illegitimate; they were just amoral and self-interested. They were not motives sincere reformers could embrace, at least not in 1917.

The progressives did not like to look at the dark side. The "deep-running consistency of the progressive mentality," David Kennedy has pointed out, was an ability "to find grounds for hopeful affirmation even in the face of unprecedented calamity." [24] They believed that there was purpose in human affairs and that people were moving forward. What Robert Moats Miller writes of Harry Emerson Fosdick applies to most other progressives as well:

> His perception of reality was coherent, ordered, purposeful, intelligible, moral. . . . This vision may accommodate a tragic sense of life; it may permit an awareness of sin and guilt; it may allow realistic descriptions of death and mutilation in the trenches. But it is not compatible with that dominant form of understanding that originated, arguably, in the application of mind and memory to the events of the Great War — it is not compatible with irony. Absent from Fosdick's perception are the absurd, the ridiculous, the outrageous, the opaque, the paranoid. [25]

The need to believe in purpose explains the progressives' counter-factual optimism — their sense that forward movement was inevitable, that good would emerge from bad, that even low motives would produce elevated results. It also explains their poor preparation for life in the twentieth century.

Woodrow Wilson understood how the progressives thought. He was one of them. He knew they had to be inspired and their idealism had to be tapped. When he said he wanted a war to end war and to make a world safe for democracy he was not a manipulator or a hypocrite. He was reflecting the needs and desires of the broad and idealistic progressive constituency that had faith in the unique and special nature of the country, that was committed to a decent, humane, and progressive world, that needed to believe its actions would contribute to that sort of world, and that needed to be assured of the cosmic importance of actions it was reluctant to take. Wilson knew that there were strategic and economic considerations in the decision to enter the war, but for him and the people he represented they were insufficiently noble to compel participation. For him, and for the progressives, American participation had to make an essential difference in the future of civilization.

Like his progressive followers, Wilson was naive regarding power politics and too optimistic about the prospects for change. He expected wonderful things to be brought forth from the horror of war. He hoped that relatively trivial changes would have far-reaching results, that free trade or a league of nations, for example, would mitigate national rivalries and selfishness. In the end, Wilson's failure to realize his grandiose expectations contributed to progressive disillusionment and the retreat from optimism to a greater extent than other failures had. When nonpartisan elections failed to produce an urban utopia or factory inspection did not deliver social justice progressives were disappointed, but it took the failure of an international crusade to bring true disillusionment. The irony is that, while his goals were unattainable, Wilson would not have called for war on the basis of lesser goals and he could not have led the country into war with less noble ends. He reflected his generation, and therein lay both his triumphs and his tragedy.

Once they made the leap of faith, the progressives threw themselves into the war effort with characteristic fervor. Many went to Europe. Women and men too old or too proud to fight donned Red Cross and YMCA uniforms and offered their services. It was the great adventure of their lives, but they seem ridiculous to us today. Drawing inspiration from legless soldiers, visiting shelled cathedrals and talking about consecrated purpose, earnestly pressing boys who hoped only to see Iowa or Georgia again to save the world for democracy—they embarrass modern readers. They were not yet embarrassed themselves.

At least the ones who went overseas were harmless. The ones who stayed at home were dangerous. They offered their fervor and their expertise to a government that used both. They helped organize industry and agriculture. They regulated labor, fuel, and capital. They helped run the draft and train the army. They propagandized and prosecuted the unwilling. They thought great ends justified their means, but they ended up being used by cynical people for illiberal purposes. They helped destroy much that was good in the country, including their own values.

In their defense, it is possible to say that the progressives were similar to other historical actors in that they did not have a very clear understanding of how things would turn out. Had the unlikely occurred, had their hopes and dreams for the war been realized, the progressives' means would have seemed reasonable. When the war failed to deliver the promised results, however, their actions took on an unattractive, even sinister cast. As Stephen Vaughn has noted in his study of the Committee on Public Information, the many progressives in the agency "believed the war had evoked a new spirit of self-sacrifice and cooperation. They were drawn to the committee in hope that they might fight society's evils and make a better world." [26] In making this fight they stretched the truth, manipulated people, and justified illiberal values, attitudes, and policies. When they recognized what they were doing they excused themselves by pointing to the ultimate goal of victory and the transformation it would entail. Only later did they recognize that their good intentions had paved the road to hell, not to heaven.

For a time, though, the great crusade for America and the world seemed to succeed. Shrewdly taking advantage of the favorable public mood and sometimes exploiting popular intolerance and hatred, prohibitionists, social purists, woman suffragists, Americanizers, and immigration restrictionists advanced their reforms. A new spirit of community, sacrifice, and social solidarity seemed to spread through the land. Men and women forgot their petty, selfish concerns and joined the service, registered for the draft, bought war bonds, contributed to the Red Cross, rolled bandages, saved food, and did dozens of other selfless things. The people seemed to become less contentious, individualistic, and jealous of their rights and more socially efficient, cooperative, disciplined, obedient to authority, and conscious of their duties. Of course, there were reasons for doubt even in the hopeful times. Unity came from fear as much as from affection. Progressives complained that Attorney General Thomas Gregory and Postmaster General Albert Sidney Burleson were too vigorous and undiscriminating in punishing dissent and that federal agents and the private vigilantes who cooperated with them punished those who complained about business or who organized workers and farmers along with those who dissented on the war. Wilson called Burleson in for a talk and the Postmaster General faced him down. The federal attorneys and agents and the main street patriots continued their crusade to make America unsafe for liberty.

Economic efficiency seemed to advance during the war. Various government agencies—such as the War Industries Board, the Food Administration, the Fuel Administration, and the War Labor Board— exercised a certain degree of plenary direction over various segments of the economy, and transportation and communications were effectively nationalized. For those optimists who did not look too closely, all of this seemed to go quite smoothly. In retrospect, even relatively efficient agencies like the Food Administration do not seem to have worked very well, but progressives in and out of the agencies tacitly agreed to praise the emperor's new garb of efficiency. Progressives also agreed that business seemed to accept government direction, capital and labor seemed to cooperate, and industry and agriculture seemed to operate more efficiently. Everything appeared to be proceeding according to the progressive plan. As they had hoped, in David W. Noble's words, "the conditions of war . . . had greatly increased the fluidity of society; they had made man's environment plastic and capable of being remolded into a new and better form."[27]

For a time, then, it appeared that the great leap of faith, the optimistic affirmation of progress, was justified. Many agreed that tremendous changes had occurred in American social and economic life. In 1918, journalist Charles Wood interviewed a variety of people regarding the permanent changes they thought would result from the war. War Labor Policies Board chairman Felix Frankfurter, engineers H. L. Gantt and Walter Polakov, and dollar-a-year industrialist Charles M. Schwab seemed to agree that scientific management, productive efficiency, and cooperation between capital and labor would characterize the postwar period. Columbia University psychologist Robert S. Woodworth observed that the war had strengthened the "herd instinct" among the American people: "The inevitable result will be to make us as a people less selfish, more social, less timid, more devoted, less cautious, more loyal, less discriminating, but more capable of co-operation." On the basis of his conversations, Wood concluded that the war had created an environment that produced tremendous changes. He believed the "great change" meant "the substitution of the motive of co-operation for the competitive motive which has ruled us in the past. It means the realization of human brotherhood; not from any sentimental scruple that we ought to be brothers, but because, in the hard realities of life, we shall have come to recognize a common aim." [28]

Most progressives, in part simply because they were progressives and in part because there did seem to be real changes in human behavior, believed that wartime developments justified their optimism. But none were more enthusiastic than scientific reformers, who revelled in the new social emphasis on efficiency, the importance of the expert, and the active state as the expression of society. Some predicted that, in the "reconstruction" period that they insisted would follow the war, the utopian, long-term goals of scientific progressivism would be realized. To many of them, a new political order seemed to be taking shape.

In 1918, Mary Parker Follett argued that a "new state" was emerging from the war, an entity that would express "true democracy," the core of which could be seen in the wartime "*will to will the common will.*" Follett believed the war had proved that progress derived from unity and from genuine cooperation, both of which depended on individual recognition and acceptance of complete social interdependence. "An individual" she said, "is one who is being created *by* society, whose daily breath is drawn *from* society, whose life is spent *for* society." It was the job of the New State—the institutional structure of which Follett left unclear—to express the social will through a distillation of the expressions of group and neighborhood wills. Follett was not a forerunner of modern pluralists, who perceive the state as a broker among contending groups. Like other scientific progressives, she believed the comprehensive social will discovered and expressed by the state both encompassed and transcended the wills of individuals and groups. For her the operation of the state was almost mystical in nature:

[The state] must appear as the great moral leader. Its supreme function is moral ordering. What is morality? The fulfilment of relation by man to man, since it is impossible to conceive an isolated man. . . . The state is the ordering of this infinite series into their right relations that the greatest possible welfare of the total may be worked out. The ordering of relations is morality in its essence and completeness. The state must gather up into itself all the moral power of its day.[29]

Others also saw great political changes arising from the war. In a two-part article in the *American Journal of Sociology*, Professor Robert Kern of George Washington University argued that the war would lead to a greater degree of government "supervision of the social order" in the public interest. Kern noted that the role of government was to serve society as a whole, regardless of the interests of the various individuals therein. The problem, as exasperated progressives had recognized, was that selfish individuals and groups made demands on government and that policies tended to emerge from the clash of self-interested groups. But the war had forced men and women to see themselves as part of an organic and interrelated society and had led them to express a truly social will through the state. Kern was pleased to see that the war was creating truly socialized people:

They . . . find satisfaction and freedom . . . in the realization of social ideals — the ideals of social democracy, social justice, social welfare, and social efficiency. The will of such a socialized person finds freedom, even though his overt activity is necessarily circumscribed by organized or institutionalized activity, because his will is not contending against, trying to thwart, the wills of others in the interest of unsocial impulses and satisfactions but has the same common purpose and tends in the same direction as the wills of the other members; for each of these socialized persons wants to be just toward the others, wants to be democratic toward the others, wants the best welfare of the others, and wants all these things efficiently realized.[30]

Like Follett, Kern foresaw a permanent system in which the individual will, as traditionally understood, was submerged. Scientific progressives who saw a new political system emerging from the war were never specific about its institutional structure or about how it would fit into the existing federal system, characterized by contentious pluralism, democracy, and distrust of power. When confronted by the stubborn realities of power and democracy, in the past, they had usually leaned on the unstable reed of voluntarism. Now they were placing their faith in a new social will, characterized by a selfless desire to cooperate, which had supposedly derived from the wartime revelation of the evils of selfish ways. In speaking of a social will, to be expressed by the state, and in derogating individual rights, scientific progressives were playing with themes that, in other countries, were woven into the fabric of fascism. They were also assuming that a temporary and ill-formed mood indicated a permanent and sweeping change. The character of a people does not change so quickly, and in the end the United States proved infertile ground for the growth of anything approaching a clear expression of a social will.

Scientific progressives believed that they could see manifestations of the social will in the economy as well as in the political system. Farmers appeared to become more efficient and seemed more cognizant of their duties as individual producers to the society of which they were parts. In order to further this spirit, reformers suggested a continuation of the county agent system, growth in the farm bureaus that supported the agents, and professionally supervised land settlement whereby rural economic and social practices could be redirected in the interests of efficiency.[31]

Industry seemed to have caught the social spirit as well, rising to higher levels of productive efficiency in response to wartime demands, and progressives hoped that this tendency would continue. In 1919, scientific management specialist H. L. Gantt argued that it was the duty of industry to serve the community by producing goods cheaply and efficiently. The war had indicated that "profit-making efficiency" among businessmen had increased over the years, but that their productive efficiency had not: "In the great emergency created by the war, our need was not for dollars but for goods, and people who had been trained for the seeking of dollars were in most cases not at all fitted for the producing of goods." It had been necessary to give greater authority to those expert at production rather than business.

In order to obtain greater production throughout industry, and thus more adequately serve the public, Gantt argued, control of all industry must be turned over to engineers. Ownership could remain in private hands, but industry must serve the public: "The community needs service first, regardless of who gets the profits, because its life depends upon the service it gets." Failure to serve the public, he warned, could lead to a bolshevik revolution: "The lesson is this: the business system must accept its social responsibility and devote itself primarily to service, or the community will ultimately make the attempt to take it over in order to operate it in its own interest." Gantt concluded by equating efficiency with morality and service with Christianity. "Christ, who was the first to understand the commanding power of service, . . . stands revealed as the first great Economist," Gantt contended, "for economic democracy is simply applied Christianity."[32] Christ was being given a heavier load all the time. It was not enough that he redeem the world; now he had to be an economist, too, toiling over some divine demand curve.

Everywhere, the enthusiasts professed to see an upsurge in what they called "democracy." The public was united and the state was expressing its will. Individuals were cooperative, disciplined, obedient, and apparently cognizant of their duties to society. And the economy was serving the public efficiently and selflessly. Selfishness, materialism, destructive individualism, and hedonism alike were submerged by the rising social spirit. "The war has destroyed much of the old society," ex-Socialist Algie Simons wrote in 1919. "Its industrial pillars of competition, private incentive, individual profit and demand and supply have been overthrown. Governmental departments have been shuffled, created and abolished like color combinations in a kaleidoscope. There is no human relation outside its influence." Simons concluded that the old "institutions have been replaced with new ones. The framework of the coming society is already in existence. We cannot go back."[33]

Within a short time these hopes seemed unrealistic and even silly. But it was consistent of progressives to see revolutions in temporary trends and gains where none really existed. For all the well-intentioned progressives embracing the war was a leap of faith that led to other leaps of faith. They had to believe the war would produce something wonderful or else admit to bankruptcy of the values by which they lived. And to do that was to question the very legitimacy of their lives.

III

By mid-1919, reality was abrading the optimistic faith that had sustained and inspired so many progressives during the war years. Their belief that the war had created a united, cooperative, socially oriented people appeared increasingly unreal. There had been a heightened degree of cooperation, unity, and sacrifice during the war, but the price for achieving it had been high. Unity had demanded either the voluntary or the involuntary suppression of dissent, and it had been enforced in part through the inculcation of a narrow and illiberal nationalism. Cooperation had been more apparent than real. Social and economic groups recognized that it was in their interest to appear cooperative, but throughout the war they jostled for preference and advantage. People sacrificed for the nation, but they usually expected to be compensated for the sacrifices they made.

At the end of the war, the enforced and artificial unity declined rapidly in a public arena characterized by intense partisanship, vicious political repression, racial and ethnic bigotry and violence, and bitter conflict between capital and labor. Some reforms, long on the progressive agenda, were realized during the war, but most of the proposals designed to achieve a more just society were deferred on the grounds of wartime exigency. Moreover, the conservative reaction that flourished during the so-called "reconstruction" period made it unlikely that social justice would be much advanced in the foreseeable future. And even some of the reforms that were advanced during the war — prohibition and immigration restriction most clearly — came in the postwar period to seem narrow and oppressive. The progressives' altruistic impulse languished due to lack of public support, while their repressive side thrived.

It was also becoming clear that the war had not led to a revolution in economic organization. A heightened measure of government control over business did not result from the war. On the contrary, the great influx of dollar-a-year volunteers into government from business sharply increased the influence of the latter over the former while greatly improving the popular image of businessmen. The war did witness an increased interest in making industry efficient and a greater respect for those engineers, of whom Herbert Hoover was the most visible, seen as the vanguards of the efficiency revolution. But this did not mean that businessmen were ready to turn control of industry over to engineers, who would then make it an instrument to serve the public interest. Hoover, who symbolized the promise of technocratic efficiency for many Americans throughout the twenties, shared the attitude of most prewar engineers that control of industry should remain in the hands of businessmen and that engineers were employees who would serve the interests of their employers. This was an attitude with which most businessmen were quite comfortable.

The idealistic hopes of progressives regarding the postwar international scene were also dashed. It was inevitable that Woodrow Wilson would be unable to satisfy all of the hopes that he had aroused—and shared—but the inevitability of his failure did not make it less painful for those who had believed in him. Everywhere they looked in the postwar years, progressives could see goals that had seemed so realizable slipping out of their grasp.

Perceptive observers began their post-mortems of progressivism while reformers like Simons were still fantasizing about the wonders the conflict had wrought. "There are many persons not pacifists and not Presidents with reputations to live up to who are facing the future with misgiving," noted *Nation* editor Harold de Wolfe Fuller in July of 1919. "This war is over and after all the sacrifices they begin to catch the lineaments of the same old world which in the past was too much with them. Thus they are left disappointed over the big price paid for the small gain if gain there was." Fuller concluded that "their feeling is . . . part of the big crop of disillusion which it has long been evident would be reaped of too great expectations." [34]

Of course, there were gains from the war. We were on the winning side, which, as many Germans would readily attest, was not a trivial matter. Our physical security was assured, at least for the foreseeable future, and we were in a position to dominate the world economy to our benefit. But these were victories of realpolitik. The progressives had wanted far more. For them, "the measure of success and satisfaction during the war was social and spiritual progress."[35] When that goal was not reached, they became disillusioned, regardless of whatever other good things the war brought.

Not only did things turn out differently from what progressives had hoped for, but the reformers themselves were implicated in the policies that had produced unfortunate results. Actions that had seemed justifiable when a golden future was in prospect produced shame among the actors when they were confronted with postwar realities. Randolph Bourne and Harold Stearns mercilessly flayed the progressives for their wartime behavior, exposing their shortcomings and probing their guilt. By serving the war effort, Stearns argued, the progressives had contributed to a narrow, intolerant, majoritarian political spirit. They had allowed themselves to be used by "our leaders [who] were not genuinely liberal in principle." They had been induced to sacrifice their principles by government, which shrewdly appealed to their vanity, their need for recognition, and their desires for honor and utility. And they had forgotten that "method and technique are subsidiary to ends and value" when they lent their expertise for odious purposes. Stearns believed that liberalism could survive the shock of war, but only if it returned to the Christian and scientific principles that underlay it:

> Liberalism cannot afford to compromise with moral categories and idealistic intentions in the field of practical action. It must continue further its pragmatic analysis of events rather than just stopping short when the analysis becomes embarrassing; it must increase rather than decrease its insistence upon scientific rigor; in politics it must continue to judge by results rather than intentions; in leadership it will pay more attention to character than to sentiment.[36]

What Stearns was asking for—that progressives function in the world without being of it, that they mold Christianity and science together—was theoretically and practically difficult but not impossible. Liberalism did not die in America, and it continued to reflect the diverse and sometimes contradictory impulses to which Stearns pointed. What did happen to progressivism, though, was that it lost that optimistic certainty that progress was good, inevitable, and unitary. And sometimes it could not even be sure what progress was.

"The liberal of 1900–1920 was an optimist," Christopher Lasch once noted; "he believed in the moral progress of the human spirit; he believed that human reason could ultimately order the world."[37] To the progressives, people were basically good and rational, they had value and dignity, they and the society in which they lived were attaining higher levels of civilization, and they were progressing morally as well as materially. When progress came into question, the whole edifice in which it was the keystone was weakened. "Disillusion with Wilson and disappointment at their own failure to protect the reform cause were not the only wounds the war inflicted on progressives," David Kennedy noted in *Over Here*. "The cruelest damage was visited on their very social philosophy, their most cherished assumptions about the reasonableness of mankind, the malleability of society, and the value of education and publicity as the tools of progress."[38]

The war made it much more difficult to maintain the belief that human progress was inevitable. It was no longer easy to see history as a chronicle of forward movement. "The liberal generation did not lose all of the past," David W. Noble points out in *The Paradox of Progressive Thought*, "but rather it lost a past, a past of inevitable progress imposed on history by a blind faith in progress."[39] When the progressives lost this past they also lost the wonderful future toward which it was leading. Liberals remained and good intentions continued, but the character of the goal became cloudy. Increasingly, liberals saw short-term steps as ends in themselves and they allied with those whose purposes were selfish rather than altruistic. More uncomfortable than ever before with their own values, they drifted toward a moral relativism that sometimes led them to embrace and celebrate hedonism, selfishness, and materialism. More than before they assumed ends justified means. Less optimistic about the possibilities of people and less respectful of them, they were more likely to embrace cynicism or elitism, rely on a manipulative state or business community, or accept communism or fascism.

The war had not destroyed the value system of the prewar generation (scientific progressives were already questioning it, albeit rather innocently), but it had made belief in that system more a matter of faith than of objective analysis. Moreover, as Edgar Kemler noted twenty years later, it had not created a satisfactory new system to replace the old:

> Since the First World War there has been a general collapse of values, of the Pollyanna spirit in politics and of the prudery in morals. The millions of men who fought and died in that war did not fight and die for democracy alone, or for a League of Nations or for the protection of little nations or for the profits of munition makers. Whether they knew it or not they also fought to overthrow the dead weight of Victorian angelicism, which has been called by some people dignity, and by others hypocrisy. In this respect they did not die in vain. If anything, they succeeded too well.[40]

All of this was not immediately apparent to American liberals in all its implications, nor was it ever clear to all of them. But in Europe, where the values of Western civilization had been under assault for some time, the devastating effect of the war on the dominant belief system was more plain. Not only was it much more evident on a continent racked by war, revolution, starvation, and disease that progress was neither inevitable nor good, but it also appeared that civilization was on the verge of collapse. "Turn where one will, one finds only that the war has worsened mankind," one author informed the readers of the *Atlantic Monthly* from Europe. "The dominion of darkness has spread over Europe, and a slimy progeny of cruelty, of bestiality, of insensibility, of egoism, of violence, of materiality, has crawled into the light of day—a noisome brood, of which it will be long before we can dispossess ourselves."[41]

The very fact of the war had exposed the weaknesses of Western civilization—its pretenses, its hypocrisies, and its contradictions. And the course of the conflict had seen a barbarism that was unparalleled in civilized memory but that was, unfortunately, to be repeated. For Franklin Giddings, who recognized that "a sense of undefined danger pervades civilization," the war and its aftermath merely proved the survival of barbarism among and within human beings. "It is a sinister element in every nation," he concluded. "It is a part of every people." [42] However true this might have been, not all people could accept it. To recognize the barbarism of people was to abandon the values of civilization. But what could be done in the face of horrible reality?

For some, the answer lay in a new system, of which bolshevism seemed the most promising at the end of the war. Others looked to some regeneration of the old values. One author argued in 1920 that the world could take comfort from the fact that most people found the war horrible. This proved the existence of "a civilised world-conscience" and was thus "a sign that righteousness still reigns in the heavens, and tends, even though baffled often, and temporarily repulsed, to reign also on earth." [43] Dean W. R. Inge of Oxford demanded nothing less than a new leap of faith: "What we need is a fixed and absolute standard of values, that we may know what we want to get and where we want to go. It is no answer to say that all values are relative and ought to change. Some values are not relative but absolute." [44]

But from where were these values to come? Science was a possible source, but it was by no means as attractive as it had been before the war. Before 1914 thoughtful people agreed that science was benevolent and that it was one of the vehicles of human progress. Material progress and moral progress were believed to parallel one another, and some — including many scientific progressives — had gone so far as to claim that the former would lead inevitably to the latter. Advanced reformers glimpsed the day when human beings and societies would govern themselves empirically. But the war showed that science was at best neutral and at worst malevolent. "On the whole the years immediately preceding the war found a world made better," a contributor to the *Atlantic Monthly* wrote from Europe in November of 1920. "Science had brought us many gifts." However, "this did not prevent us from turning science to our own and to our neighbor's hurt, . . . from battering down the Temple of Life, painfully erected stone by stone, with the battering ram of knowledge. Progress is a reality," this author concluded in terms seldom heard in the West before 1914; "but it turns upon itself like a serpent. It pursues a splendid path, and then suddenly swings round, and we are worse than our fathers." [45]

It was clear that material progress had outrun moral progress. As scientist and editor Edwin Slosson put in the *Independent*, "the last few years have made it manifest that in our civilization the mechanical forces have got ahead of the moral forces. Man is mounted on a bigger horse than he can ride."[46] Indeed, many wondered whether moral progress had occurred at all. "Until the Great War few would have disputed that civilized man had become much more humane, much more sensitive to the sufferings of others, and so more just, more self-controlled, and less brutal in his pleasure and in his resentments," Dean Inge pointed out in his post-mortem on progress. But Inge went on to note that young Europeans had committed atrocities of the sort not seen on the continent since the Thirty Years War.[47] When barbarism remained vital in human nature, when no moral progress was apparent, material progress threatened humanity. In a remarkable article in 1920, H. F. Wyatt predicted that the harnessing of atomic energy would soon give people the opportunity to destroy the human race. In that situation, the absence of moral progress equal to material advances would be catastrophic. Wyatt posited a race between "the soul of man, upward-striving but animal-tied, and the giant non-moral force, science":

> If the second advance faster than the first, then the magic which might have made the earth almost a paradise will convert it first into a hell and later perhaps into a wilderness. Either mankind will be consigned once more to a state of savagery, whence the long and toilsome labor of ascent must be recommenced, or, not inconceivably, our kind may perish off the face of the globe, possibly to be replaced, after millions or tens of millions of years of evolution, by some other species of living entity, bird or beast or even insect, in which the process of the ages has developed a thinking brain.[48]

People were recognizing once again that character was the most important factor in progress, that moral advancement was more important than material advancement, and that the latter would not lead inevitably to the former. Presumably, these developments should have led people to turn to Christianity for the absolute values that seemed so important, but that did not occur. The leading Christian denominations in the West had become so closely identified with national war efforts and so committed to them, and they had so completely absorbed the optimistic views of progress current in the late nineteenth and early twentieth centuries, that they were ill prepared for the great disillusionment that followed the war. They were simply too much a part of Western civilization to fill the void.[49]

In the United States the Social Gospel movement was weakened and challenged to the point that liberals could no longer presume to speak for American Protestantism. The Social Gospelers who had enthusiastically supported the war were denigrated in the postwar disillusionment, and their optimistic hopes seemed silly. Their assumptions about human beings, progress, and civilization—so in step with the prewar spirit—seemed very much out of place after 1918. They were challenged by fundamentalists, who resumed their attack on science, theological modernism, the Social Gospel, and secular reform, all of which they saw as related. What had been a swell in dissent against liberal Protestantism before the war became a tidal wave afterward, largely because the war seemed to strengthen conservative positions. Progress did not seem inevitable, people did not appear to be basically good, human beings were not conforming more closely to the Golden Rule and the law of love. American Protestants split more clearly into two broad wings. While some, disillusioned and confused, tried to salvage the prewar liberal faith, others expressed a more individualistic, pessimistic, and traditional fundamentalism. Challenged and weakened by increasing secularism before 1914, confused and divided Protestants were not well circumstanced to offer social leadership afterward.

IV

The First World War did not end progressivism in America, but it provides us with a useful perspective from which to survey the decline of some beliefs that had sustained American reformers for some time. The faith in progress, the belief in human possibilities, the assurance that people were becoming more civilized, and the vision of a utopian future had all been challenged before the war. Progressives had seen their values advance toward social realization in the early and mid-teens, but their destination seemed always to elude them. Many of them hoped that the war would arrest the slide and allow them to realize their goals, but it could not because it contradicted all that they believed. It was their greatest leap of faith, and it failed—as it had to fail—to a degree that their lesser leaps could not. After the war, they found themselves betrayed by reality, clinging to ideals that seemed almost completely irrelevant to modern life. Neither religion nor science provided very useful guides for living or promised a future that was at once credible and attractive. When the beliefs that had guided them were shattered, some progressives rejected reform, embracing materialism, hedonism, or cynicism. Others kept the faith, ignoring the massive and horrible reality of war as they had ignored other troubling realities earlier. Still others fashioned a more cynical liberalism that assumed that people were selfish, materialistic, and hedonistic and that pointed to no glorious future. Reform, in some guise or another, continued, but it was never the same after the war. The Victorian world could not survive that conflict, and no movement rooted so deeply in that world could survive either.

THE FAILURE OF SUCCESS

It will help to understand the new world, which
someday must be, to go into this story of the world
that was; the world of hope, the era of faith, when
men . . . went out to do battle with forces of evil, won
their fights and made the gains for the world which
are not lost to-day. . . . It was a fight for justice
because men believed in justice and they believed in
justice because they had faith in the brotherhood of
man and the fatherhood of God.

W ILLIAM A LLEN W HITE

In America we have created a new race, with healthy
physiques, sometimes beautiful bodies, but empty
minds: people who have accepted life as an alternation of meaningless routine with insignificant sensation. They deny because of their lack of experience
that life has any other meanings or values or possibilities.

L EWIS M UMFORD

The wistful lines above, penned by William Allen White in his preface
to Brand Whitlock's autobiography, capture the complex attitude of
many progressive reformers in the 1920's.[1] A sense of loss is there, a
recognition that what had been was gone, destroyed by the war or the
defects of human character or the stubborn conservatism of institutions. For some — Whitlock was one — the loss and the disillusionment
were so deep that public life became something to be avoided. But a
sense of accomplishment is there too, and some progressives continued
to press in the new decade for the old reforms or for reforms that fit

the old patterns. But most of all, there is a sense of disjuncture and discontinuity there, a notion that the *was* differed sharply from the *is*, that the "new world" contrasted starkly with "the world that was." It is particularly remarkable that his sense of discontinuity came not in the atomic age, or as the result of the holocaust, or after the rise of the dictators, but just a few years after the end of the progressive era. White prefaced Whitlock's book not in 1945, or 1935, but in 1925.

The wistfulness, the sense of loss, and the feeling of discontinuity expressed by so many progressives during the twenties is remarkable, because, on the surface, that decade showed how successful they had been. Everywhere their impact was discernable. Government on the local and state levels was more honest and more efficient—if not always more responsible or more humane—than it had been at any time since the Civil War. "First, and perhaps foremost," Hoyt Warner noted in one state study of progressivism, "the Ohio reformers clearly elevated the tone and stature of government, both city and state. . . . These reformers gave vitality to the ideal that public office is a public trust and to the corollary principle that the people's business is to be conducted as efficiently and honestly as possible."[2] What was true in Ohio apparently held for California as well: "If the progressive did nothing else, he gave California honest and decent government," George Mowry concluded in his classic study of reform in the Golden State. "That in itself, in the light of the state's history, was a major achievement."[3]

In the modern day we take this progressive accomplishment for granted. We are used to relatively efficient and honest—and boring—public administration. By contrast, boss rule seems rather exciting. Filtered through the gauze of time, the bosses often appear as fun-loving, roguish scamps. We forget that they maintained their power by perverting the political process and that they lived by theft and corruption and pandering.

We are less likely to forget the progressive achievement of making government a more vital and visible factor in American life, though in our more conservative and distrustful times we see that as a distinctly mixed blessing. Government was more interventionist after the progressive era than it had been previously. The hopes of scientific progressives for an administrative state were not fully realized, but government was more deeply involved in regulation, coordination, and planning in the economy than had ever been the case before. The dream of social justice remained elusive, but government did accept a measure of responsibility to ameliorate some of the grossest injustices in American society. The perfect correspondence of Christianity and government was not effected, but the latter did take more responsibility to enforce morality. If these general trends were too nebulous to provide satisfaction, reformers could justly point to a variety of economic, social, and political reforms realized in the heady days after 1910 and generally accepted by the resurgent conservatives after 1920.

Business seemed to have changed as well. Corporate spokesmen proclaimed a "New Era" that promised the achievement of many of the things progressives had wanted. Businessmen gave notice that they were now recognizing their responsibilities to the society of which they were parts. Cooperation was going to characterize their relationships with competitors, and they were determined to serve the wants and needs of consumers. Scientific administration and management promised to unlock the abundance of industrialism and create a universal and never-ending prosperity. Welfare capitalism would diminish industrial strife, unite workers and employers, and prove that the bosses cared seriously about their employees. Business, it seemed, was at once becoming more scientific and more Christian, and society was the beneficiary.

The apparent success of reform satisfied some progressives, but many recognized—or sensed, at least—that ephemeral successes masked a deep failure to realize the essence of reform. For most progressives— particularly those whose analyses and solutions of social problems were Christian in nature—specific reforms were less important as ends in themselves than as tangible signs of alterations in human character. Those who believed in the individual, in his or her goodness, progress, and ability to attain higher levels of civilization, had received some serious shocks in the years before 1920, and little happened during the twenties to rebuild their faith.

Public behavior—in business and government, for example— seemed more elevated, but it was difficult to tell where sincere behavioral changes ended and cynical, manipulative hypocrisy began. Government was, perhaps, more honest, but genuine devotion to the public interest seemed more elusive in 1925 than it had been in 1910. Self-interested individuals and groups fought among themselves for favors—beneficial tariff rates, subsidies, contracts, price supports, and whatever else government had to give—sometimes taking the trouble to masquerade as devotees of the public interest and sometimes not. Conceptions of justice, decency, and duty were eclipsed by the demands of raw power.

Business showed mainly that it had learned to cover its public flank. The trappings of the New Era were less signs of sincere alterations of business behavior than they were tools for creating a favorable public image. Efficiency, once a vehicle for criticizing business, was fashioned into a tool for defending it. God, too, was appropriated by the corporate community and was transformed into the first businessman, a prophet of abundance, a being as interested in distributing material goods as in redeeming humankind. Business was showing brilliantly that its means were flexible. Only its ends—power and profit—did not change.

All of this was difficult for progressives to understand, because they had always seen behavior as indicative of character and they had usually taken the individual at his or her word. Their innocence made the hypocrisy of their adversaries effective. But if they did not perfectly understand what was going on in public life, they had a fairly clear picture of what was happening in private life. Rampant hedonism, selfishness, and materialism, which were supposed to be cured by the values of private life, now engulfed it, threatening the family, the church, and the community. And the forces dominating economic and political life assured the people that self-indulgence and antisocial behavior were approved by the co-equal authorities, science and Christianity. The sort of individual feared by the Victorians—selfish, hedonistic, materialistic, antisocial, alienated, restrained only by fear or self-interest—had emerged in full bloom by the twenties.

The individual had let the progressives down. He and she seemed capable of physical self-improvement and material advancement. Reformation of character to serve humankind or the public interest seemed beyond the individual's grasp and, more disturbing, outside his or her interest. Perhaps it was because the idea of service to humanity sounded hypocritical from the lips of some and embarrassing from the lips of others. It was harder to speak with much conviction about human dignity and duty and progress when the din of European battlefronts still echoed in the world's ears. The society in which the progressives were fated to continue to exist received its tone from those who lived in the short term and for themselves, who had few transcendent values and little interest in acquiring any. "In America we have created a new race, with healthy physiques, sometimes beautiful bodies, but empty minds: people who have accepted life as an alternation of meaningless routine with insignificant sensation," Lewis Mumford complained in 1940. "They deny because of their lack of experience that life has any other meanings or values or possibilities."[4]

In the confusion of values and the deterioration of standards that followed the war all sorts of people — Benito Mussolini, Calvin Coolidge, Babe Ruth, Rudolph Valentino, Charles Lindbergh, Al Capone — could become celebrities. Our impersonal industrial society needed individual heroes; it simply lacked the ability to define and apply standards for them. Most progressives were ill prepared for a world without values. Those without values were ill prepared for the horrors on the horizon. "When the history of Western civilization will have been written, it will probably appear that we have lived in a Corrupt Age (1920–1940) comparable to nothing since the Renaissance," Edgar Kemler wrote in 1941. "The creeds now flourishing are the most naked and the least exalted that man can believe in. They presuppose not that man is made in the likeness of God, replete with dignity, tolerance and rationality, but that he is simply the highest anthropoid, wallowing in racial egotisms, greed, power, and sensuality. These," Kemler concluded, "are the least exalted beliefs that a man can have."[5] This was not a world in which most progressives could feel very happy or comfortable.

I

Historians must make history simpler than it was, for accurately to recreate the complexity of the past would be to make it hopelessly confusing and unusable. In order to simplify it, we break history into manageable chunks, using decades, wars, presidential administrations, depressions, and the like as beginning and ending points. Human experience is similar to a continuous film, but we like it better as a series of short subjects.

For many years the conventional knowledge about progressivism was that it began around 1900 and that it had ended by 1920. The film ran out, to be replaced by another short subject entitled "The Roaring Twenties." Then along came Arthur Link, who pointed out that progressive reforms continued to have a vital existence during the twenties and that progressives continued to fight for more. Others drew on and expanded Link's insights, and even Herbert Hoover, damned for years as a mossback conservative, was refurbished as a "forgotten progressive." [6]

It is good to be reminded that continuity is as characteristic of history as is change, but the old school was not totally wrong. Clearly, something was quite different about reform after 1920. What was different was that the special commitment and optimism of prewar reform was gone. Progressive reformers lived on into the twenties, and many of them remained committed to particular progressive reforms, but the special, essential character of prewar progressivism ceased to exist.

The progressive coalition had started to unravel even before World War I. Scientific progressivism challenged the Christian variety, moralistic reformers irritated more realistic ones, policy differences belied rhetorical unity, economic and social interest groups became more assertive, and failures of optimistic hopes led to division and disillusionment. The war intensified the disintegrating forces, and after it was over the progressive coalition could not be recreated. Or, perhaps more accurately and significantly, many of the important figures in progressive reform were unwilling to attempt to recreate the coalition. Hoyt Warner explains the situation in Ohio:

> When peace returned there was no co-ordinated effort to revive the progressive movement in Ohio. Some of the former leaders refused to consider entering politics again because they wished to pursue careers . . . and earn a competence for their families. . . . Coupled with this desire was the feeling that their personal sacrifice was no longer justified because the people were tired of political and economic reform. . . . [Others held the belief] that

the main outline of their program was complete. . . . Perhaps a more fundamental reason for their declining interest in reform at home was the fact that they lacked the intensive ideological commitment to the cause that sustained the first crusaders.[7]

There was, then, a failure of will at the top as well as a disintegration at the bottom. The central problem was the absence of an "intensive ideological commitment," but this was due less to the characteristics of individual reformers than it was to the horrible damage the war had done to the premises of progressivism. It was understandable that men and women who had been drawn to progressivism by faith in the individual and belief in progress before 1914 might well have lost their enthusiasm for reform in the years that followed. Ideals of any kind came into disrepute during the twenties. The core beliefs of civilization had been misused, abused, and tarnished by 1920, and they never recovered their former vitality or their ability to unite and inspire people. "Where would the human race be were it not for the ideals of men?," asked Edward Bok in 1924. "It is idealists, in a large sense, that this old world needs today."[8] The old idealists were still around, it was just that the ideals were hard to sustain. As a consequence, ex-progressives were returning "to self after wandering through a wilderness of altruism." A dying Walter Weyl perceived a natural evolution in liberal "thought and action, from intense preoccupation with the affairs of humanity, to self—self-culture, self-indulgence."[9] Those turning to the self were not likely to fulfill the need Bok perceived.

The decay of idealism was reflected in the deterioration of Christian progressivism as a viable reform force. Growing secularization in America was one factor in minimizing Christian influence, but more important was the division among Christians themselves. Fundamentalism, battening even before the war on the failure of the Social Gospel and the dissatisfaction of many churchgoers with it, thrived in the environment of the postwar years. Fundamentalists tended to be more pessimistic, more oriented toward the individual, and less inclined to humanize Christ than liberals, but they had cooperated in reform ventures before the war. During the twenties they continued to be involved in reform, but in the context of the times their efforts appeared intolerant and defensive. Support for moral order, opposition to prostitution, and the upholding of prohibition all seemed narrow and reactionary in the altered social climate. Opposition to the teaching of evolution seemed an hysterical response to the modern age. And the leading Protestant reform organization, the imperfectly understood Ku Klux Klan, had a bigoted and vicious hue.[10] The times had changed, and what had been reform a few years before had now become reaction. In a drifting age, when traditional values were discredited, measures that had once been accepted as uplifting and civilizing seemed punitive and intolerant.

Of course, there were other Christians, of the advanced Social Gospel type, who continued to be liberals in the New Era. They fought against child labor and for social insurance and marched in behalf of Sacco and Vanzetti and did the other liberal things. And no self-respecting reform committee existed that did not include at least one liberal minister. But the fact was that reform no longer seemed a Christian imperative. Moreover, as a result of the reshuffling of Christian progressivism, liberals became wary of explicitly religious support for reformers and distrustful of those who brought religious considerations into policy questions.

The excision of the Christian component from liberalism was unfortunate for a number of reasons. It denuded reform of its enthusiastic, crusading flavor. "After 1920, reform became simply 'liberalism,'" Ferenc Szasz has noted. "It was carried on by dedicated men and women, but seldom with the earlier sense of exuberance. . . . When the Protestant ministers abandoned their attempts to establish the Kingdom of God in America, they took with them a mood which proved impossible to replace." Szasz concludes that "when the spirit died, so too did Progressivism."[11] In addition, reform lost its most powerful public appeal and its strongest potential adhesive when it became separated from Christianity. Christian concepts united the public more perfectly and appealed to it more completely than could any others. Nothing else—not science, nor nationalism, nor some vague commitment to the public interest—would ever work as well. Christianity also imparted a legitimacy to policies that nothing else could. Whether the marriage between liberalism and Christianity was necessarily good for the latter—which must transcend politics, policies, and even the nation to fulfill its role—is an open question. But the day when Christianity and liberalism were separated was a sad one for reform in this country, for it cost it much of its force, power, and idealism.

Scientific progressivism lived on into the postwar period, or at least its spirit did. It survived in part because experts had skills that were increasingly necessary to government in an ever more complex age. As a consequence, professional administration and governmental management made great strides during the twenties. And politicians, whether conservative or liberal, paid homage to the canons of expertise and efficiency.

Many of the popular heroes of the age were men who were masters of technique, specialists who were honored for what they did rather than for their characters. Herbert Hoover, Henry Ford, Charles Lindbergh, Sinclair Lewis' fictional Martin Arrowsmith, even Babe Ruth were celebrated for their mastery of technique.[12] Other attributes might be attached to them—devotion to science above materialism, personal morality, Christian values, or whatever—but their mastery of technique was the necessary element in their fame. For some, it was also sufficient. "He liked Mussolini as much as Lenin and Henry Ford as much as either dictator," one of Lincoln Steffens' biographers says of him. "What communism, fascism, and American business efficiency shared was a rationalized—Steffens would say 'scientific'—society. This was the real challenge to the old, moralistic, corrupt world."[13]

Problems lay just under the surface. Their apparent acceptance by the political system obscured the experts' lack of power in it. They were still under the control of others, and their expertise functioned mainly to serve those with power. Most of them came to accept this, but Walter Lippmann still hoped the experts could get real authority. He suggested in *Public Opinion* in 1922 that experts could never assume their rightful place as shapers of policy until they achieved the ability to shape public opinion. To Lippmann's mind, representative government and democracy had failed. "Representative government," he held, "cannot be worked successfully, no matter what the basis of election, unless there is an independent, expert organization for making the unseen facts intelligible to those who have to make the decisions." And he argued that "it is no longer possible . . . to believe in the original dogma of democracy; that the knowledge needed for the management of human affairs comes up spontaneously from the human heart." [14]

The "human heart," the conscience, or the basic goodness of people was undependable. People were driven by prejudices, they thought in stereotypes, and they were easily manipulated by the powerful and cynical forces that controlled the media and directed public opinion. Lippmann called for the creation of a powerful "intelligence bureau" that would generate the "facts" on which policymakers would act and that would thus control public policy. The operation of this agency would make for better government, and Lippmann made it clear that this would not be democratic government. The purpose of the bureau, he pointed out, "is not to burden every citizen with expert opinions on all questions, but to push that burden away from him towards the responsible administrator. . . . The demand for the assistance of expert[s] . . . comes not from the public, but from men doing public business, who can no longer do it by rule of thumb." [15]

In *Public Opinion*, many of the undercurrents of prewar scientific progressivism surfaced. Contempt for the people, impatience with democratic institutions, self-conscious realism, and arrogant elitism paraded beside a childlike faith in the expert and a toadyistic devotion to men with political and economic power. Covering it all was a veneer of innocence, a belief that somehow people with power would turn it over to experts and that they would use it to serve the public interest. Lippmann the pragmatist had learned little from experience.

Another aspect of prewar scientific progressivism that became more pronounced during the 1920's was its occupational nature. Scientific progressives had always been embarrassed by any indications of sentiment, spontaneity, moralism, or even excitement from within their ranks. They were tough-minded professionals, after all, experts who did not need hearts because they had heads. This mantle was consciously, and not always honestly, assumed, but it was true that one could more easily restrain his or her enthusiasm when the goal was the development of a more efficient accounting system for a sanitation department than when it was the realization of the Kingdom of God in America.

The occupational tendency embedded in professionalism became much more pronounced as reformers created bureaucracies and ensconced themselves in them. Maintenance and expansion of their day-to-day functions became important, and the mundane questions of paid vacations and retirement plans took precedence over the more universal goals scientific progressives had once pursued. This tendency could be seen throughout government. In social work, for example, which had attracted both Christian and scientific progressives, professionals drawn more to an occupation than to a calling came to dominate. When that occurred, the dynamism and excitement of the prewar years drained away, as did the enthusiasm of reformers who still operated in response to the imperatives of the heart. "As settlements like the rest of the social effort became professionalized," Vida Scudder remembered, "my interest . . . waned a little." [16] In his memoir, written at the end of the New Deal period, New York social worker Edward Devine hoped that the idea that "the spirit of social work is the spirit of brotherhood, the spirit of science, the spirit of the Sermon on the Mount" could be rekindled, but it probably could not have been. [17] Scientific progressives hoped to make reform a job rather than an adventure, and in this one effort, at least, they succeeded too well.

Reformers who still believed that alterations in public policy could and should be made faced an increasingly pluralistic, interest-group-oriented political system after 1920. The development of active interest groups had presented progressives with problems in the prewar period, and American politics became much more group-oriented after the war. Politicians accepted interest-group competition as the new paradigm for political behavior, even though they continued to justify their actions by invoking the public interest. They recognized that the old, pre-1900 system was gone, and they adjusted to the new system as practical people do. In time, it became difficult for them to respond to individual political demands or to broad public pressures unless they were tied to clear and recognizable organizations. Rather than seeing groups as threats to their independence, politicians vied with one another for the right to represent them or to broker among them. Eventually, government even found it necessary to create interest groups to which it would in turn respond.

Progressives reacted to the developing political situation in a variety of ways. Otis Graham has shown that many ex-reformers rejected the

New Deal because they believed that the pluralistic, interest-group politics to which Franklin Roosevelt responded and that he in turn encouraged was dividing the American people.[18] But Roosevelt was merely the messenger, carrying the bad news of the modern age. And interest-group politics was bad news to many who believed in social unity, in selfless public service and citizenship, and in the notion that there was a public interest separate from and superior to the interests of particular individuals or groups.

Some progressives made their peace with the new situation and participated in the emerging political configuration, creating reform interest groups or cooperating with existing ones. In this process, what liberals defined as reform changed dramatically. Before World War I most reforms, whether they especially benefitted particular groups or not, were supported by relatively broad and amorphous public coalitions. Unorganized middle-class people provided the base of support for prohibition, woman suffrage, economic regulation, and social welfare because they believed these changes would serve the public interest. After the war, liberal reforms could be seen much more clearly to benefit particular social or occupational groups. Labor, farmers, ethnic and racial minorities moved into the reform vanguard, demanding favors not on the basis of justice or the public interest but simply on the grounds that they had the political clout to get what they wanted. The unorganized and amorphous middle-class core of American progressivism drifted away from reform, sometimes into a narrow and intolerant reaction.

The development of interest-group liberalism was not necessarily bad. It did reflect growing self-confidence among traditionally weak and inarticulate people, and it was an understandable response to the condescension that reformers often showed. Still, the alienation of much of the unorganized middle class from liberalism made that class much more vulnerable to the conservative forces of wealth and power. Eschewing any but a rhetorical commitment to the public interest, self-interested reform groups implicitly accepted the values of selfishness, materialism, and hedonism so vibrant in American life. For all their own self-limiting conservatism, most progressives had believed at least that something different could be wrought out of the system. The farm and labor organizations in the forefront of reform during the twenties were interested not in something different, but merely in getting a larger share of what existed.

It was also true that something fine and noble went out of our political system when we ignored the possibility of a public interest and when we chose to appeal to human selfishness and materialism rather than to altruism. When we determined that we should either ignore people with ideals or manipulate them, when we determined to control people through appeals to their selfishness, when we decided to make public policy on the basis of cynical appraisals of wealth and political power unleavened by any altruistic sentiments, we entered an age that was as ignoble and dehumanizing as it was modern. The greatness of a nation must be measured both by the nobility of its ideals and by the degree to which it approximates those ideals in reality. By either measure, the United States has had precious little reason to be proud since the end of the progressive era.

II

Politics was one area of public behavior in the twenties in which the failure of progressivism was clear. Individual successes—legislation passed, reforms realized, cleaner government, expert administrators— camouflaged but could not hide the failure to realize an exalted vision. The presence of the signposts of a selfless, altruistic, united society in which people were motivated by love and a desire to serve the public interest clearly did not prove that such a society really existed. In retrospect, we have often seen the signposts as false, or as ends in themselves, or we have assumed that they were meant to lead to the reality that emerged. Most of the progressives knew better. They knew that specific actions had not had the consequences they desired, and they recognized that the signs did not reflect reality.

In society as in politics progressive hopes were dashed. The threats to the family, the church, and the community they had glimpsed before the war came into full view afterward. Private institutions that were supposed to civilize behavior by infusing public life with private values were threatened by a rising tide of selfishness, materialism, hedonism, and lawlessness. The confident notion of earlier years that private institutions would civilize public life was forgotten; the question of the hour was whether the former would even survive. In their anxiety to defend family, church, and community, many progressives drifted from defensive reform to aggressive reaction. In the process they showed how changing times and circumstances could twist aspirations and sour ideals.

Business behavior during the twenties also showed that specific signs of progressive success obscured a larger failure. On the surface, it appeared that business had transformed itself, that it was operating in a selfless, socially responsible manner, that it was devoted to industrial cooperation and service to workers and consumers. This was the New Era, in which a mature business system promised universal prosperity and freedom from economic insecurity. And yet it is clear in retrospect that American business remained devoted to power and profits, first and foremost, and that this devotion was only occasionally compatible with a commitment to American society. The progressive reformers failed to transform business into an ethical and selfless engine for public service, and in the end even the superficial signs of transformation were seen to be false.

The apparent alterations in business behavior were impressive. Instead of resisting science, businessmen seemed to embrace it. Scientific management, scientific administration, and scientific personnel work were all apparently accepted readily. As Daniel Nelson has noted, "by the end of the war scientific management and personnel work had achieved a degree of popularity and acceptability that earlier proponents would not have foreseen in their most euphoric moments." Science was leading to a "new factory system" in which advanced technology, professional management, and a tightly controlled work force contributed to high productive efficiency, material abundance, and impressive corporate benefits.[19] Instead of being seen as foot-dragging opponents of industrial progress, businessmen came to be viewed as trailblazers of efficiency. In the popular literature of the day dozens of corporate leaders were squeezed into the pattern cut initially for Henry Ford and were thus portrayed as selfless pioneers of efficiency providing abundance to the people under the capitalistic system.

The twenties was the heyday—insofar as public attention was concerned, at least—of welfare capitalism. Corporations trumpeted their efforts on behalf of employees — paid vacations, stock options, worker input in management decisions, profit sharing, health and welfare benefits, retirement plans, and so forth. And these efforts, like those more explicitly designed to increase efficiency, enjoyed broad public approval. "Welfare capitalism . . . enjoyed growing intellectual, social, and political support among nonbusiness groups," two recent students of the development of the American welfare state have noted. "Hesitant and partial as businessmen's innovations might be, theirs remained the most active role in the provision of welfare services. The very weakness of public and trade union response to the human problems of a complex industrial age accented entrepreneurial achievement and legitimized corporate purpose."[20] Businessmen, it seemed, were finally accepting their responsibility to their workers just as they had accepted their responsibility to consumers.

Businessmen had the best of two worlds during the twenties. Celebrated as scientifically advanced stewards to the community, they were also returned to a place of honor in American Christianity. The public religious rehabilitation of businessmen had started during the late teens, and it proceeded rapidly after the war. A significant milepost along the way was Roger Babson's *Religion and Business*, published in 1920.

Babson, a statistician and head of a major accounting firm, interpreted Christianity in such a way as to make it a much more comfortable faith for some businessmen than it had been in the hands of advanced Social Gospelers. He argued that Christ favored the efficient and productive. "If Jesus were here to-day," he assured his readers, "He would give His greatest rewards to the scientist, the inventor, . . . and those who are trying to make two blades of grass grow where only one grew before." It followed that Christ, contrary to long-standing popular belief, actually encouraged materialism. "The thing which bothered Jesus in connection with material possessions was that those who came to Him were not interested in producing more but rather in a redistribution of what was already produced."[21]

Having cleansed Christ of any taint of socialism and having lined him up on the side of materialism, Babson sought to enlist the churches in the same cause. He argued that religion made men more efficient and productive and that such was the best measure of its value. "The

best religion is that which makes its people most efficient, most productive, most useful, and most worth while. This is the test which
men demand in business and our religion must pass the same test."
Ultimately, Babson believed, the religion that best met this business
standard would prove its superiority — or the superiority of its com-
municants — because it would rule the world. "The domination of the
world should go to the people of the best religion, but the truth is that
the people who ultimately dominate the world will have proven which
is the best religion." [22] The efficient rather than the meek would inherit
Babson's earth.

Religion and Business was a clear sign of the times, and an indication
of how different those times were from the progressive period that
preceded them. After being an implicit threat to capitalism, Christianity was again being twisted into an adjunct of it. Babson was willing
to say a word for the old notions — that the wealthy enjoyed God's
favor and that they were stewards of their wealth — but he added the
rather modern and "scientific" idea that their supposed productivity,
efficiency, and ability to provide material abundance to the community
rendered businessmen superior. In an abundant, technologically advanced, capitalistic society, materialism was receiving religious sanction and those who controlled and provided material wealth were
gaining spiritual stature. Babson was quite willing to bind religion to
materialistic capitalism and to judge the former by the standards of the
latter. Progressive distinctions were being forgotten, and priorities were
being reversed.

Bruce Barton was a better-known reconciler of Christian and business values. His books *The Man Nobody Knows* and *The Book Nobody
Knows* were popular during the twenties, and historians since have
seen them as representative of the ethos of that decade. They were
that, but they were also responses to a generation of Christian criticism of business and attempts to renew the businessman's religious
credentials.

Barton's life represents an instructive twentieth-century evolution.
The son of a minister, Barton attempted to make Christ more relevant
to modern life with *A Young Man's Jesus*, published in 1914. During
the twenties he became a highly successful and innovative advertising
executive, and in the thirties the streams of liberal religion, conserva-

tive economics, and media savvy flowed together into a political career that saw Barton become one of Franklin D. Roosevelt's best-known congressional critics. Barton's popular religious works during the twenties showed how the tools of Protestant modernism—depiction of a personal and relevant Christ, Biblical analysis based in part on the analyst's experience, and the emphasis on the human characteristics of God—could be used to buttress business as easily as they had been used earlier to criticize it.

In *The Man Nobody Knows* Barton turned Christ into a being quite familiar and flattering to businessmen. He became the consummate organization man, able to mold disparate individuals into an effective working unit, and a great advertiser whose skills led to the spread of Christianity. Equally important, he enjoyed the self-confidence necessary for the success of any business venture. As Christ became more like a businessman he became less like a god. Barton made him a fallible being who changed his mind and saw the error of his ways. He was portrayed as a self-made man and compared with other self-made entrepreneurs. (Apparently Barton did not think Christ's status as the son of God gave him any particular advantage over his competitors.) And he was interpreted as approving self-interest as long as it was leavened by the ideal of service. Because he was so like a businessman, Christ's pronouncements and activities seemed to Barton to be worthy of the attention of men of affairs. "Every one of His conversations, every contact between His mind and others," Barton noted, "is worthy of the attentive study of any sales manager." [23] This was high praise, indeed.

In *The Book Nobody Knows*, a sequel to *The Man Nobody Knows* and a response to its popularity, Barton applied his treatment to the entire Bible. Once again, the holy figures of antiquity were portrayed in a modern light. God was a fallible figure who erred in bringing the Great Flood. Abel was lazy because he did not farm. Christ was a political and economic conservative who encouraged service and recommended the power of positive thinking. Barton even tried to get Eve off the hook for her part in the original sin, arguing, among other things, that "the fruit was good to eat—she had an eye to food values." [24] In a society in which people increasingly lived to consume, Eve's aptitude seemed to Barton an important exonerating factor.

It is easy to see why historians delight in quoting Barton and lampooning him, but he was much more than a buffoonish period piece in a frivolous decade. He was engaged in an effort to reconcile corporate capitalism with Christianity, and he was using the tools of liberal Protestantism to do it.[25] Success in his endeavor would enhance the legitimacy of business and defuse much of the critical potential of religion. The reconciliation of business and religion generally took place, and the bulk of the churches have not been alienated from corporate America since 1920. Even during the Great Depression, when public questioning of business was intense, little of the criticism was Christian in nature. And today American corporations and right-wing Protestants are yoked together tightly in a conservative coalition, even though the former represent the most potent social threats to the self-restraint the latter are trying to inculcate. Bruce Barton could not have foreseen this outcome, but there is little reason to believe he would have been terribly unhappy about it.

To many modern readers the pronouncements of Bruce Barton and other spokesmen for the New Era seem pompous and hypocritical. But they expressed a kind of conservative utopianism and even a sense of consecration. Barton, Hoover, publicist Ivy Lee, financier John Jacob Raskob, industrialist Gerard Swope, and even Calvin Coolidge, among others, pointed to a bright future that they outlined in terms familiar to progressives. A benevolent capitalism would provide more prosperity and security to workers than bolshevism ever could. A productive and efficient industry, presided over by stewards of the public interest, would assure an increasing material abundance for the nation. "The humane, rationalized corporation," led by men devoted to public service, would be "the chief instrument of social progress" and spiritual regeneration both here and abroad.[26] "Two things are clear," argued enlightened capitalist Edward Filene in 1924. "The first is that business in order to be good business must itself be conducted as a public service. The second is that the finest possible public service of business men is that rendered in and through the private businesses of the world."[27]

The leaders of the business community during the New Era had learned from the controversies of the progressive period. One of the things they had learned was the importance of public opinion and the necessity of responding to it. Often they discovered that a rhetorical response was sufficient, that old values and old behavior could survive and even thrive if dressed in new clothes. "Businessmen succeeded in molding progressive programs to their own ends," Paul Glad pointed out some years ago; "they also succeeded in adapting progressive rhetoric to their own uses."[28]

The New Era showed that adaptability and flexibility remained the most prominent characteristics of corporate capitalism in America. "Manufacturers and merchants are learning that to succeed permanently they must talk service," Roger Babson noted in a revealing remark, "whatever may be their . . . opinions."[29] The conversion of businessmen was not exclusively rhetorical, but the fact remained that for virtually every businessman the measure of success was still profits rather than service. For a time the latter was one means to the former, but it was never an end in itself. "I have always dealt with matters of social justice, coöperation, and general welfare, not on the basis of philanthropy or paternalism," argued Filene, "but as essential factors in the development of successful business." Filene and other spokesmen for enlightened selfishness saw service, the public interest, sometimes even the Golden Rule as highly compatible with profits, but there was never any question where their emphasis lay. "Good social policies," said Filene, "are the surest recipe for big and continuous profits."[30]

The spokesmen for the New Era were not especially swinish or duplicitous men. They believed in business and they believed in public service and they thought the two could be reconciled. Most progressives, as well, had thought that there was no necessary contradiction in the notion of a capitalist economy that simultaneously generated profits, served the public interest, and operated by the law of love. Perhaps a degree of service capitalism was achieved during the twenties, but hard times revealed the contradiction at the heart of the ideal. Businessmen then were torn in two directions. Either they could pursue the course of the heart, selflessly sacrificing for others, or they could follow their heads, doing whatever was necessary to assure their own survival and prosperity. There was no real contest here. Willing captives of a system that had given them economic and social dominion, they conformed to its most honored values, individual self-interest and materialism. And so, in the early years of the Great Depression, the institutional manifestations of the service ideal, devotion to the public interest, and fealty to the law of love were less and less compatible with self-interest and were thus jettisoned.

The image of a progressive, service-oriented capitalism continued even after its reality faded away. Many businessmen had recognized before 1920 that a favorable public opinion was essential to the economic and political health of business. Some believed this demanded changes in business behavior, while others stressed that favorable public opinion would come if business merely changed its image. Its influence on the public media and its ability to hire professionals in advertising and public relations seemed to put the corporate community in a good position to create a favorable image. During the New Era, Edward Bernays elaborated a strategy for the creation of an attractive public image detached from reality.

Bernays, a nephew of Sigmund Freud, worked as a theatrical press agent before World War I. During the twenties he became a leading advertising and public relations professional (among other public services, he helped popularize cigarette smoking by portraying it as a habit of the fashionable) and an intellectual giant in the relatively new and inchoate field of corporate public relations. Like many others, Bernays had been fascinated by the ability of the government to manipulate public opinion during the war. After the war, as he remembered in his autobiography, business rushed to apply "wartime propaganda methods to launching peacetime services or products." [31] The growing significance of public opinion led Bernays to attempt a sophisticated and practical explanation of it in his 1923 book, *Crystallizing Public Opinion*. "The most significant social, political and industrial fact about the present century is the increased attention which is paid to public opinion, not only by individuals, groups or movements that are dependent on public support for their success," Bernays pointed out, "but also by men and organizations which until very recently stood aloof from the general public and were able to say, 'The public be damned.' " [32]

The events of the progressive period had illustrated the importance of public opinion and had created a need for the "public relations counsel," whose function was similar to that of an "attorney — to advise his client and to litigate his causes for him." [33] Bernays' portrayal of the public relations counsel as attorney was a significant modification of Ivy Lee's conception of the counsel as an ombudsman serving the client and the public simultaneously. Both attorneys and ombudsmen are professionals, but the former much more clearly serve their employers and do so without making moral judgments regarding their clients' behavior or purposes. Bernays had developed a much more realistic understanding of the function of professionals in the corporate capitalist system.

The constant importance of public opinion demanded the full-time use of public relations professionals. It was not enough that the public relations counsel "bring his clients by chance to the public's attention" or that he merely "extricate them from difficulties into which they have already drifted," he must "advise his clients how positive results can be accomplished." Positive results could be accomplished best by projecting a favorable image, and the best way to do that was by shaping an image that "enlist[ed] established points of view." "The actual experience of the public relations counsel shows," Bernays pointed out, "that the cause he represents must have some group reaction and tradition in common with the public he is trying to reach." [34] Hence, if the public values efficiency, service, the public interest, or Christian ethical values, the wise corporation will stress its devotion to these things. This functions both to give the corporation a favorable image —with the economic and political benefits that entails—and to disarm critics by appropriating the terms of their criticism. Moreover, though the public relations/advertising counsel might prefer that the image be matched by reality, favorable public opinion in the modern age was much more dependent on the former that it was on the latter.

When we view business in the twenties we can see again how apparent progressive successes masked a larger failure. Business had apparently changed, at least partially in response to progressive pressure. The New Era, with its stress on service, cooperation, efficiency, and welfare capitalism, seemed to show the success of progressive efforts, as did the high level of corporate attention to public opinion. And yet the system remained—as it had to remain—motivated primarily by profit, and any values that came into conflict with profits were forgotten. What the business community did not forget was the political and economic importance of a favorable public image, and it continued to cultivate that, often cynically and hypocritically. Clearly, the progressives had stimulated hypocrisy by raising a standard of virtue that demanded a payment of tribute by vice. In view of what they wanted to do, this was not much.

III

Analyses of progressivism, which seemed often to assume the character of post-mortems, began early on. The reformers experienced the uncomfortable sensation of having their successes and failures judged while they still lived; many even joined in the effort. The world in which they lived appeared so different from that "world of hope" in which they had thrived that analytical perspective did not seem too difficult to acquire. They generally agreed with most analysts that they were reformers, not radicals. This is how most historians have judged them as well. They did not, generally, favor a reordering of social values. Instead, they hoped to universalize social values that already existed, pressing them into every area of life. Nor did they favor an alteration in the control or distribution of economic power. For them, individual character and individual behavior were more important than institutions. Neither did they want a dramatic revolution in the institutions of American political life. They merely wanted the existing ones to work as they should.

As it originally developed, progressivism was a revitalization movement. Progressives hoped to force public behavior to conform to the standards of civilized Christian conduct that governed private life. Confronted by a corrupt and vicious public life, progressives demanded that it conform to the selfless and altruistic standards that governed private behavior. They believed it could so conform, regardless of its formal institutional structure, because they believed in the basic goodness of the individual and the inevitability of progress toward ever higher levels of civilization.

Scientific progressives argued that revitalization could not take the form simply of altering public reality to fit private values. They believed that both private and public values had to be altered and that both private and public life had to become more empirical and efficient. Still, despite their self-conscious realism and modernism, scientific progressives shared the Christian progressive faith in the individual and progress and the Christian progressive repugnance for antisocial selfishness and materialism.

In the end, a sort of revitalization took place. Unfortunately, it happened in a way that thoughtful progressives certainly abhorred. Instead of public values conforming to private values, or both being altered together, the public values of individualism, materialism, and hedonism triumphed in public as well as private life. In the process basically selfless and socially oriented concepts such as those of Christian ethics or publicly interested science were twisted in such a way as to justify the very selfishness, materialism, and hedonism that they had previously threatened. Reforms did not do what they were supposed to do, people did not justify the faith progressives had in them, progress did not turn out to be either inevitable or good, and established institutions and behavior patterns proved flexible, durable, and resistant to change.

Today the progressives and what they tried to do seem distant, quaint, even silly. We are sure they were wrong to concentrate on human character instead of institutions, while we do nothing to change either. We see spiritual poverty and hypocrisy in their society, while we overlook the bankruptcy of our own. We believe that they were wrong to assume that the individual was good, rational, and capable of improvement. We assume that the individual is controlled not by altruism, but by instinct, force, or selfishness. We expect people to be selfish, antisocial, materialistic, and self-indulgent, and we feel cynical pride when they meet our expectations. We believe moral progress is a joke, as perhaps we should in the light of all that has happened since 1914. All we can look forward to is more things and greater self-indulgence; a better, more spiritually satisfying society seems out of the question. We cannot agree about what is moral, or whether morality even exists. To some of us, morality is a codeword for repression and intolerance, and for others it is an excuse for these things. We cannot see how genuine commitment to standards of value might help free us from our own cynicism and from those who manipulate us and might help us create a more decent and humane society. The progressives failed, and failed badly, but the magnitude of their failure matched the nobility of their effort. It is unlikely that we, who understand their failure so clearly, will ever repeat their errors. But neither will we ever engage in an undertaking so noble.

NOTES

I

1. Shailer Mathews, *New Faith for Old: An Autobiography* (New York: Macmillan, 1936), p. 6

2. Raymond Blaine Fosdick, *Chronicle of a Generation: An Autobiography* (New York: Harper and Brothers, 1958), p. 2.

3. Frederic C. Howe, *The Confessions of a Reformer* (Chicago: Quadrangle, 1967; published originally by Charles Scribner's Sons, 1925), pp. 17–18.

4. Hutchins Hapgood, *A Victorian in the Modern World* (New York: Harcourt, Brace, 1939), p. vii.

5. My understanding of Victorian culture and its social functions draws heavily on Daniel Walker Howe's essay, "Victorian Culture in America," in his edited collection of essays, *Victorian America* (Philadelphia: University of Pennsylvania Press, 1976), pp. 3–28.

6. George Fredrickson, *The Inner Civil War: Northern Intellectuals and the Crisis of the Union* (New York: Harper and Row, 1968).

7. Howe, "Victorian Culture in America," p. 28.

8. Nathan G. Hale Jr., *Freud and the Americans: The Beginnings of Psychoanalysis in the United States, 1876–1917* (New York: Oxford University Press, 1971), p. 25

9. For the inculcation of moral principles by one fraternal organization, see Lynn Dumenil, *Freemasonry and American Culture, 1880–1930* (Princeton, N.J.: Princeton University Press, 1984).

10. Robert Wiebe, *The Search for Order, 1877–1920* (New York: Hill and Wang, 1967), p. 40.

11. Daniel Walker Howe, "American Victorianism as a Culture," *American Quarterly* 27 (1975): 528.

12. George Hubbard, "How and Where to Begin Reform," *New Englander* 52 (Feb. 1890): 109.

13. James Turner, *Without God, Without Creed: The Origins of Unbelief in America* (Baltimore: Johns Hopkins University Press, 1985), p. 217.

14. Frances Power Cobbe, "Secular Changes in Human Nature," *The Forum* 9 (April 1890): 175 and 171.

15. Graham Taylor, *Pioneering on Social Frontiers* (New York: Arno, 1976; published originally by the University of Chicago Press, 1930), p. viii.

16. See Jerry Israel, ed., *Building the Organizational Society: Essays on Associational Activities in Modern America* (New York: Free Press, 1972), and Samuel P. Hays, *The Response to Industrialism, 1885–1914* (Chicago: University of Chicago Press, 1957), as well as Wiebe, *The Search for Order.*

17. H. Wayne Morgan, *Unity and Culture: The United States, 1877–1900* (Baltimore: Penguin, 1971), pp. 16–17.

18. Henry George, *Progress and Poverty: An Inquiry into the Cause of Industrial Depressions and of Increase of Want with Increase of Wealth: The Remedy* (New York: Henry George, 1879).

19. James B. Gilbert, *Work Without Salvation: America's Intellectuals and Industrial Alienation, 1880–1910* (Baltimore: Johns Hopkins University Press, 1977), p. 22.

20. Theodore Roosevelt, *The Autobiography of Theodore Roosevelt: Condensed from the Original Edition, Supplemented by Letters, Speeches, and Other Writings*, ed. Wayne Andrews (New York: Charles Scribner's Sons, 1958), p. 222.

21. Edward Chase Kirkland, *Dream and Thought in the Business Community, 1860–1900* (Chicago: Quadrangle, 1964), p. 21.

22. Gilbert, *Work Without Salvation*, p. 12.

23. Jean B. Quandt, *From the Small Town to the Great Community: The Social Thought of Progressive Intellectuals* (New Brunswick, N.J.: Rutgers University Press, 1970), p. 17.

24. Daniel T. Rodgers, *The Work Ethic in Industrial America, 1850–1920* (Chicago: University of Chicago Press, 1978), p. 28.

25. The alteration of the ideal family in the nineteenth century, and the implications of that development for women especially, is detailed in Carl Degler's *At Odds: Women and the Family in America from the Revolution to the Present* (New York: Oxford University Press, 1980), esp. pp. 144–209.

26. The literature dealing with the domestic ideal is abundant. See especially Barbara Welter, "The Cult of True Womanhood, 1820–1860," *American Quarterly* 18 (1966): 151–174, Nancy F. Cott, *The Bonds of Womanhood: "Woman's Sphere" in New England, 1780–1835* (New Haven, Conn.: Yale University Press, 1977), and Kathryn Kish Sklar, *Catherine Beecher: A Study in American Domesticity* (New Haven, Conn.: Yale University Press, 1973), as well as Degler, *At Odds.*

27. Elaine Tyler May, *Great Expectations: Marriage and Divorce in Post-Victorian America* (Chicago: University of Chicago Press, 1980), p. 46.

28. Gwendolyn Wright, *Moralism and the Model Home: Domestic Architecture and Cultural Conflict in Chicago, 1873–1913* (Chicago: University of Chicago Press, 1980), p. 21.

29. Viviana A. Rotman Zelizer, *Morals and Markets: The Development of Life Insurance in the United States* (New York: Columbia University Press, 1979), p. 117.

30. Robert T. Handy, *The Protestant Quest for a Christian America, 1830–1930* (Philadelphia: Fortress Press, 1967), pp. 6–7.

31. Turner, *Without God, Without Creed*, p. 199, and Paul Carter, *The Spiritual Crisis of the Gilded Age* (DeKalb: Northern Illinois University Press, 1971). For the impact of Darwinism see Cynthia Eagle Russett, *Darwin in America: The Intellectual Response, 1865–1912* (San Francisco: W. H. Freeman, 1976).

32. My interpretation of Henry Ward Beecher draws heavily on William G. McLoughlin, *The Meaning of Henry Ward Beecher: An Essay on the Shifting Values of Mid-Victorian America, 1840–1870* (New York: Knopf, 1970), and Clifford E. Clark Jr., *Henry Ward Beecher: Spokesman for a Middle-Class America* (Urbana: University of Illinois Press, 1978).

33. Clark, *Henry Ward Beecher*, p. 187.

34. Lyman Abbott, *Reminiscences* (Boston: Houghton Mifflin, 1915), p. 127.

35. Carter, *Spiritual Crisis of the Gilded Age*, p. 83.

36. My understanding of Dwight L. Moody is drawn primarily from James F. Findlay Jr., *Dwight L. Moody: American Evangelist, 1837–1899* (Chicago: University of Chicago Press, 1969).

37. Sandra Sizer, "Politics and Apolitical Religion: The Great Urban Revivals of the Late Nineteenth Century," *Church History* 48 (March 1979): 86.

38. Findlay, *Dwight L. Moody*, p. 284.

39. Sizer, "Politics and Apolitical Religion," pp. 81–98.

40. Matthews, *New Faith for Old*, pp. 20–38.

41. Martin E. Marty, *Righteous Empire: The Protestant Experience in America* (New York: Harper and Row, 1970), p. 161.

42. Nathan Irvin Huggins, *Protestants Against Poverty: Boston's Charities, 1870–1900* (Westport, Conn.: Greenwood, 1971), p. 79.

43. See Roy Lubove, *The Professional Altruist: The Emergence of Social Work as a Career, 1880–1930* (Cambridge, Mass.: Harvard University Press, 1965).

44. Paul Boyer, *Urban Masses and Moral Order in America, 1820–1920* (Cambridge, Mass.: Harvard University Press, 1978), p. 149. See also Kenneth

L. Kusmer, "The Functions of Organized Charity in the Progressive Era: Chicago as a Case Study," *Journal of American History* 60 (Dec. 1973): 657–678.

45. See, for example, Thomas Bender, *Toward an Urban Vision: Ideas and Institutions in Nineteenth-Century America* (Lexington: University Press of Kentucky, 1975).

46. Eric Goldman, *Rendezvous with Destiny: A History of Modern American Reform* (New York: Vintage, 1956), p. 82, and Sidney Fine, *Laissez-Faire and the General-Welfare State: A Study of Conflict in American Thought, 1865–1901* (Ann Arbor: University of Michigan Press, 1956), p. 118.

47. For a particularly good example refer to the case of Edward Judson in Joan Jacobs Brumberg, *Mission for Life: The Story of the Family of Adoniram Judson, the Dramatic Events of the First American Foreign Mission, and the Course of Evangelical Religion in the Nineteenth Century* (New York: Free Press, 1980). See also Henry F. May, *Protestant Churches and Industrial America* (New York: Harper and Row, 1967).

48. Louis Galambos, with the assistance of Barbara Barrow Spence, *The Public Image of Big Business in America, 1880–1940: A Quantitative Study in Social Change* (Baltimore: Johns Hopkins University Press, 1975), p. 56.

49. Andrew Carnegie, *The Gospel of Wealth and Other Timely Essays*, ed. Edward Chase Kirkland (Cambridge, Mass.: Belknap Press of Harvard University, 1962), pp. 14, 25, and 23.

50. Ibid., p. 28

51. United States House of Representatives, *The Housing of Working People: Eighth Special Report of the Commissioner of Labor*, 53rd Congress, 3rd Session, Executive Document no. 354 (Washington, D.C.: Government Printing Office, 1895), p. 419.

52. Jacob Riis, *How the Other Half Lives: Studies Among the Tenements of New York* (New York: Hill and Wang, 1957; published originally by Charles Scribner's Sons, 1890), p. 4.

53. Hace Sorel Tischler, *Self-Reliance and Social Security, 1870–1917* (Port Washington, N.Y.: Kennikat, 1971), p. 70.

54. My understanding of Pullman is drawn primarily from Stanley Buder, *Pullman: An Experiment in Industrial Order and Community Planning, 1880–1930* (New York: Oxford University Press, 1967). In *The Model Company Town: Urban Design Through Private Enterprise in Nineteenth-Century New England* (Amherst: University of Massachusetts Press, 1984), John S. Garner argues convincingly that Pullman was not a typical model company town. It was, however, the best-known model community in the country.

55. Carroll D. Wright, "May a Man Conduct His Business as He Please?," *The Forum* 18 (Dec. 1894): 432.

2

1. Robert Graves, *Claudius the God and His Wife Messalina* (New York: Harrison Smith and Robert Haas, 1935), p. 523.

2. Charles Sheldon, *His Life Story* (New York: George H. Doran, 1925), pp. 81–82.

3. Robert M. LaFollette, *LaFollette's Autobiography: A Personal Narrative of Political Experiences* (Madison, Wisc.: LaFollette, 1913), p. 163.

4. David P. Thelen, *The New Citizenship: Origins of Progressivism in Wisconsin, 1885–1900* (Columbia: University of Missouri Press, 1972).

5. Henry George, *Progress and Poverty: An Inquiry into the Cause of Industrial Depressions and of Increase of Want with Increase of Wealth: The Remedy* (New York: Modern Library, 1929), pp. 4–5.

6. My interpretation of Henry George draws largely on John L. Thomas, *Alternative America: Henry George, Edward Bellamy, Henry Demarest Lloyd and the Adversary Tradition* (Cambridge, Mass.: Harvard University Press, 1983).

7. George, *Progress and Poverty*, p. 562.

8. B. O. Flower, *Progressive Men, Women, and Movements of the Past Twenty-Five Years* (Boston: New Arena, 1914), p. 80.

9. Edward Everett Hale, *How They Lived at Hampton: A Study of Practical Christianity, Applied in the Manufacture of Woollens* (Boston: J. Stillman Smith, 1888), p. 266.

10. Thomas, *Alternative America*, p. 237.

11. Edward Bellamy, *Looking Backward, 2000–1887* (New York: New American Library, 1960; published originally by Ticknor, 1888), p. 99.

12. A vigorous recent criticism of Bellamy's system is Arthur Lipow's *Authoritarian Socialism in America: Edward Bellamy and the Nationalist Movement* (Berkeley: University of California Press, 1982).

13. For vagueness among Nationalists see Mary A. Hill, *Charlotte Perkins Gilman: The Making of a Radical Feminist, 1860–1896* (Philadelphia: Temple University Press, 1980), pp. 173–174.

14. Steven Kesselman, *The Modernization of American Reform: Structures and Perceptions* (New York: Garland, 1979).

15. James B. Weaver, *A Call to Action: An Interpretation of the Great Uprising, Its Source and Causes* (Des Moines: Iowa Printing, 1892), pp. 392, 441, and 442.

16. In his *Knights of the Golden Rule: The Intellectual as Christian Social Reformer in the 1890s* (Lexington: University Press of Kentucky, 1976), Peter J. Frederick stresses the way in which the impending end of the century strengthened the moralistic tendencies of the reformers.

17. Henry Demarest Lloyd, *Wealth Against Commonwealth* (New York: Harper, 1894), p. 504.

18. Ibid., p. 514.

19. Ibid., p. 512, 7, and 509–510.

20. Ibid., p. 518.

21. Ibid., p. 526.

22. Ronald C. White Jr., "Beyond the Sacred: Edgar Gardner Murphy and a Ministry of Social Reform," *Historical Magazine of the Protestant Episcopal Church* 49 (March 1980): 60.

23. Charles Howard Hopkins, *The Rise of the Social Gospel in American Protestantism, 1865–1915* (New Haven, Conn.: Yale University Press, 1940), p. 321. For recent, variant views of the Social Gospel see Gary Scott Smith, *The Seeds of Secularization: Calvinism, Culture, and Pluralism in America, 1870–1915* (Grand Rapids, Mich.: Christian University Press, 1985), and Ferenc Morton Szasz, *The Divided Mind of Protestant America, 1880–1930* (University: University of Alabama Press, 1982).

24. Robert M. Crunden, *Ministers of Reform: The Progressives' Achievement in American Civilization, 1889–1920* (New York: Basic Books, 1982), p. 40.

25. Graham Taylor, *Pioneering on Social Frontiers* (New York: Arno, 1976), pp. 109–110.

26. Henry F. May, *Protestant Churches and Industrial America* (New York: Harper and Row, 1967), p. 116.

27. Josiah Strong, *Our Country: Its Possible Future and Its Present Crisis* (New York: Baker and Taylor for the American Home Missionary Society, 1885), p. 104.

28. Ibid., pp. 123, 93, 106, and 120.

29. Ibid., p. 211.

30. Josiah Strong, *The New Era: Or, The Coming Kingdom* (New York: Baker and Taylor, 1893), pp. 240 and 313–314.

31. Washington Gladden, *Recollections* (Boston: Houghton Mifflin, 1909), p. 61.

32. Ibid., p. 38.

33. Washington Gladden, *Applied Christianity: Moral Aspects of Social Questions* (Boston: Houghton Mifflin, 1886), p. 112.

34. Ibid., pp. 100 and 37.

35. Ibid., p. 180.

36. Shailer Mathews, *The Social Teaching of Jesus: An Essay in Christian Sociology* (New York: George H. Doran, 1897), p. 209.

37. George D. Herron, *The New Redemption: A Call to the Church to Reconstruct Society According to the Gospel of Christ* (New York: Thomas Y. Crowell, 1893), pp. 29, 30, and 38.

38. George D. Herron, *The Christian Society* (New York: Johnson Reprint, 1969; published originally by F. H. Revell, 1894), p. 36.

39. George D. Herron, *The Christian State: A Political Vision of Christ* (New York: Johnson Reprint, 1968; published originally by Thomas Y. Crowell, 1895), pp. 198 and 64.

40. For the impact of the social gospel on the churches, see, especially, Aaron Ignatius Abell, *The Urban Impact on American Protestantism, 1865–1900* (Hamden, Conn.: Archon, 1962), and Hopkins, *The Rise of the Social Gospel.*

41. Brenda K. Shelton, *Reformers in Search of Yesterday: Buffalo in the 1890's* (Albany: State University of New York Press, 1976), p. 25.

42. Crunden, *Ministers of Reform.*

43. William Allen White, *The Autobiography of William Allen White* (New York: Macmillan, 1946), p. 325.

44. Charles M. Sheldon, *In His Steps: Or, What Would Jesus Do?* (Grand Rapids, Mich.: Zondervan, 1967; published originally by Advance, 1896).

45. May, *Protestant Churches and Industrial America,* p. 210.

46. William T. Stead, *If Christ Came to Chicago!: A Plea for the Union of All Who Love in the Service of All Who Suffer* (Chicago: Laird and Lee, 1894), p. 72.

47. The development of social science as a response to the "crisis of authority" in the late nineteenth century is explored especially fruitfully by Thomas L. Haskell in his book, *The Emergence of Professional Social Science: The American Social Science Association and the Nineteenth-Century Crisis of Authority* (Urbana: University of Illinois Press, 1977).

48. Lester Frank Ward, *Dynamic Sociology,* Vol. I (New York: Johnson Reprint, 1968; published originally by D. Appleton, 1883), p. 14.

49. Richard Hofstadter, *Social Darwinism in American Thought* (Boston: Beacon Press, 1955).

50. Mary Furner, *Advocacy and Objectivity: A Crisis in the Professionaliza-*

tion of American Social Science, 1865–1905 (Lexington: University Press of Kentucky, 1975).

51. C. R. Henderson, "Business Men and Social Theorists," *American Journal of Sociology* 1 (Jan. 1896): 390.

52. For an interesting exploration of this theme see John Rutherford Everett, *Religion in Economics: A Study of John Bates Clark, Richard T. Ely, Simon N. Patten* (Morningside Heights, N.Y.: King's Crown Press, 1946). In *American Sociology: Worldly Rejections of Religion and Their Direction* (New Haven, Conn.: Yale University Press, 1985), Arthur J. Vidich and Stanford M. Lyman emphasize the heavily Christian orientation of American sociology at the turn of the century.

53. Richard T. Ely, *Social Aspects of Christianity, and Other Essays* (New York: Thomas Y. Crowell, 1889), p. 57.

54. Ibid., pp. 20–21.

55. Ibid., p. 53, 6, and 73.

56. Richard T. Ely, *The Social Law of Service* (New York: Eaton and Mains, 1896), pp. 58 and 128.

57. Richard T. Ely, *Ground Under Our Feet: An Autobiography* (New York: Macmillan, 1938), p. 136.

58. Ely, *Social Law of Service*, p. 181.

59. For examples see Thelen, *The New Citizenship*, and Steven L. Piott, *The Anti-Monopoly Persuasion: Popular Resistance to the Rise of Big Business in the Midwest* (Westport, Conn.: Greenwood, 1985).

60. Hopkins, *The Rise of the Social Gospel*, p. 121.

61. Paul Boyer, *Urban Masses and Moral Order in America, 1820–1920* (Cambridge, Mass.: Harvard University Press, 1978), p. 122.

62. David P. Thelen, *Robert M. LaFollette and the Insurgent Spirit* (Boston: Little, Brown, 1976), p. 25.

63. Lincoln Steffens, *The Autobiography of Lincoln Steffens* (New York: Harcourt, Brace, 1931), p. 215.

64. Charles Parkhurst, *Our Fight with Tammany* (New York: Charles Scribner's Sons, 1895), pp. 131 and 20.

65. James B. Crooks, *Politics and Progress: The Rise of Urban Progressivism in Baltimore, 1895–1911* (Baton Rouge: Louisiana State University Press, 1968), and Ross E. Paulson, *Radicalism and Reform: The Vrooman Family and American Social Thought, 1837–1937* (Lexington: University Press of Kentucky, 1968).

66. Richard L. McCormick, *From Realignment to Reform: Political Change in New York State, 1893–1910* (Ithaca, N.Y.: Cornell University Press, 1981), pp. 60–61.

67. For a strong defense of municipal government in the late nineteenth century, see Jon C. Teaford, *The Unheralded Triumph: City Government in America, 1870-1900* (Baltimore: Johns Hopkins University Press, 1984).

68. Boyer, *Urban Masses and Moral Order*, p. 169.

69. For an exploration of attitudes and relationships within the municipal reform coalition in Chicago see David Paul Nord, "The Paradox of Municipal Reform in the Nineteenth Century," *Wisconsin Magazine of History* 66 (Winter 1982-1983): 128-142.

70. Judd Kahn, *Imperial San Francisco: Politics and Planning in an American City, 1897-1906* (Lincoln: University of Nebraska Press, 1979).

71. Jacob Riis, *How the Other Half Lives: Studies Among the Tenements of New York* (New York: Hill and Wang, 1957), p. 207.

72. B. O. Flower, *Civilization's Inferno: Or, Studies in the Social Cellar* (Boston: Arena, 1893), pp. 28 and 213.

73. For the Salvation Army see Herbert A. Wisbey Jr., *Soldiers Without Swords: A History of the Salvation Army in the United States* (New York: Macmillan, 1956), and Norris Magnuson, *Salvation in the Slums: Evangelical Social Work, 1865-1920* (Metuchen, N.J.: Scarecrow, 1977).

74. Vida D. Scudder, *On Journey* (New York: E. P. Dutton, 1937), p. 84.

75. For Jane Addams and the social settlement movement see, especially, Christopher Lasch, *The New Radicalism in America, 1889-1963: The Intellectual as a Social Type* (New York: Vintage, 1965), Allen F. Davis, *Spearheads for Reform: The Social Settlements and the Progressive Movement, 1890-1914* (New York: Oxford University Press, 1967) and *American Heroine: The Life and Legend of Jane Addams* (New York: Oxford University Press, 1973), and Daniel Levine, *Jane Addams and the Liberal Tradition* (Madison: Historical Society of Wisconsin, 1971).

76. Jane Addams, *Twenty Years at Hull-House* (New York: Macmillan, 1912), p. 122.

77. Davis, *Spearheads for Reform*, p. 27.

78. Melvin G. Holli, *Reform in Detroit: Hazen S. Pingree and Urban Politics* (New York: Oxford University Press, 1969).

79. Frederic C. Howe, *The Confessions of a Reformer* (Chicago: Quadrangle, 1967).

80. Samuel M. Jones' welfare capitalist activities are detailed in his *Letters of Love and Labor: A Series of Weekly Letters Addressed and Delivered to the Working-Men of the Acme Sucker Rod Company, Toledo, Ohio, During the Summer and Fall of 1901*, Vol. II (Toledo, Ohio: Franklin Printing and Engraving, 1901).

81. Samuel M. Jones, *The New Right: A Plea for Fair Play Through a More*

Just Social Order (New York: Eastern Book Concern, 1899), pp. 478, 407–408, 231, and 240.

82. Ibid., pp. 58 and 246.

83. Albert Bushnell Hart, "Are Our Moral Standards Shifting?," *The Forum* 18 (Jan. 1895): 514.

84. "1903," *The Independent* 55 (Jan. 1, 1903): 53.

85. Anthony F. C. Wallace, "Revitalization Movements," *American Anthropologist* 58 (1956): 265.

86. Josiah Strong, *Religious Movements for Social Betterment* (New York: Baker and Taylor, 1900), pp. 12–13.

87. Washington Gladden, *The Christian Pastor and the Working Church* (New York: Charles Scribner's Sons, 1898), p. 48. William G. McLoughlin applies Wallace's revitalization concept to the Social Gospel movement in his *Revivals, Awakenings, and Reform: An Essay on Religion and Social Change in America, 1607–1977* (Chicago: University of Chicago Press, 1978).

88. L. G. Powers, "Modern Social Reform and Old Christian Ideals," *Yale Review* 6 (Feb. 1898): 430.

89. Francis Greenwood Peabody, *Jesus Christ and the Social Question: An Examination of the Teaching of Jesus in Its Relation to Some of the Problems of Modern Social Life* (New York: Grosset and Dunlap, 1900), p. 9.

90. B. O. Flower, "Laying the Foundations for a Higher Civilization: A Survey and a Forecast," *The Arena* 25 (Feb. 1901): 180.

3

1. Frederic C. Howe, *The Confessions of a Reformer* (Chicago: Quadrangle, 1967), p. 17.

2. Early interpreters who lambasted progressives for their moralism include John Chamberlain, *Farewell to Reform, Being a History of the Rise, Life and Decay of the Progressive Mind in America* (New York: Liveright, 1932), and Richard Hofstadter, *The Age of Reform: From Bryan to F.D.R.* (New York: Knopf, 1955). John Whiteclay Chambers II, *The Tyranny of Change: America in the Progressive Era, 1900–1917* (New York: St. Martin's, 1980), and William L. O'Neill, *The Progressive Years: America Comes of Age* (New York: Dodd, Mead, 1975), apply the modernization thesis to the progressives.

3. Paul Boyer, *Urban Masses and Moral Order in America, 1820–1920* (Cambridge, Mass.: Harvard University Press, 1978), p. 196.

4. William Allen White, "The Golden Rule," *Atlantic Monthly* 96 (Oct. 1905): 441.

5. Arthur S. Link and Richard L. McCormick, *Progressivism* (Arlington Heights, Ill.: Harlan Davidson, 1983), pp. 8–9.

6. Jane Addams, *Democracy and Social Ethics* (Cambridge, Mass.: Harvard University Press, 1964; published originally by Macmillan, 1902), p. 4.

7. Robert M. Crunden, *Progressivism* (Cambridge, Mass.: Schenkman, 1977), p. 75.

8. Robert M. Crunden, *Ministers of Reform: The Progressives' Achievement in American Civilization, 1889–1920* (New York: Basic Books, 1982), p. ix.

9. Arthur Twining Hadley, *Standards of Public Morality* (New York: Macmillan, 1907), p. 13.

10. Charles Williams, "The Final Test of Christianity," *McClure's Magazine* 26 (Dec. 1905): 223 and 225.

11. Washington Gladden, *Recollections* (Boston: Houghton Mifflin, 1909), p. 313.

12. Jane Addams, *Newer Ideals of Peace* (New York: Macmillan, 1911), p. 138.

13. White, "The Golden Rule," p. 443.

14. Ferenc M. Szasz, "The Stress on 'Character and Service' in Progressive America," *Mid-America* 63 (1981): 145–156.

15. Editorial, "Morality, Half and Whole," *The Outlook* 79 (April 1, 1905): 775.

16. Walter Rauschenbusch, *Christianity and the Social Crisis* (New York: Macmillan, 1907), p. 65.

17. Lincoln Steffens, *The Shame of the Cities* (New York: Peter Smith, 1948; published originally by McClure, Phillips, 1904), p. 3.

18. J. Allen Smith, *The Spirit of American Government* (Cambridge, Mass.: Harvard University Press, 1965; published originally by Macmillan, 1907), p. 363.

19. Steffens, *The Shame of the Cities*, p. 10.

20. Fremont Older, *My Own Story* (Oakland, Calif.: Post-Enquirer, 1925), p. 96.

21. LeRoy Ashby, *Saving the Waifs: Reformers and Dependent Children, 1890–1917* (Philadelphia: Temple University Press, 1984).

22. Samuel Zane Batten, *The Christian State: The State, Democracy and Christianity* (Philadelphia: Griffith and Rowland, 1909), p. 381.

23. Ross E. Paulson, *Radicalism and Reform: The Vrooman Family and American Social Thought, 1837–1937* (Lexington: University Press of Kentucky, 1968), pp. 77–78.

24. Charles Zahniser, *Social Christianity: The Gospel for an Age of Social Strain* (Nashville: Advance, 1911), p. 106.

25. Jane Addams, *Twenty Years at Hull-House* (New York: Macmillan, 1912), p. 139.

26. Rauschenbusch, *Christianity and the Social Crisis*, p. 351.

27. Crunden, *Ministers of Reform*, p. 165.

28. Philip Loring Allen, "The Moral Wave and the Average Man," *The Outlook* 83 (Aug. 11, 1906): 839.

29. Rauschenbusch, *Christianity and the Social Crisis*, pp. 376–377.

30. Franklin Spencer Edmonds, "Some Social Effects of a Reform Movement," *Annals of the American Academy of Political and Social Science* 28 (Nov. 1906): 52.

31. Washington Gladden, *The Church and Modern Life* (Boston: Houghton Mifflin, 1908), p. 150.

32. Walter Rauschenbusch, *Christianizing the Social Order* (New York: Macmillan, 1912), p. 313.

33. Rauschenbusch, *Christianity and the Social Crisis*, p. 315.

34. Ida M. Tarbell, *All in the Day's Work: An Autobiography* (New York: Macmillan, 1939), p. 26.

35. Frank Parsons, *The City for the People: Or, The Municipalization of the City Government and of Local Franchises* (Philadelphia: C. F. Taylor, 1901), p. 99.

36. Robert M. LaFollette, *LaFollette's Autobiography: A Personal Narrative of Political Experiences* (Madison, Wisc.: LaFollette, 1913), pp. 352–353.

37. William Jackson Armstrong, "Political Economy and Present-Day Civilization: A Criticism," *The Arena* 38 (Nov. 1907): 495.

38. Rauschenbusch, *Christianity and the Social Crisis*, p. 265.

39. Otis Kendall Stuart, "Business Honesty and—Honesty," *The Independent* 55 (March 19, 1903): 677.

40. Editorial, "The Economic Restraints of Religion," *The Independent* 54 (Oct. 16, 1902): 2490.

41. Florence Kelley, *Modern Industry in Relation to the Family, Health Education, Morality* (New York: Longmans, Green, 1914), p. 128.

42. Chauncey Brewster, *The Kingdom of God and American Life* (New York: Thomas Whittaker, 1912), p. 135.

43. Frank D. Bentley, "Survival of the Fittest in the Coming Age," *The Arena* 27 (March 1902): 252.

44. Charles D. Williams, *A Valid Christianity for To-Day* (New York: Macmillan, 1909), p. 11.

45. Robert Wiebe, *Businessmen and Reform: A Study of the Progressive Movement* (Cambridge, Mass.: Harvard University Press, 1962), p. 9.

46. Robert M. Crunden, "George D. Herron in the 1890's: A New Frame of

Reference for the Study of the Progressive Era," *Annals of Iowa* 42 (Fall 1973): 112.

47. Editorial, "Some Things Gained," *The Outlook* 83 (May 26, 1906): 152.

48. Roy Lubove, *The Progressives and the Slums: Tenement House Reform in New York City, 1890-1917* (Pittsburgh: University of Pittsburgh Press, 1962), p. 207. For the National Consumers' League as a social feminist organization see William L. O'Neill, *Everyone Was Brave: A History of Feminism in America* (Chicago: Quadrangle, 1971).

49. Kelley, *Modern Industry*, p. 132.

50. Charles N. Glaab, "John Burke and the Progressive Revolt," in Thomas W. Howard, ed., *The North Dakota Political Tradition* (Ames: Iowa State University Press, 1981), p. 63.

51. Roland G. Usher, "The Ethics of Business," *Atlantic Monthly* 110 (Oct. 1912): 453-454.

52. George W. Alger, *Moral Overstrain* (Boston: Houghton, Mifflin, 1906), p. 18.

53. See, for example, Samuel P. Hays, *Conservation and the Gospel of Efficiency: The Progressive Conservation Movement, 1890-1920* (Cambridge, Mass.: Harvard University Press, 1959), and Wiebe, *Businessmen and Reform.*

54. Gabriel Kolko, *The Triumph of Conservatism: A Reinterpretation of American History, 1900-1920* (Chicago: Quadrangle, 1967). See also James Weinstein, *The Corporate Ideal in the Liberal State, 1900-1918* (Boston: Beacon Press, 1968).

55. Frederic C. Howe, *The City: The Hope of Democracy* (Seattle: University of Washington Press, 1967; published originally by Charles Scribner's Sons, 1905), p. 30.

56. Parsons, *The City for the People*, p. 172.

57. Daniel Levine, *Jane Addams and the Liberal Tradition* (Madison: Historical Society of Wisconsin, 1971), p. 128.

58. Robert Hunter, *Poverty* (New York: Macmillan, 1904), p. 63.

59. Ibid., pp. 63-64.

60. Ben B. Lindsey and Rube Borough, *The Dangerous Life* (New York: Liveright, 1931), pp. 102 and 188.

61. Boyer, *Urban Masses and Moral Order*, p. 224.

62. Delos F. Wilcox, *The American City: A Problem in Democracy* (New York: Macmillan, 1911), pp. 140 and 170.

63. Jean B. Quandt, *From the Small Town to the Great Community: The Social Thought of Progressive Intellectuals* (New Brunswick, N.J.: Rutgers University Press, 1970).

64. John F. McClymer, *War and Welfare: Social Engineering in America,*

1890-1925 (Westport, Conn.: Greenwood, 1980), p. 16.

65. Don S. Kirschner, "The Ambiguous Legacy: Social Justice and Social Control in the Progressive Era," *Historical Reflections* 2 (Summer 1975): 69–88.

66. Howe, *The City: Hope of Democracy*, p. 45.

67. Brand Whitlock, "The City and Civilization," *Scribner's Magazine* 52 (Nov. 1912): 633, and *Forty Years of It* (New York: D. Appleton, 1925), p. 205. For Whitlock's inspirational vision see also Shirley Leckie, "Brand Whitlock and the City Beautiful Movement in Toledo, Ohio," *Ohio History* 91 (1982): 5–36.

68. Edward W. Bemis, "Public Service," in *Morals in Modern Business: Addresses Delivered in the Page Lecture Series, 1908, Before the Senior Class of the Sheffield Scientific School, Yale University* (New Haven, Conn.: Yale University Press, 1909), p. 106.

69. Daniel Aaron, *Men of Good Hope: A Story of American Progressives* (New York: Oxford University Press, 1961).

70. Prestonia Martin, *Is Mankind Advancing?: The Most Important Question in the World* (New York: Baker and Taylor, 1910).

71. Guglielmo Ferrero, *Ancient Rome and Modern America: A Comparative Study of Morals and Manners* (New York: G. P. Putnam's Sons, 1914).

72. Dana W. Bartlett, *The Better City: A Sociological Study of a Modern City* (Los Angeles: Neuner, 1907), p. 171.

73. Scott Nearing, *Social Religion: An Interpretation of Christianity in Terms of Modern Life* (New York: Macmillan, 1903), p. xvi.

74. Rauschenbusch, *Christianizing the Social Order*, p. 7.

75. William Dean Howells, "Editor's Study," *Harper's Monthly Magazine* 126 (Feb. 1913): 478.

76. John Graham Brooks, "Signs of Progress," *The Chautauquan* 50 (May 1908): 354.

77. Editorial, "The Problem of Modern Barbarism," *The Independent* 55 (June 25, 1903): 1524–1525.

78. Smith, *The Spirit of American Government*, p. 363.

79. Editorial, "Is It Not a Moral Awakening?," *World's Work* 22 (July 1911): 14554.

80. Thorstein Veblen, "Christian Morals and the Competitive System," *International Journal of Ethics* 20 (Jan. 1910): 185.

81. Clyde Griffen, "The Progressive Ethos," in Stanley Coben and Lorman Ratner, eds., *The Development of an American Culture* (Englewood Cliffs, N.J.: Prentice-Hall, 1970), p. 149.

82. Ferenc M. Szasz, "The Progressive Clergy and the Kingdom of God," *Mid-America* 55 (1973): 18.

83. Edgar Kemler, *The Deflation of American Ideals: An Ethical Guide for New Dealers* (Seattle: University of Washington Press, 1941), p. 122.

84. White, "The Golden Rule," 441.

4

1. John Dewey and James Hayden Tufts, *Ethics* (New York: Henry Holt, 1908), p. 334.

2. Walter Lippmann, *A Preface to Politics* (New York: Mitchell Kennerley, 1913), p. 108.

3. Newton Marshall Hall, *Civic Righteousness and Civic Pride* (Boston: Sherman, French, 1914), p. 43.

4. Frederick A. Bushee, "Science and Social Progress," *Popular Science Monthly* 79 (Sept. 1911): 251.

5. Charles E. Rosenberg, *No Other Gods: On Science and American Social Thought* (Baltimore: Johns Hopkins University Press, 1976), p. 3.

6. For the compulsive altruism of the Victorian value system see Robert M. Crunden, *Ministers of Reform: The Progressives' Achievement in American Civilization, 1889–1920* (New York: Basic Books, 1982). Arthur S. Link and Richard L. McCormick emphasize the complementary nature of Christian and scientific progressivism in practice in *Progressivism* (Arlington Heights, Ill.: Harlan Davidson, 1983). For the smooth transition from the Christian to the scientific point of view in one discipline see Arthur J. Vidich and Stanford M. Lyman, *American Sociology: Worldly Rejections of Religion and Their Direction* (New Haven, Conn.: Yale University Press, 1985).

7. United States Senate, *Industrial Relations: Final Report and Testimony Submitted to Congress by the Commission on Industrial Relations, Created by the Act of August 23, 1912*, 64th Congress, 1st Session, Document no. 415 (Washington, D.C.: Government Printing Office, 1916), Vol. 4, p. 3330.

8. Herbert Croly, *The Promise of American Life* (New York: E. P. Dutton, 1963; published originally by Macmillan, 1909), p. 106.

9. Walter Lippmann, *Drift and Mastery: An Attempt to Diagnose the Current Unrest* (Englewood Cliffs, N.J.: Prentice-Hall, 1961; published originally by Mitchell Kennerley, 1914), p. 116.

10. Edward Alsworth Ross, *Social Control: A Survey of the Foundations of Order* (New York: Macmillan, 1901), p. 87.

11. Charles Horton Cooley, *Human Nature and the Social Order* (New York: Charles Scribner's Sons, 1902), pp. 1 and 392–393.

12. Ibid., p. 12.

13. Edward Alsworth Ross, *Sin and Society: An Analysis of Latter-Day Inequity* (Boston: Houghton Mifflin, 1907), p. 51.

14. Albion Small, "The Evolution of a Social Standard," *American Journal of Sociology* 20 (July 1914): 15.

15. Croly, *The Promise of American Life*, p. 139.

16. Ross, *Sin and Society*, p. 75.

17. Ibid., p. 141.

18. Frank B. Vrooman, *The New Politics* (New York: Oxford University Press, 1911), p. 172.

19. Ibid., p. 272.

20. Samuel P. Hays, *Conservation and the Gospel of Efficiency: The Progressive Conservation Movement, 1890–1920* (Cambridge, Mass: Harvard University Press, 1959), and Samuel Haber, *Efficiency and Uplift: Scientific Management in the Progressive Era, 1890–1920* (Chicago: University of Chicago Press, 1964).

21. Haber, *Efficiency and Uplift*, p. 55.

22. David Starr Jordan, "Unrest and Progress," *The Independent* 72 (Aug. 8, 1912): 312.

23. Edward W. Bemis, "Public Service," in *Morals in Modern Business: Addresses Delivered in the Page Lecture Series, 1908, Before the Senior Class of the Sheffield Scientific School, Yale University* (New Haven, Conn.: Yale University Press, 1909), p. 126.

24. Simon N. Patten Jr., "Is Christianity Ethics or Religion?," *The Independent* 70 (March 30, 1911): 656.

25. Jordan, "Unrest and Progress," p. 314.

26. James B. Gilbert, *Work Without Salvation: America's Intellectuals and Industrial Alienation, 1880–1910* (Baltimore: Johns Hopkins University Press, 1977), pp. 149 and 155.

27. See David B. Danbom, *The Resisted Revolution: Urban America and the Industrialization of Agriculture, 1900–1930* (Ames: Iowa State University Press, 1979).

28. For the eugenics movement see Donald K. Pickens, *Eugenics and the Progressives* (Nashville: Vanderbilt University Press, 1968), and Hamilton Cravens, *The Triumph of Evolution: American Scientists and the Heredity-Environment Controversy, 1900–1941* (Philadelphia: University of Pennsylvania Press, 1978).

29. Judith A. Merkle, *Management and Ideology: The Legacy of the International Scientific Management Movement* (Berkeley: University of California Press, 1980), p. 40.

30. Edwin T. Layton Jr., *The Revolt of the Engineers: Social Responsibility and the American Engineering Profession* (Cleveland: Case Western Reserve University, 1971), p. viii, and Haber, *Efficiency and Uplift*, p. 28.

31. Louis D. Brandeis, *Business — A Profession* (Boston: Small, Maynard, 1914), pp. 2–3.

32. George S. Morison, *The New Epoch: As Developed by the Manufacture of Power* (New York: Arno, 1972; published originally by Houghton Mifflin, 1912), p. 43.

33. For manager's views of the manipulative potential of scientific management see Harry Braverman, *Labor and Monopoly Capital: The Degradation of Work in the Twentieth Century* (New York: Monthly Review, 1974), and David Montgomery, *Workers' Control in America: Studies in the History of Work, Technology, and Labor Struggles* (Cambridge, Eng.: Cambridge University Press, 1979).

34. U.S. Senate, *Industrial Relations*, Vol. 3, p. 2682.

35. Reinhard Bendix, *Work and Authority in Industry: Ideologies of Management in the Course of Industrialization* (New York: Wiley and Sons, 1956), p. 279.

36. David F. Noble, *America by Design: Science, Technology, and the Rise of Corporate Capitalism* (New York: Knopf, 1979), p. 264.

37. Ibid., p. 292.

38. Lippmann, *Preface to Politics*, p. 155.

39. U.S. Senate, *Industrial Relations*, Vol. 1, pp. 1008–1009, and Edward M. House, *Philip Dru, Administrator: A Story of Tomorrow, 1920–1935* (New York: B. W. Huebsch, 1912), pp. 57–58.

40. Morison, *The New Epoch*, p. 3, and Walter Weyl, *The New Democracy: An Essay on Certain Political and Economic Tendencies in the United States* (New York: Macmillan, 1912), p. 191.

41. See T. J. Jackson Lears, "From Salvation to Self-Realization: Advertising and the Therapeutic Roots of the Consumer Culture, 1880–1930," in Richard Wightman Fox and T. J. Jackson Lears, eds., *The Culture of Consumption: Critical Essays in American History, 1880–1980* (New York: Pantheon, 1983).

42. Simon N. Patten, *The New Basis of Civilization*, ed. Daniel M. Fox (Cambridge, Mass.: Belknap Press of Harvard University, 1968; published originally by Macmillan, 1907), p. 186.

43. Daniel M. Fox, *The Discovery of Abundance: Simon N. Patten and the Transformation of Social Theory* (Ithaca, N.Y.: Cornell University Press, 1967), p. 51.

44. Simon N. Patten, *The Theory of Social Forces*, Supplement to the *Annals of the American Academy of Political and Social Science* (Philadelphia: American Academy of Political and Social Science, 1896), p. 84.

45. Simon N. Patten, *The Social Basis of Religion* (New York: Macmillan, 1911).

46. Fox, *The Discovery of Abundance*, p. 64.

47. Daniel Nelson, *Frederick W. Taylor and the Rise of Scientific Management* (Madison: University of Wisconsin Press, 1980), p. 168.

48. Layton, *The Revolt of the Engineers*, p. 66.

49. Noble, *America by Design*, pp. xxii-xxiii.

50. Margaret W. Rossiter, "The Organization of the Agricultural Sciences," in Alexandra Oleson and John Voss, eds., *The Organization of Knowledge in Modern America, 1860–1920* (Baltimore: Johns Hopkins University Press, 1979), p. 241. For an extended discussion of scientific progressivism and agriculture see Danbom, *The Resisted Revolution*.

51. Dwight Waldo, *The Administrative State: A Study of the Political Theory of American Public Administration* (New York: Ronald Press, 1948), p. 32.

52. Richard L. Watson Jr., *The Development of National Power: The United States, 1900–1919* (Boston: Houghton Mifflin, 1976), p. 69.

53. Bradley Robert Rice, *Progressive Cities: The Commission Government Movement in America, 1901–1920* (Austin: University of Texas Press, 1977), p. xi.

54. Samuel P. Hays highlights, and overemphasizes, business involvement in municipal reform in his article "The Politics of Reform in Municipal Government in the Progressive Era," *Pacific Northwest Quarterly* 55 (Oct. 1964): 157–169. See also Martin J. Schiesl, *The Politics of Efficiency: Municipal Administration and Reform in America, 1800–1920* (Berkeley: University of California Press, 1977).

55. John R. Commons, *Myself: The Autobiography of John R. Commons* (Madison: University of Wisconsin Press, 1964; published originally by Macmillan, 1934), p. 152.

56. Hall, *Civic Righteousness and Civic Pride*, p. 57.

57. Louis Filler, *Appointment at Armageddon: Muckraking and Progressivism in the American Tradition* (Westport, Conn.: Greenwood, 1976), p. 355.

58. Haber, *Efficiency and Uplift*, pp. 54–55.

59. William Graebner, *Coal-Mining Safety in the Progressive Period: The*

Political Economy of Reform (Lexington: University Press of Kentucky, 1976),
p. 163.

60. Weyl, *The New Democracy*, pp. 276 and 279.

61. Lippmann, *Drift and Mastery*, pp. 148.

62. Edward Alsworth Ross, "The Rules of the Game," *Atlantic Monthly*
100 (Sept. 1907): 326.

63. Croly, *The Promise of American Life*, p. 400.

64. Vrooman, *The New Politics*, p. 165.

65. Lippmann, *Preface to Politics*, p. 51.

66. Croly, *The Promise of American Life*, p. 178.

67. Morton White, *Social Thought in America: The Revolt Against Formalism*
(Boston: Beacon Press, 1957).

68. David Hollinger, "The Problem of Pragmatism in American History,"
Journal of American History 67 (June 1980): 105.

69. Franklin H. Giddings, "The Greatest Reformative Period in the History
of the World," *Munsey's Magazine* 38 (Nov. 1907): 177.

70. Lippmann, *Preface to Politics*, pp. 31–32.

71. Ibid., p. 200.

72. Ibid., p. 225.

73. Tufts, *Ethics*, p. 186.

74. Lippmann, *Preface to Politics*, pp. 120–121.

75. See, for example, David W. Noble, *The Paradox of Progressive Thought*
(Minneapolis: University of Minnesota Press, 1958), and David Marcell,
*Progress and Pragmatism: James, Dewey, Beard, and the American Idea of Prog-
ress* (Westport, Conn.: Greenwood, 1974).

76. Lippmann, *Drift and Mastery*, p. 155.

77. Benjamin Parke DeWitt, *The Progressive Movement: A Non-partisan,
Comprehensive Discussion of Current Tendencies in American Politics* (Seattle:
University of Washington Press, 1968; published originally by Macmillan,
1915), p. 320.

78. Steven Diner, *A City and Its Universities: Public Policy in Chicago,
1892–1919* (Chapel Hill: University of North Carolina Press, 1980), p. 153.

79. Schiesl, *The Politics of Efficiency*, p. 131.

80. See Herbert Croly, *Progressive Democracy* (New York: Macmillan, 1914).

81. DeWitt, *The Progressive Movement*, p. 338.

82. Editorial, "The Reformer," *New Republic* 1 (Dec. 12, 1914): 8–9.

83. James A. Nuechterlein, "The Dream of Scientific Liberalism: The *New
Republic* and American Progressive Thought, 1914–1920," *Review of Politics*
42 (April 1980): 169.

84. Clyde Griffen, "The Progressive Ethos," in Stanley Coben and Lorman Ratner, eds., *The Development of an American Culture* (Englewood Cliffs, N.J.: Prentice-Hall, 1970), p. 140. See also Vidich and Lyman, *American Sociology*.

85. E. D. H. Klyce, "Scientific Management and the Moral Law," *The Outlook* 99 (Nov. 18, 1911): 663. James H. Moorhead argues in "The Erosion of Postmillennialism in American Religious Thought, 1865–1925," *Church History* 53 (March 1984): 61–77, that even conservative churches adopted new administrative techniques and strove for organizational efficiency in the early years of the century.

86. William H. Allen, *Efficient Democracy* (New York: Dodd, Mead, 1907), p. 5.

87. O. W. Firkins, "The Cult of the Passing Hour," *Atlantic Monthly* 113 (May 1914): 664.

5

1. Mary Kingsbury Simkhovitch, *The City Worker's World in America* (New York: Arno and the New York Times, 1971; published originally by Macmillan, 1917), pp. 43–44.

2. Dana Bartlett, *The Better Country* (Boston: C. M. Clark, 1911), p. 501.

3. Editorial, "Have We Advanced?," *Scientific American* 114 (Feb. 19, 1916): 192.

4. Editorial, "Happy New Year!," *The Outlook* 105 (Dec. 27, 1913): 873.

5. David W. Levy, *Herbert Croly of the New Republic: The Life and Thought of an American Progressive* (Princeton, N.J.: Princeton University Press, 1985), p. 160.

6. Gerald Stanley Lee, *Inspired Millionaires: A Forecast* (Garden City: Doubleday, Page, 1914; published originally by Mount Tom Press, 1908), pp. 294–295.

7. Editorial, "The Year and the Years," *The Outlook* 99 (Dec. 30, 1911): 1040.

8. Gilbert Holland Montague, "The Ethics of Trust Competition," *Atlantic Monthly* 95 (March 1905): 414.

9. Roland G. Usher, "The Ethics of Business," *Atlantic Monthly* 110 (Oct. 1912): 447.

10. Saul Engelbourg, *Power and Morality: American Business Ethics, 1840–1914* (Westport, Conn.: Greenwood, 1980), p. xii.

11. Edward D. Page, "The Morals of Trade in the Making," in *Morals in*

Modern Business: Addresses Delivered in the Page Lecture Series, 1908, Before the Senior Class of the Sheffield Scientific School, Yale University (New Haven, Conn.: Yale University Press, 1909), pp. 8–9 and 11.

12. Walter Lippmann, *Drift and Mastery: An Attempt to Diagnose the Current Unrest* (Englewood Cliffs, N.J.: Prentice-Hall, 1961; published originally by Mitchell Kennerley, 1914), p. 36.

13. Louis Brandeis, *Business — A Profession* (Boston: Small, Maynard, 1914), p. 2–3.

14. Walter Lippmann, *A Preface to Politics* (New York: Mitchell Kennerley, 1913), p. 57.

15. Brandeis, *Business — A Profession*, p. 321.

16. Henry Holt, "Competition," in *Morals in Modern Business*, p. 68.

17. Ibid., p. 68.

18. Lee, *Inspired Millionaires*, p. 303.

19. Ibid., p. 301.

20. Editorial, "Ethics in the Air," *Century Magazine* 71 (Dec. 1905): 329.

21. Author unknown, "Prosperity and Business Morals," *World's Work* 12 (July 1906): 7777.

22. John Graham Brooks, *An American Citizen: The Life of William Henry Baldwin, Jr.* (Boston: Houghton Mifflin, 1910), p. 112.

23. Morrell Heald, *The Social Responsibilities of Business: Company and Community, 1900–1960* (Cleveland: Case Western Reserve University Press, 1970), p. 33.

24. Melvin I. Urofsky, *Big Steel and the Wilson Administration: A Study in Business-Government Relations* (Columbus: Ohio State University Press, 1969), p. 2.

25. United States Senate, *Industrial Relations: Final Report and Testimony Submitted to Congress by the Commission on Industrial Relations, Created by the Act of August 23, 1912*, 64th Congress, 1st Session, Document no. 415 (Washington, D.C.: Government Printing Office, 1916), Vol. 8, pp. 7598–7599.

26. James Weinstein, *The Corporate Ideal in the Liberal State, 1900–1918* (Boston: Beacon Press, 1968), p. x.

27. George W. Perkins, "Business: The Moral Question," *World's Work* 2 (June 1911): 14470.

28. Stuart D. Brandes, *American Welfare Capitalism, 1880–1940* (Chicago: University of Chicago Press, 1976), pp. 5–6.

29. Gerald G. Eggert, *Steelmasters and Labor Reform, 1886–1923* (Pittsburgh: University of Pittsburgh Press, 1981), p. xiv.

30. Gerd Korman, *Industrialization, Immigrants and Americanizers: The View From Milwaukee, 1866–1921* (Madison: Historical Society of Wisconsin, 1967), p. 83.

31. J. A. Biddle, "The New Business Conscience," *The Outlook* 97 (Jan. 21, 1911): 133.

32. Interview, "The Awakening Conscience in the Business World as Viewed by the New Secretary of Commerce," *Current Opinion* 54 (May 1913): 399.

33. Graham Taylor, "Socializing Commercial Ethics," *The Survey* 25 (Jan. 14, 1911): 640–641, and Gerald Stanley Lee, "Advertising Goodness," *Everybody's Magazine* 28 (Feb. 1913): 151.

34. See, for example, Charles Edward Jefferson, "The Christian in Business," *Woman's Home Champion* 44 (April 1917): 14, and George H. Cushing, "The Dollar Value of Moral Fiber in Business," *Illustrated World* 27 (April 1917): 203–208.

35. Lippmann, *Drift and Mastery*, pp. 43–44.

36. Ida M. Tarbell, *All in the Day's Work: An Autobiography* (New York: Macmillan, 1939), pp. 287–295. See also Lincoln Steffens, *The Autobiography of Lincoln Steffens* (New York: Harcourt, Brace, 1931), pp. 851–853.

37. Engelbourg, *Power and Morality*, p. 129.

38. Testimony of Thomas E. Donnelley in U.S. Senate, *Industrial Relations*, Vol. 4, pp. 3430–3431.

39. U.S. Senate, *Industrial Relations*, Vol. 4, p. 3401.

40. Donnelley, in ibid., p. 3431.

41. Mansel G. Blackford, "Scientific Management and Welfare Work in Early Twentieth Century American Business: The Buckeye Steel Castings Company," *Ohio History* 90 (1981): 252–253.

42. Brandeis, *Business — A Profession*, p. 11–12.

43. See, for example, Brooks Adams, *The Theory of Social Revolutions* (New York: Macmillan, 1913).

44. Engelbourg, *Power and Morality*, p. 130.

45. Richard Tedlow, *Keeping the Corporate Image: Public Relations and Business, 1900–1950* (Greenwich, Conn.: J.A.I. Press, 1979), p. xvi.

46. Ibid., p. 14.

47. Paul Kleppner, *The Cross of Culture: A Social Analysis of Midwestern Politics, 1850–1900* (New York: Free Press, 1970), Richard Jensen, *The Winning of the Midwest: Social and Political Conflict, 1888–1896* (Chicago: University of Chicago Press, 1971), Samuel T. McSeveney, *The Politics of Depression: Political Behavior in The Northeast, 1893–1896* (New York: Oxford University Press, 1972), Robert W. Cherny, *Populism, Progressivism, and*

the Transformation of Nebraska Politics, 1885–1915 (Lincoln: University of Nebraska Press, 1981), and Richard L. McCormick, *From Realignment to Reform: Political Change in New York State, 1893–1910* (Ithaca, N.Y.: Cornell University Press, 1981).

48. McCormick, *From Realignment to Reform*, pp. 151–152.

49. David P. Thelen, *Robert M. LaFollette and the Insurgent Spirit* (Boston: Little, Brown, 1976), p. 21.

50. George E. Mowry, *The California Progressives* (Chicago: Quadrangle, 1963), p. 101.

51. Henry L. Stimson and McGeorge Bundy, *On Active Service in Peace and War* (New York: Harper and Brothers, 1947), p. 81.

52. William Rainsford, *The Story of a Varied Life: An Autobiography* (Garden City: Doubleday, Page, 1922), p. 353.

53. Mowry, *The California Progressives*, p. 217.

54. Thelen, *Robert M. LaFollette*, p. 99.

55. John Whiteclay Chambers II, *The Tyranny of Change: America in the Progressive Era, 1900–1917* (New York: St. Martin's, 1980), p. 138.

56. William L. O'Neill, *Everyone Was Brave: A History of Feminism in America* (Chicago: Quadrangle, 1971), p. 126.

57. Otis L. Graham Jr., *An Encore for Reform: The Old Progressives and the New Deal* (New York: Oxford University Press, 1967), p. 38.

58. Albion W. Small, "The Evolution of a Social Standard," *American Journal of Sociology* 20 (July 1914): 14–15.

59. Herbert Croly, *Progressive Democracy* (New York: Macmillan, 1914), p. 199.

60. For the Pittsburgh Survey and its importance see Clarke A. Chambers, *Paul U. Kellogg and the Survey: Voices for Social Welfare and Social Justice* (Minneapolis: University of Minnesota Press, 1971). For an overview of rural social surveys see Hal S. Barron, "Rural Social Surveys," *Agricultural History* 58 (April 1984): 113–117.

61. Charles Ferguson, *The Religion of Democracy: A Manual of Devotion* (San Francisco: D. P. Elder and Morgan Shephard, 1900).

62. Charles Ferguson, *The Great News* (New York: Mitchell Kennerley, 1915), p. 23.

63. Ferguson, *The Religion of Democracy*, p. 19.

64. Ferguson, *The Great News*, p. 198.

65. F. Stuart Chapin, "Moral Progress," *Popular Science Monthly* 86 (May 1915): 470–471.

66. Madison Grant, *The Passing of the Great Race: Or, The Racial Basis of European History* (New York: Charles Scribner's Sons, 1916), p. 228.

67. David B. Danbom, *The Resisted Revolution: Urban America and the Industrialization of Agriculture, 1900–1930* (Ames: Iowa State University Press, 1979), pp. 75–96.

68. Shailer Mathews, *The Individual and the Social Gospel* (New York: Laymen's Missionary Movement, 1914), p. 78.

69. William O'Neill, *Divorce in the Progressive Era* (New Haven, Conn.: Yale University Press, 1967), p. 260.

70. In *Anti-intellectualism in American Life* (New York: Vintage, 1962), Richard Hofstadter argued that women were so closely identified with reform that it was stigmatized as a feminine activity. He believed this did not change until the aggressively masculine Theodore Roosevelt became identified with reform.

71. Mark Thomas Connelly, *The Response to Prostitution in the Progressive Era* (Chapel Hill: University of North Carolina Press, 1980), p. 88. See also Ruth Rosen, *The Lost Sisterhood: Prostitution in America, 1900–1918* (Baltimore: Johns Hopkins University Press, 1982).

72. See Richard Wightman Fox and T. J. Jackson Lears, eds., *The Culture of Consumption: Critical Essays in American History, 1880–1980* (New York: Pantheon, 1983).

73. William E. Carson, *The Marriage Revolt: A Study of Marriage and Divorce* (New York: Hearst's International·Library, 1915), pp. 461 and 86.

74. Ibid., p. 468.

75. Charlotte Perkins Gilman, *Women and Economics: A Study of the Economic Relation Between Men and Women as a Factor in Social Evolution*, ed. Carl N. Degler (New York: Harper and Row, 1966; published originally by Small, Maynard, 1898), and Olive Schreiner, *Woman and Labor* (New York: Frederick A. Stokes, 1911).

76. See Ellen Key, *The Century of the Child* (New York: G. P. Putnam's Sons, 1909).

77. David Kennedy, *Birth Control in America: The Career of Margaret Sanger* (New Haven, Conn.: Yale University Press, 1970), p. 69. See also Nathan G. Hale Jr.'s *Freud and the Americans: The Beginnings of Psychoanalysis in the United States, 1876–1917* (New York: Oxford University Press, 1971).

78. Paul Moore Strayer, *The Reconstruction of the Church: With Regard to Its Message and Program* (New York: Macmillan, 1915), pp. vii–viii.

79. James H. Leuba, *The Belief in God and Immortality: A Psychological, Anthropological and Statistical Study* (Boston: Sherman, French, 1916).

80. William G. McLoughlin, *Revivals, Awakenings, and Reform: An Essay on Religion and Social Change in America, 1607–1977* (Chicago: University of

Chicago Press, 1978), p. 156. See also Shailer Mathews, *New Faith for Old: An Autobiography* (New York: Macmillan, 1936), p. 102.

81. Bruce Barton, *A Young Man's Jesus* (Boston: Pilgrim Press, 1914).

82. Elwood Worcester, Samuel McComb, and Isador H. Coriat, *Religion and Medicine: The Moral Control of Nervous Disorders* (New York: Moffat, Yard, 1908), p. 7, and Elwood Worcester and Samuel McComb, *The Christian Religion as a Healing Power: A Defense and Exposition of the Emmanuel Movement* (New York: Moffat, Yard, 1909), p. 8.

83. Rainsford, *The Story of a Varied Life*, p. 376.

84. Mathews, *New Faith for Old*, p. 151.

85. Jacob Henry Dorn, *Washington Gladden: Prophet of the Social Gospel* (Columbus: Ohio State University Press, 1966), pp. 399–401.

86. See Ferenc Morton Szasz, *The Divided Mind of Protestant America, 1880–1930* (University: University of Alabama Press, 1982). For conservative Protestant involvement in the Social Gospel movement see Gary Scott Smith, "The Cross and the Social Order: Calvinist Strategies for Social Improvement, 1870–1920," *Fides et Historia* 17 (Fall–Winter 1984): 39–55.

6

1. Charles Edward Russell, *After the Whirlwind: A Book of Reconstruction and Profitable Thanksgiving* (New York: George H. Doran, 1919), pp. 268–269.

2. Stuart I. Rochester, *American Liberal Disillusionment in the Wake of World War I* (University Park: Pennsylvania State University Press, 1977), p. 102.

3. Lewis Mumford, *Faith for Living* (New York: Harcourt, Brace, 1940), p. 222.

4. Rochester, *American Liberal Disillusionment*, p. 103.

5. Herbert Hoover, *The Memoirs of Herbert Hoover: Years of Adventure, 1874–1920* (New York: Macmillan, 1951), p. 136.

6. Henry F. May, *The End of American Innocence: A Study of the First Years of Our Time, 1912–1917* (Chicago: Quadrangle, 1964), p. 361.

7. Franklin H. Giddings, "The Larger Meanings of the War," *The Survey* 33 (Nov. 7, 1914): 144.

8. Bradley A. Fiske, "The Mastery of the World," *North American Review* 202 (Oct. 1915): 523.

9. Charles A. Ellwood, "The Social Problem and the Present War," *American Journal of Sociology* 20 (Jan. 1915): 487.

10. Fiske, "The Mastery of the World," p. 525.

11. Paul Moore Strayer, *The Reconstruction of the Church: With Regard to Its Message and Program* (New York: Macmillan, 1915), p. xi.

12. Washington Gladden, "The Unescapable Law," *The Independent* 88 (Nov. 13, 1916): 279.

13. Joseph Alexander Leighton, "Culture, Ethics, and the War," *The Forum* 53 (March 1915): 346–347.

14. Ellwood, "The Social Problem and the Present War," p. 488.

15. Victor S. Yarros, "Human Progress: The Idea and the Reality," *American Journal of Sociology* 21 (July 1915): 17.

16. Robert L. Duffus, "Progress—1917," *New Republic* 11 (July 14, 1917): 298–299.

17. Editorial, "Does the War Disprove Progress?," *The Nation* 100 (June 17, 1915): 674.

18. W. W. Campbell, "Science and Civilization," *Science* N.S. 42 (Aug. 20, 1915): 228 and 237.

19. Robert Yerkes, "Progress and Peace," *Scientific Monthly* 1 (Nov. 1915): 196.

20. Yarros, "Human Progress," pp. 28–29.

21. Samuel McChord Crothers, "The Enlargement of the Family Ideal," *Proceedings of the National Conference of Charities and Corrections at the Forty-Second Annual Session Held in Baltimore, Maryland, May 12–19, 1915* (Chicago: Hildmann Printing, 1915), p. 38.

22. Rochester, *American Liberal Disillusionment*, p. 40.

23. Ellwood, "The Social Problem and the Present War," pp. 500–502.

24. David M. Kennedy, *Over Here: The First World War and American Society* (New York: Oxford University Press, 1980), p. 51.

25. Robert Moats Miller, *Harry Emerson Fosdick: Preacher, Pastor, Prophet* (New York: Oxford University Press, 1985), p. 79.

26. Stephen Vaughn, *Holding Fast the Inner Lines: Democracy, Nationalism, and the Committee on Public Information* (Chapel Hill: University of North Carolina Press, 1980), pp. 23–24.

27. David W. Noble, *The Paradox of Progressive Thought* (Minneapolis: University of Minnesota Press, 1958), p. 48.

28. Charles W. Wood, *The Great Change: New America as Seen by Leaders in American Government, Industry and Education Who Are Remaking Our Civilization* (New York: Boni and Liveright, 1918), pp. 155 and 212.

29. Mary Parker Follett, *The New State: Group Organization the Solution of*

Popular Government (New York: Longmans, Green, 1918), pp. 49, 67, and 333.

30. Robert R. Kern, "The Supervision of the Social Order," *American Journal of Sociology* 24 (Jan. 1919): 449.

31. David B. Danbom, *The Resisted Revolution: Urban America and the Industrialization of Agriculture, 1900–1930* (Ames: Iowa State University Press, 1979), pp. 97–119.

32. H. L. Gantt, *Organizing for Work* (New York: Harcourt, Brace and Howe, 1919), pp. 23, 24, 5, 15, and 108.

33. Algie M. Simons, *The Vision for Which We Fought: A Study in Reconstruction* (New York: Macmillan, 1919), p. 182.

34. Harold de Wolfe Fuller, "Has Civilization Failed?," *Weekly Review* 1 (July 5, 1919): 165.

35. Rochester, *American Liberal Disillusionment*, p. 52.

36. Harold Stearns, *Liberalism in America: Its Origin, Its Temporary Collapse, Its Future* (New York: Boni and Liveright, 1919), pp. 24, 180, and 146–147. For Randolph Bourne see Carl Resek, ed., *War and the Intellectuals: Essays by Randolph S. Bourne, 1915–1919* (New York: Harper and Row, 1964).

37. Christopher Lasch, *The American Liberals and the Russian Revolution* (New York: McGraw-Hill, 1972), p. vii.

38. Kennedy, *Over Here*, p. 90.

39. Noble, *Paradox of Progressive Thought*, p. 33.

40. Edgar Kemler, *The Deflation of American Ideals: An Ethical Guide for New Dealers* (Seattle: University of Washington Press, 1941), p. 9.

41. Sisley Huddleston, "The Menace of the World," *Atlantic Monthly* 125 (May 1920): 594.

42. Franklin H. Giddings, "The Supreme Menace," *The Independent* 101 (March 17, 1920): 470 and 472.

43. H. F. Wyatt, "The Race: Death or Life?," *Nineteenth Century* 138 (Nov. 1920): 866.

44. W. R. Inge, *The Idea of Progress* (Oxford: Clarendon Press, 1920), p. 32.

45. Sisley Huddleston, "The Human Spirit in Shadow," *Atlantic Monthly* 126 (Nov. 1920): 606.

46. Edwin E. Slosson, "This Changing World," *The Independent* 106 (Sept. 24, 1921): 139.

47. Inge, *The Idea of Progress*, pp. 22–23.

48. Wyatt, "The Race," p. 858.

49. A thoughtful exploration of the impact of the war on the churches is Reinhold Niebuhr's "What the War Did to My Mind," *Christian Century* 45 (Sept. 27, 1928): 1161–1163.

1. William Allen White, Preface, in Brand Whitlock, *Forty Years of It* (New York: D. Appleton, 1925), n.p.

2. Hoyt Landon Warner, *Progressivism in Ohio, 1897–1917* (Columbus: Ohio State University Press, 1964), p. 483.

3. George E. Mowry, *The California Progressives* (Chicago: Quadrangle, 1963), p. 300.

4. Lewis Mumford, *Faith for Living* (New York: Harcourt, Brace, 1940), p. 38.

5. Edgar Kemler, *The Deflation of American Ideals: An Ethical Guide for New Dealers* (Seattle: University of Washington Press, 1941), p. 7.

6. Arthur S. Link, "What Happened to the Progressive Movement in the 1920's?," *American Historical Review* 64 (1959): 833–851; Joan Hoff Wilson, *Herbert Hoover: Forgotten Progressive* (Boston: Little, Brown, 1975).

7. Warner, *Progressivism in Ohio*, pp. 482–483.

8. Edward Bok, *The Americanization of Edward Bok: The Autobiography of a Dutch Boy Fifty Years Later* (New York: Charles Scribner's Sons, 1924), p. 429.

9. Walter E. Weyl, "Tired Radicals," in his *Tired Radicals and Other Papers* (New York: B. W. Huebsch, 1921), p. 12.

10. For progressive aspects of the Klan see William D. Jenkins, "The Ku Klux Klan in Youngstown, Ohio: Moral Reform in the Twenties," *The Historian* 41 (Nov. 1978): 76–93. My own research, included in my unpublished manuscript, "Progressivism and the Ku Klux Klan in Denver, 1912–1925," shows the connection between reform voters and the Klan in that city.

11. Ferenc M. Szasz, "The Progressive Clergy and the Kingdom of God," *Mid-America* 55 (1973): 20.

12. For some interesting observations on some aspects of heroism in the twenties see "Martin Arrowsmith: The Scientist as Hero," in Charles E. Rosenberg's *No Other Gods: On Science and American Social Thought* (Baltimore: Johns Hopkins University Press, 1976).

13. Robert Stinson, *Lincoln Steffens* (New York: Frederick Ungar, 1979), p. 120.

14. Walter Lippmann, *Public Opinion* (New York: Harcourt, Brace, 1922), pp. 31 and 248–249.

15. Ibid., p. 399.

16. Vida D. Scudder, *On Journey* (New York: E. P. Dutton, 1937), p. 164.

17. Edward T. Devine, *When Social Work Was Young: Personal Recollections of the Time—Some Forty Years Ago—When Organized Charities, Public Relief*

Agencies, Social Settlements, and Others Were Developing What Has Come to Be Called Social Work (New York: Macmillan, 1939), p. 158.

18. Otis L. Graham Jr., *An Encore for Reform: The Old Progressives and the New Deal* (New York: Oxford University Press, 1967), p. 174.

19. Daniel Nelson, *Frederick W. Taylor and the Rise of Scientific Management* (Madison: University of Wisconsin Press, 1980), p. 201.

20. Edward Berkowitz and Kim McQuaid, *Creating the Welfare State: The Political Economy of Twentieth-Century Reform* (New York: Praeger, 1980), p. 56.

21. Roger Babson, *Religion and Business* (New York: Macmillan, 1920), pp. 18 and 102.

22. Ibid., pp. 118 and 116–117.

23. Bruce Barton, *The Man Nobody Knows* (Indianapolis: Charter Books, 1962; published originally by Bobbs-Merrill, 1925), p. 72.

24. Bruce Barton, *The Book Nobody Knows* (Indianapolis: Bobbs-Merrill, 1926), pp. 234–235.

25. For Barton's use of liberal Protestantism see Leo P. Ribuffo, "Jesus Christ as Business Statesman: Bruce Barton and the Selling of Corporate Capitalism," *American Quarterly* 33 (1981): 206–231.

26. Stuart D. Brandes, *American Welfare Capitalism, 1880–1940* (Chicago: University of Chicago Press, 1976), p. 28.

27. Edward A. Filene, *The Way Out: A Forecast of Coming Changes in American Business and Industry* (Garden City: Doubleday, Page, 1925), p. 281.

28. Paul W. Glad, "Progressives and the Business Culture of the 1920's," *Journal of American History* 53 (June 1966): 80.

29. Babson, *Religion and Business*, p. 204.

30. Filene, *The Way Out*, pp. 11 and 42.

31. Edward L. Bernays, *Biography of an Idea: Memoirs of Public Relations Counsel Edward L. Bernays* (New York: Simon and Schuster, 1965), p. 205.

32. Edward L. Bernays, *Crystallizing Public Opinion* (New York: Liveright, 1923), p. 34.

33. Ibid., p. 50.

34. Ibid., pp. 52, 87, and 118.

INDEX

Abbott, Lyman, 23, 24
Acme Sucker Rod Company, 74
Addams, Jane, 72-73, 79, 83, 84, 88, 103, 107
Alger, George W., 99
American Protective Association, 39
Armour, Philip D., 61
Arrowsmith, Martin, 227

Babson, Roger, 233-234, 237
Baer, George F., 154
Baker, Newton, 45
Baltimore, Maryland, 67
Bartlett, Dana, 150
Barton, Bruce, 189, 234-236
Beard, Charles, 139
Beecher, Henry Ward, 23-24, 25, 46
Behaviorism, 122-123
Bellamy, Edward, 41, 47-49, 51, 79, 80, 139
Bemis, Edward, 106-107
Berkman, Alexander, 44
Bernays, Edward, 238-239
Bok, Edward, 225
Bolshevik Revolution, 41
Bourne, Randolph, 212
Brandeis, Louis D., 124, 129, 135, 157, 158, 168, 179
Brooks, John Graham, 109, 161
Bryan, William Jennings, 83, 93, 94, 175
Buckeye Steel Castings Company, 167
Buffalo, New York, 59
Bureau of Municipal Research of New York, 132

Burleson, Albert Sidney, 205
Bushee, Frederick A., 112, 114
Business: changing behavior of, 153-169; during the 1920's, 232-240; public relations and, 169-170, 238-240

California, 220
Calvinism, 22, 24, 56
Campbell, W. W., 199
Capone, Al, 223
Carnegie, Andrew, 31-33
Carnegie Steel Company, 43-44
Carson, William, 185-186
Catholicism, 25, 31, 39, 53, 54
Chapin, F. Stuart, 181
Charity organization societies, 27
Chicago, Illinois, 61, 72
Children, 104-105
Christian progressives: and economic behavior, 89-100; ideas of, 80-89; and municipal reform, 100-107; and politics, 98-99; successes and failures of, 107-111
Civil War, 8, 172
Clark, John Bates, 62
Cleveland, Grover, 43, 44
Cleveland, Ohio, 73-74
Cobbe, Frances Power, 10-11
Coeur d'Alene, Idaho, 44
Committee on Public Information, 204
Commons, John R., 133
Cooke, Morris Llewellyn, 126, 131
Cooley, Charles Horton, 117
Coolidge, Calvin, 223, 226

Cripple Creek, Colorado, 44
Croly, Herbert, 116, 118, 137, 138, 143, 179
Cubberly, Ellwood, 135

Darwinism, 16, 21
Denver, Colorado, 104
Depression of 1893, 35, 41–44, 66, 77, 154
Depression of 1930's, 236, 238
Detroit, Michigan, 73–74
Devine, Edward, 229
Dewey, John, 113, 135, 139
DeWitt, Benjamin Parke, 141, 144
Duffus, Robert, 198

Eastern Rate Case, 135
Edmonds, Franklin Spencer, 89
1890's: crisis of, 38–44; municipal
    reform during, 66–76; Protestantism
    during, 52–61; and "revitalization,"
    76–79; social criticism during, 49–52
Ellwood, Charles, 195, 197, 201
Ely, Richard, 63–65, 146
Emmanuel Movement, 189
Engineering. See Scientific management
Eugenics, 123, 181

Family: Christian Progressives and,
    183–187; Victorian, 18–20
Federal Council of Churches, 187
Ferguson, Charles, 179–180, 189
Ferrero, Guglielmo, 108, 196
Field, Marshall, 61
Filene, Edward, 169, 236–237
Filene family, 168
Fiske, Bradley, 195, 196
Flower, Benjamin Orange, 46, 71, 79, 83
Follett, Mary Parker, 206–207
Ford, Henry, 127, 130, 166, 169, 227, 232
Fosdick, Harry Emerson, 202
Fosdick, Raymond Blaine, 3, 4
Frankfurter, Felix, 205

Freud, Sigmund, and Freudianism, 137, 149, 186–187, 238
Frick, Henry Clay, 44
Friendly visitors, 28
Fuller, Harold de Wolfe, 211

Gantt, Henry L., 131, 205, 208–209
Gary, Elbert, 161
George, Henry, 15, 41, 44–46, 48–49, 139
Georgia, 43
Giddings, Franklin, 63, 140, 195, 214
Gilman, Charlotte Perkins, 186
Gladden, Washington, 23, 41, 56–57, 78, 79, 80, 84, 89, 97, 146, 196
Gould, E. R. L., 33
Grant, Madison, 181–182
Gregory, Thomas, 204

Hadley, Arthur Twining, 83–84
Hale, Edward Everett, 47, 51
Hall, Newton, 133–134
Hapgood, Hutchins, 5
Hart, Albert Bushnell, 76
Herron, George D., 58–59, 90, 96
Hibbard, John B., 166
Hill, Octavia, 28, 72
Holmes, Oliver Wendell, Jr., 139
Holt, Henry, 158
Home. See Family
Homestead, Pennsylvania, 43
Hoover, Herbert, 130, 192, 194, 211, 224, 227, 236
House, Edward, 129
Howe, Frederick C., 4, 9, 80–81, 101, 106, 107
Howells, William Dean, 10
Hubbard, George, 10
Hunter, Robert, 103

Inge, W. R., 215, 216

James, William, 139
Johnson, Tom, 45, 73–74

Jones, Samuel M. ("Golden Rule"), 74–76, 79, 83, 127, 164
Jordan, David Starr, 120–121
Judaism, 25, 31, 53

Kansas, 43
Kansas City, Missouri, 66
Kelley, Florence, 94, 97–98
Kellogg, Paul U., 179
Kemler, Edgar, 110–111, 214, 223
Kern, Robert, 207
Key, Ellen, 186
Ku Klux Klan, 104, 226

LaFollette, Robert M., 41, 93, 94, 174, 175
Lee, Gerald Stanley, 154, 159–160, 165–166
Lee, Ivy, 236, 239
Leighton, Joseph Alexander, 197
Lenin, Vladimir, 227
Lewis, Sinclair, 227
Lindbergh, Charles, 223, 227
Lindsey, Ben B., 104–105, 107
Lippmann, Walter, 113–114, 116, 128, 136, 137, 140–141, 157, 158, 166, 179, 227–228
Lloyd, Henry Demarest, 50–52, 61, 67, 80, 83, 139
Lombroso, Cesare, 108

Martin, Prestonia, 107–108, 196
Mathews, Shailer, 25, 58, 183, 190
McDowell, Mary E., 112, 115
Mead, George Herbert, 135
Milwaukee, Wisconsin, 133
Moody, Dwight L., 23, 24–25, 46
Morgan, J. P., and the House of Morgan, 161, 192
Morison, George, 125, 129
Mormonism, 154
Muckraking, 85–86
Mumford, Lewis, 193, 219, 223
Mussolini, Benito, 223, 227

National Cash Register Company, 36, 164
National Civic Federation, 160, 162
National Consumers' League, 94, 97–98
Nationalist clubs, 48
Nearing, Scott, 108
Nelson, Nelson Olson, 36, 164
New Deal, 178, 230
New Era, 221, 222, 236–237, 238, 239–240
New Orleans, Louisiana, 39
New York City, 67
North Dakota, 43, 98

Ohio, 45, 220, 224
Older, Fremont, 86

Page, Edward D., 156
Parkhurst, Charles, 67
Parsons, Frank, 92, 102
Patten, Simon, 62–63, 121, 129–130, 146
Patterson, John, 35, 164
Peabody, Francis Greenwood, 78
Perkins, George W., 161, 162, 163–164, 171
Pingree, Hazen, 73–74
Pittsburgh Survey, 179
Polakov, Walter, 205
Political system: changing nature of, after 1890, 172–174; effects of progressive reforms on, 174–177; increasing importance of interest groups in, 177–179; after 1920, 229–231
Populism, 43, 49, 60, 172
Post, Louis, 45
Powers, L. G., 78
Pragmatism, 115, 138–142
Progressive reform, accomplishments of, 220–222
Protestant churches: poverty and, 27–29; in Victorian society, 20–27; wealthy and, 29–35

Pullman, George, 34–35, 61, 164
Pullman Palace Car Company, 44

Rainsford, William, 176, 190
Raskob, John Jacob, 236
Rauschenbusch, Walter, 85, 88, 90, 93, 94, 108
Recession of 1914, 177
Redfield, William C., 165
Reform Darwinism, 62
Riis, Jacob, 34, 71
Rockefeller, John D., 16, 50, 92, 97
Roosevelt, Franklin D., 230, 235
Roosevelt, Theodore, 16, 83, 98, 147, 151, 175, 176, 179, 195
Ross, Edward A., 63, 116, 117–118, 128, 137, 146
Ruef, Abe, 86
Russell, Charles Edward, 192, 193
Ruth, Babe, 223, 227

Salvation Army, 25, 71–72
Schreiner, Olive, 186
Schwab, Charles M., 205
Scientific management, 122–132, 179, 221
Scientific progressives: and efficiency, 119–121, 123–132; ideas of, 112–119; during the 1920's, 227–229; and public administration, 132–145, 179; public resistance to, 182–183; relationship with Christian progressives, 145–149
Scudder, Vida, 71–72, 229
Secular humanism, 190
Settlement houses, 72–73, 106
Sheldon, Charles M., 38, 39–40, 41, 60–61
Simkhovitch, Mary Kingsbury, 150
Simons, Algie, 209, 211
Single tax, 45
Slossen, Edwin, 216
Small, Albion, 62, 118, 178

Smith, Adam, 128
Smith, J. Allen, 86, 109, 139
Social Darwinism, 31, 62
Social Gospel, 11, 24, 25, 63–65, 77, 152, 217; development of, 52–59; fundamentalism and, 225–226; impact of, 59–61; Protestant challenges to, 187–191
Social science in the 1890's, 61–65
Spanish-American War, 39
Spencer, Herbert, 62
Standard Oil Company, 50, 75, 97
Stead, William T., 61, 67
Stearns, Harold, 212–213
Steffens, Lincoln, 67, 83, 85–86, 166, 227
Stewardship, 31–35
Stimson, Henry, 176
Strayer, Paul Moore, 188, 196
Strong, Josiah, 41, 54–56, 77
Sunday, Billy, 190
Swope, Gerard, 236

Tarbell, Ida, 83, 91–92, 94, 166
Taylor, Frederick Winslow, 123, 126, 127, 130, 131, 149, 166
Taylor, Graham, 11–12, 53–54, 146, 165
Toledo, Ohio, 74
Toynbee Hall, 72
Tufts, James Hayden, 113

Union for Practical Progress, 67
Union for Public Good, 67
United States Food Administration, 205
United States Fuel Administration, 205
United States Steel, 161, 165

Valentino, Rudolph, 223
Veblen, Thorstein, 109, 139
Victorian culture: place of religion in, 20–26; poverty and, 26–29; progressives and, 3–5; threats to, 12–20; values of, 4–12

Vrooman, Frank, 118, 119, 137
Vrooman family, 67

Ward, Lester Frank, 62, 139
War Industries Board, 205
War Labor Board, 205
Weaver, James B., 49
Welfare capitalism, 34–36, 164–169, 221, 232–233
Weyl, Walter, 129, 136, 225
White, William Allen, 60, 80, 82, 84, 111, 219, 220
Whitlock, Brand, 106, 107, 219, 220
Wilcox, Delos, 105
Williams, Charles D., 84, 95–96
Wilson, Woodrow, 83, 151, 175, 176, 179, 192, 202–203, 211

Wisconsin, 42, 66, 93
Women: changing roles of, 183–187; and domestic ideal, 18–19
Wood, Charles, 205–206
Woodworth, Robert S., 205–206
Worcester, Elwood, 189
World War I: progressives' disillusionment with, 210–217; progressives' hopes for, 200–210; progressives' reaction to, 194–200
Wright, Carroll D., 35
Wyatt, H. F., 216

Yerkes, Robert, 199
Young, Owen D., 166
Young Men's Christian Association, 25, 34